BENJAMIN BRITTEN'S 'HOLY THEATRE':
FROM OPERA-ORATORIO TO THEATRE-PARABLE

BARBARA A. DIANA

London
Travis & Emery

Benjamin Britten's 'Holy Theatre':
from Opera-Oratorio to Theatre Parable

© Barbara Diana 2011.

Hardback: 978-1-84955-118-2   Paperback: 978-1-84955-119-9

First published by
Travis & Emery Music Bookshop
17 Cecil Court, London, WC2N 4EZ, United Kingdom.
(+44) 20 7240 2129
neworders@travis-and-emery.com

*To Philip Langridge,
unforgettable Aschenbach
and Grimes*

Benjamin Britten's Holy Theatre: From Opera-Oratorio to Theatre-Parable

TABLE OF CONTENTS

Copyright acknowledgements	p.8
Introduction	p.9
CHAPTER 1: BEFORE *GRIMES*	p.15
1.1 The Auden Years	p.16
1.2 The GPO Film Unit	p.18
1.3 Political Consciousness	p.23
1.4 Radio Days	p.26
1.5 Political Theatre	p.32
1.6 An American Interlude	p.37
1.7 Finding the Form Best-Suited	p.55
CHAPTER 2: THE POET'S MIND	p.60
2.1 'A Useful Part of the Borough'	p.62
2.2 Parable-Art	p.65
2.3 Portrait of the Artist as a Gay Man	p.67
2.4 The Child's Lost Power of Sight	p.70
2.5 'Only in Peace I Can Be Free'	p.72
2.6 Communication	p.74
2.7 The Holy Stage	p.76
CHAPTER 3: THE COMPOSER AS A DRAMATIST, IMPRESARIO, LIBRETTIST	p.80
3.1 Peter Grimes, Peter Grimes, Peter Grimes...	p.80
3.2 Opera Consciousness	p.83
3.3 A New Opera Company	p.86
3.4 The Method of Work	p.93

CHAPTER 4: WHY DOES LUCRETIA DIE? p.101
4.1 The Libretto p.102
4.2 Opera-Oratorio p.112
4.3 Harnessing Songs to Human Tragedy p.119
4.4 Lucretia p.130
4.5 The Suicide p.138
4.6 The First Parable p.144

CHAPTER 5: SACRED AND PROFANE p.150
5.1 Chamber Drama p.152
5.2 Church Drama p.155
5.3 Church Parable p.164
5.4 Holy Theatre p.181
5.5 Theatre Parable p.183

CHAPTER 6: THE TASTE OF KNOWLEDGE p.185
6.1 The Literary Source: *Der Tod in Venedig* p.188
6.2 The Libretto p.196
6.3 The Musico-Dramatic Structure p.200
6.4 Didactic Theatre p.208
6.5 Apollo and Dionysus p.211
6.6 'Does Beauty lead to Wisdom?' p.214

Conclusions p.224
Selected bibliography p.227

ABSTRACT

Benjamin Britten's works for the stage developed from the traditional late nineteenth-century romantic opera structure of *Peter Grimes* to the experimental format of the church parables and of *Death in Venice*, his last opera. At the core of this development seems to have been Britten's intention to use the stage as a pulpit to express his philosophical views. Such views influenced his aesthetic vision, and he explored new musico-dramatic possibilities in order to find a form suitable to communicate his message in the most effective way. His efforts were mainly directed to attempt a fusion of the epic, lyric and dramatic narrative modalities into a form that can be qualified as belonging to what contemporary drama theorists define as 'holy theatre'.

This study examines the development of Britten's philosophical views, mainly through the analysis of his own writings, from his early involvement with Left wing activism during the thirties through to his more spiritually oriented objectives after the war, and essays an assessment of how these influenced his creative choices. Particular attention has been given to the definition of Britten's 'method of work' when theatre is involved, to ascertain his overall responsibility for the final product.

The results of this analysis are then used to support alternative readings of two of his most controversial works for the stage, *The Rape of Lucretia* and *Death in Venice*, works that lie at the opposite ends of his operatic output. The similarities between some of the unusual dramaturgical features shared by these works, features that are also found in some of his non-dramatic works, are proofs of the consistency of his artistic vision throughout his development.

COPYRIGHT ACKNOWLEDGEMENTS

The quotations from the diaries, letters and other writings of Benjamin Britten are © copyright the Trustees of the Britten–Pears Foundation and may not be further reproduced without the written permission of the Trustees.

NOTE TO THE READER

The present work was originally submitted as a dissertation in accordance with the regulations for the degree of Doctor of Philosophy, University of London

INTRODUCTION

> *However useful attentive reading of operatic scores may be,*
> *it is the theatre which ultimately reveals the truth*
> *(F.Noske, The Signifier and the Signified)* [1]

In his obituary for Benjamin Britten Michael Tippett, recalling the triumph of *Peter Grimes*, writes: 'For Britten himself, this triumph meant something more than the immediacy of being an internationally recognised composer. It meant for him that he was now willing in himself, and indeed, determined to be, within the twentieth century, a professional opera composer'.[2] The fact that Britten succeeded in becoming an opera composer is beyond argument. In the thirty-year span of his career he wrote sixteen original works for the stage, together with a couple of adaptations: few musicians this century have been so prolific and so successful in the field of opera. In the minds of both critics and audience he seems to be, principally, a dramatic composer. Although this may not be a noteworthy fact, the subtext of Tippett's affirmation is that there is something quite exceptional in being a professional opera composer 'within the twentieth century'. And, we could add, 'in England'.

AN ENGLISH OPERA COMPOSER

The general condition of opera in England was not particularly healthy, especially at the end of the Second World War.[3] Christopher Headington points out that, at the time of the success of *Peter Grimes*, 'there was

---

[1] NOSKE 1990, p.viii
[2] As quoted in BLYTH 1981, p.69.
[3] About the problem of opera in England see WHITE 1972 and 1985.

indeed no tradition of writing operas: there was no tradition among audiences of wanting to see contemporary operas'.[4] Even so, Britten decided to concentrate almost all his energies on the creation of opportunities for a contemporary English opera, to the point that he founded his own opera company[5] and, later, his own Festival. Understanding the complexity and difficulties in the management of such an adventure is important if we want to have a clear vision of the kind of pressures the composer faced. For someone devoted to his personal career as much as Britten seems to have been, to persist in the production of a genre that apparently had no market demand or solid tradition might not have been the most advantageous move. After all, by 1944 he was the most successful English composer of his generation; W.H. Auden had dubbed him 'the white hope of music',[6] he was internationally renowned even before the extraordinary impact of *Grimes*, he had been commissioned to write a symphonic work by the Japanese government,[7] and the composition of the opera itself had been possible thanks to a commission from the Koussevitsky Foundation. Some critics have suggested that there was 'some fundamental incompatibility between the composer and purely instrumental form which only became fully apparent after the composition of his first successful opera'.[8] But a close look at Britten's catalogue makes it difficult to accept such a theory, even if we only consider his output up to *Grimes*, in which purely instrumental works, whether chamber of orchestral, account for more than 50% of the titles: in addition to the internationally successful *Variations on a Theme by Frank Bridge* op.10 (first performed at the Salzburg Festival), he had produced amongst other works the *Piano Concerto* op.13, the *Violin Concerto* op.15, the *First String Quartet* op.25, the *Prelude and fugue for 18 part string orchestra* op. 29 and the *Sinfonia da Requiem* op.20.[9] And if we survey his vocal works, which at the time included the choral variations *A boy was born* op.3, *Les illuminations* op.18, the *Michelangelo Sonnets* op.22, *A Ceremony of Carols* op.28 and the

---

[4] HEADINGTON 1981, p.9.
[5] The English Opera Group, founded at the end of 1946, of which Britten was artistic director.
[6] MITCHELL 1981, p.161.
[7] The commission of *Sinfonia da Requiem* was quite a complicated business, and resulted in a 'diplomatic' incident: Britten based the work on the Requiem Mass, as known in the Christian tradition, and the Japanese government, considering this an offence to their own religion, rejected the work. For a detailed account on the work and its genesis see KISHINAMI 1998.
[8] WHITTALL 1982, p.107.
[9] See BANKS 1999.

Serenade op.31, it appears that Britten had no need or compulsion to concentrate on such an 'uncomfortable' genre as opera. On the contrary, if we consider the problems that arose during the production of *Peter Grimes*, one might expect that, after having experienced what writing and staging operas was like, Britten would have been more than happy to return to the composition of song-cycles.[10] Instead, with the English Opera Group, he started a policy of 'educating' the audiences, in order to create demand where there was apparently no interest.[11] Furthermore, he ventured on writing one of the most controversial and possibly misunderstood of his works, *The Rape of Lucretia*, exploring the experimental dimension of 'chamber opera'.

This sudden change of direction, and the composer's strong determination to concentrate on the theatrical medium, should give rise to some curiosity on the part of the exegete. It is quite clear that Britten was fascinated with opera, which he himself described as 'the most exciting of musical forms'.[12] Nonetheless, he did not immediately write another 'grand opera', which was indeed what the majority of the audience was expecting and hoping for. *The Rape of Lucretia* is a chamber opera for eight singers and thirteen instruments, set in pre-republican ancient Rome. All the late-romantic elements of the first opera disappear, to give way to a highly stylised and concise 'moral meditation' in the form of a ritualistic theatrical experience. Lucretia had a mixed reception, by which the composer appears to have been quite disappointed.[13] The importance of the work, easily outshone by the gigantic success of its predecessor, seems to have been generally underestimated in the context of Britten criticism. But as Mervyn Cooke suggests, in the opera's 'subject matter and dramaturgy', if it is comprehended correctly, lies a clue for understanding the composer's operatic development.[14]

It appears that comprehension can only exist in the context of a frame of

---

[10] Arnold Whittall remarks: 'The preparations for the first production were anything but happy, and appear to have been the kind of experience which could have permanently deterred a composer less familiar than Britten with the stresses, strains, prejudices and tantrums of life in the theatre' (1982, p.112).

[11] See Eric Crozier's artistic manifesto of the English Opera Group, in CROZIER 1946.

[12] BRITTEN 1946, p.8.

[13] A few days after the first performance he wrote to a friend: 'I used to think that the days when one could shock people were over — but now I've discovered that being simple and considering things spiritual of importance, produces violent reactions'. (HOLST 1966, p.44).

[14] COOKE 1987, *The Prophecy of Lucretia*, pp.54–55.

reference, which cannot be absolute. Nonetheless, a collection of facts can help us to create a relatively objective background against which data can be interpreted in a way which is necessarily subjective and personal: in this sense, I believe in a humanistic approach to criticism. At the same time, believing that every work of art needs to be confronted in its own aesthetic terms, I think it is important in the first instance to clarify the artistic and aesthetic context that produced Britten's operas. This can lead not only to a different reading of the individual works, but also to a better understanding of the composer's personal philosophy. Britten seems to be a particularly ambiguous case, because of his apparent shyness in making aesthetic statements and his declared clumsiness in the medium of words. In an age as artistically self-conscious as the twentieth century, where it is common practice for artists to be apologists for themselves, he stands out for his apparent lack of manifestos. But he wrote more words than is generally appreciated, and some of his writings hide interesting clues which can be of great relevance for a critical approach. While an artist may not always be the best exegete of his own work, it could be argued that he knows better than anybody else what he is trying to do with it. Thus, one of my objects in the context of this enquiry has been to examine all of Britten's writings, especially those concerned with theatre and the function of art, in an attempt to clarify the composer's poetics.

SHARING THE MESSAGE

Amongst the interesting concepts that have emerged, of particular relevance seems Britten's concern with the concept of communication. In an interview with Murray Schafer in 1963, the composer, talking about music and communication, said: 'If I did not communicate I would consider I had failed'[15]. The Oxford English Dictionary defines 'to communicate' as 'to give to another as a partaker; to impart, transmit or exchange thoughts, feelings, etc., successfully. Thus it seems that for Britten music is not an end, but a means: it is his chosen personal way to share his thought. The assumption here is that the nature of such thought is essentially extramusical.

The recent developments of 'new musicology' and of its ramifications have made Britten a good subject for gay studies. Comparisons and

---

[15] SCHAFER 1963, p.124

associations between Britten and his characters are found in the critical literature since the reception of *Grimes*,[16] to the point that some critics have felt uneasy in dealing with operas like *Lucretia* or *A Midsummer Night's Dream*, where the heterosexual behaviour can hardly be misinterpreted.[17] This development, together with the public acknowledgement of the sexual basis of Britten's lifelong partnership with Peter Pears, has produced the development of a literature where apparently the interest is more on the personal life of the creator than on the work of art: Britten's operas are interpreted as metaphors of the composer's social and psychological situation. The results of such investigations are then placed in the context of his musical language: thus, tonal ambiguity and a fascination with Eastern music become a reflection of Britten's unease with his own personal condition. And although readings have been produced on the basis of this kind of approach, it seems that very little autonomy in making aesthetic decisions is left to the composer, who sometimes appears to be no more than a victim of his own frustrated unconscious. There is no doubt that 'who he was' determined in a strong way his artistic expression, but I have found it more interesting to study what he felt he wanted to say.

Indeed, what could have been the composer's intentions seems to have excited very little interest. One is often left with the image of a very gifted craftsman who wrote operas for opera's sake, and who used theatre as an outlet for the expression of his inner psychological struggle. As I have argued before, this does not seem the case to me, and I believe that the conscious choices of an artist can be relevant to interpretation. Stressing the relevance of his particular stylistic choices, I think that for Britten opera maintained its original ethical mission as an archetypal form of theatre with a moral and social responsibility. It may be possible to say that, along the same lines as W.H. Auden, a major influence on the composer, he viewed theatre as a pulpit and the operatic metaphor as a parable.[18] The later development of his theatrical output can easily support such a reading. But I believe that this idea of theatre applies to earlier works as well, and was in fact a major influence on the direction

---

[16] See for example KELLER 1995.

[17] Peter Pears points out that Britten 'was really much more interested in the beauty, and therefore the danger, that existed in any relationship between human beings – man and woman, man and man – the sex didn't really matter' (interviewed in Tony Palmer's television film *A time there was*, 1980).

[18] See below, Chapter 2, section 2.

he took. His struggle for artistic freedom seems to me a sign of his need to 'discover the form best suited to deal with the theme that mattered most to him'.[19] I believe that, taking in consideration his stylistic choices amongst other elements, it is possible to identify in Britten's dramatic output a coherent line of development which reflects his search for a philosophical answer to the problems he was faced with, and for an ideal musico-dramatic form, best suited to the message he meant to convey. Approaching the works I consider relevant in this context I hope to be able to show the interaction between aesthetic intentions and dramatic result. My aim is not the exhaustive study of a single work, but the attempt to bring attention to recurrent features of the works which may justify an overall perspective on Britten's theatre. I believe that this approach may be particularly fruitful in the reading of two works that seem to have been quite problematic, *The Rape of Lucretia* and *Death in Venice*. Ultimately I am interested in the composer 'as a thinker', and I believe that the modalities through which the thought is expressed help us in reaching a clarification of its content. I trust that the conclusions we can draw from this enquiry may bring further light on Britten's artistic and personal philosophy, which personally I consider one of the most intriguing and fruitful of the twentieth century.

---

[19] WHITTALL 1982, p.96.

CHAPTER 1
BEFORE *GRIMES*

The story is well known. Self-exiled in America, Britten suffered an acute attack of homesickness after reading an article by E.M. Forster on George Crabbe. To find some relief, he bought a copy of the poem *The Borough*, and started planning an opera scenario based on the character of Peter Grimes. Only a few months later, Britten showed the plan to Serge Koussevitsky, who commissioned the work that was going to rescue English opera from its long sleep.

Peter Grimes is indeed a turning point in Britten's development: probably a masterpiece, certainly an amazing achievement for a composer then at the beginning of his thirties and who had never written a 'grand' opera before. There are not many 'opera composers' whose first work is still considered to be their best achievement in the genre. Interestingly enough, one could argue that *Grimes* is more a final product than a new start. It is the culmination of a long period of apprenticeship in which Britten had consolidated not only his craftsmanship, but also his artistic personality.

When Michael Tippett says that it is with *Grimes* that Britten decided to become a professional opera composer,[20] he may simply be stating the obvious. But the roots of such a decision do not lie simply in *Grimes*'s international success, or in the fact that with this work the young composer had discovered that vocal music was his true vocation. Had

---
[20] As quoted in BLYTH 1981, p.69.

public acclaim been the motive behind his choice to write for the theatre, he would probably have written another work in the same tradition as *Grimes*, as most of the public and the critics were expecting from him. But Britten's artistic conscience saw a different path before him: 'Some people seem to want another *Grimes*, and still another! But they are mistaken if they expect me to give it to them. I have different challenges before me and I respond to them'.[21]

I believe that some of these challenges were not exclusively concerned with musical problems of a technical nature. They were born out of deep beliefs about the rôle of the artist in society, and related to the position of art in everyday life. Britten always seemed eager to justify his status as a creative artist, and I believe that by the end of 1945 he had developed a personal answer to the question of the importance of creative work within society, with a particular bias towards the importance of theatre.

THE AUDEN YEARS

The roots of his beliefs can be recognised in the very intense period between 1935 and 1939, before he moved to America. In the critical literature those years are often defined as 'the Auden years',[22] and indeed the English poet had a great impact on the composer's world: they collaborated on a number of projects, as well as documentaries, radio broadcasts and theatre productions. Auden's texts are prominent in the early vocal output of Britten. Talking about this period Britten himself would admit, later on: 'I was terrifically under Auden's influence at that time'.[23] He would also specify: 'I was certainly influenced by Auden personally, but never musically'.[24] Certainly Auden opened to Britten a new world of political and artistic consciousness that proved to be extremely fruitful, and that the composer never really left behind.

When we are dealing with the ambiguous concept of influence, it may be useful to keep in mind the clarification that Rose Rosegard Subotnik proposes about the problem of relationship, in her understanding of it

---

[21] SCHAFER 1963, p.121.
[22] On the subject of the Britten and Auden collaboration, see also WHITE 1983, ch.2 'Collaboration with W.H. Auden'", pp.28–33; KENNEDY 1981, in particular ch.4 'Auden & Co.', pp.16–23; and MITCHELL 1981.
[23] OSBORNE 1963, p.95.
[24] WARRACK 1964, p.28.

through 'an analytical dynamic': 'the process of viewing both terms as simultaneously prior to each other, in the sense that the thinker's definition of each term is understood to condition the definition of the other in the very act of being conditioned by that other'.[25] To paraphrase her definition in this context, clearly Britten could have been influenced by Auden, or anybody else, only in the measure of his understanding, and therefore subjectively in relation to his own receptivity towards an idea. We are therefore not talking so much about other people's ideas in relation to Britten, but rather about Britten's own interpretation of these ideas. The fact that he responded to these, or that he was involved with them, is clearly a reflection of his own thought.

It is Britten's reaction to the problems posed by Auden's aesthetic views that may be of relevance in this context, and such relevance is strictly related to Britten's adoption, or non-adoption, of Auden's ideas. In the case of his relationship with Auden it is interesting to note that later their stylistic ideals revealed themselves to be very far apart, and their divergences became more and more difficult to mediate, to the point that Britten aborted any further artistic collaboration. I consider it relevant to look at those Auden years not so much in terms of Auden's 'influence' on Britten's works,[26] but because I believe that through an understanding of the artistic and intellectual experiences of those years we can trace a coherent line of development which allows us a consistent reading of later works in the light of a precise aesthetic of art in general and of music theatre in particular. Notwithstanding the importance of Auden's presence, there was much more in those excitingly creative years,[27] a period which I believe may be interesting to discuss in some detail. It will be particularly fruitful to look at it keeping in mind some aspects of Britten's later development, not strictly in terms of musical language, but rather, in a broader sense, of his philosophy of art.

---

[25] SUBOTNIK 1990, p.xxiv. On the subject of influence see also KORSYN 1991: although it deals with a different context, it nonetheless reinforces the concept of 'influence' in terms of reaction, a reaction whose character heavily depends on the subjective 'interpretation' of ideas on the part of the 'influenced'.

[26] This was the subject of JENNINGS 1979, where the author expresses the questionable concept of 'Britten's synthesis of Auden's stylistic, philosophical and social attitudes in his emerging musical style'. I believe that it was exactly on matters of style that the artistic collaboration between the two came to an impasse.

[27] More detailed studies about this period of Britten's creative development can be found in MITCHELL 1981 and REED, PHILIP 1987.

THE GPO FILM UNIT

At the beginning of 1935 Britten, who was looking for a job, had an interview with the BBC. There was an opportunity for him to be hired there, although he was not completely happy about it.[28] Through Edward Clark's secretary he was put in touch with Alberto Cavalcanti, a film producer who was looking for a composer. Cavalcanti was part of a team of intellectuals and artists, led by John Grierson, engaged in the production of documentary films under the auspices of the General Post Office: they were the GPO Film Unit. Cavalcanti was in charge of the soundtracks of a new documentary, *The King's Stamp*.

The project that followed, about coal miners, had nothing to do with the Post Office, but Grierson and his staff were allowed a certain freedom in making films of general interest.[29] It is important to keep in mind the role of film, and especially documentary film: in the thirties, a time when television was still more experimental than popular, the newsreel was an important means of propaganda. Documentaries were shown in cinemas and hired out to educational organisations. By those making them these films were seen as educational devices for the development of criticism and social change, certainly not as agents of conformism. Such was the agenda for most of the documentaries of the GPO Film Unit, as it is made quite clear in a number of articles in periodicals such as *Sight and Sound* and *Cinema Quarterly*, signed not only by Grierson, but by many of his collaborators; Britten himself wrote a couple of articles in *World Film News*, a GPO publication.[30] Grierson, who is seen as 'the father of the documentary',[31] expounded some of his idea on the subject:

---

[28] In his diary he writes: 'There is a probability of me going there for a whole time job! Ugh!' (quoted in CARPENTER 1992, p.63).

[29] The history and programme of the GPO Film Unit are certainly too complex to be dealt in full in the present context. For an outstanding assesement of Grierson's significance see AITKEN 1992.

[30] 'Soviet opera at B.B.C.: Shostakovich "Lady Macbeth"', *World Film News* 1/1 (1936) (reprinted in *Tempo* 120 (1977) ; '"As you like it" Walton's music', *World Film News* 1/7 (1936).

[31] MITCHELL 1981, p.59.

Table 1: Britten's Incidental Music for Documentaries and Film[32]

Title	Studio	Collaborators	Year
The King's Stamp	GPO	W. Coldstream	1935
Coal Face	GPO	W.H. Auden	1935
Telegrams	GPO		1935
CTO: The Story of the Central Telegraph Office	GPO	Stuart Legg	1935
The Tocher	GPO	A. Cavalcanti	1935
Gas Abstract	GPO		1935
Negroes [never released]	GPO	W. Coldstream, Auden	1936
Men Behind the Meters	GPO	Arthur Elton	1935
Dinner Hour	GPO	Arthur Elton	1935
How the Dial Works	GPO	Ralph Elton, Rona Morris	1935
Conquering Space	GPO	Stuart Legg	1935
Sorting Office	GPO	Harry Watt	1935
The Savings Bank	GPO	Stuart Legg	1935
The New Operator	GPO	Stuart Legg, J. Grierson	1935
Night Mail	GPO	J. Grierson, W.H. Auden	1936
Love from a Stranger [feature film]	Capitol Films	Rowland Victor Lee	1936
Peace of Britain	Strand Films	Paul Rotha	1936
Around the Village Green	TID	M. Grierson, E. Spice	1936
Men of the Alps	GPO	A. Cavalcanti, H. Watts	1936
Message from Geneva	GPO	A. Cavalcanti	1936
Four Barriers	GPO	A. Cavalcanti, H. Watts	1936
The Savings of Bill Blewitt	GPO	H. Watts, J. Grierson	1936
The Way to the Sea	Strand Films	Paul Rotha, W.H. Auden	1936
Book Bargain	GPO	Norman McLaren	?1937
Calendar of the Year	GPO	A. Cavalcanti, Auden	1937
Line to the Tschierva Hut	GPO	A. Cavalcanti, J. Grierson	1937
Money A Pickle	GPO	R. Hassingham	[?1938]
Advance Democracy	Realistic Film	Ralph Bond, Basil Wright	1938
The Instruments of the Orchestra	Crown Film Unit	Montagu Slater	1945/46

---

[32] The data in this table are mainly derived from REED, PHILIP 1987, and EVANS, JOHN 1987, pp.131–144, although they have been integrated from other various sources. KELLER 1950, p.250, mentions another documentary, *Village Harvest*, which I have not been able to identify even with the help of the staff at the Britten–Pears Library in Aldeburgh; it does not seem to be another title for *Around the Village Green*, as Keller mentions both.

The documentary idea was not basically a film idea at all, and the film treatment it inspired only an incidental aspect of it. The medium happened to be the most convenient and exciting available to us. The idea itself, on the other hand, was a new idea for public education: its underlying concept that the world was in a phase of drastic change affecting every manner of thought and practice, and the public comprehension of the nature of that change vital. There it is, exploratory, experimental and stumbling, in the films themselves: from the dramatization of the workman and his daily work to the dramatization of modern organization and the new corporate elements in society to the dramatization of social problems: each a step in the attempt to understand the stubborn raw material of our modern citizenship and wake the heart and the will to their mastery. Where we stopped short was that, with equal deliberation, we refused to specify what political agency should carry out that will or associate ourselves with any one of them. Our job specifically was to wake the heart and the will: it was for political parties to make before the people their own case for leadership.[33]

The concept that seems of particular relevance here in relation to Britten's later development is the rôle of the artist as an educator, politically aware, but not necessarily politically committed. It seems to me that Britten will simply apply the same basic principles to a different medium, opera: his work will remain 'specifically to wake the heart and the will', not to offer a solution, which is a politician's job. In a way, there is an echo of a similar idea in the caption on the title page of the *War Requiem*: 'All a poet can do today is warn', although probably in 1935 Britten was still untouched by the shadow of bitter helplessness that one can feel in Owen's remark.

It is not difficult to see how Britten might have been fascinated by the environment of the GPO Unit, with its unusually explicit aesthetic ethos, and by Grierson's 'creative treatment of actuality': there was a very strong element of activism in the GPO work. Grierson himself would say: 'I look on cinema as a pulpit and use it as a propagandist'.[34] He was not alone in his belief: 'It was precisely the educative purpose – the dissemination of facts, the stimulation of civic responsibilities, the countering of misleading,

---

[33] HARDY 1979, p.113.
[34] Quoted in MITCHELL 1981, p.60.

or slanted, information from other influential sources – that was among the principal aims of many of those associated with the GPO Film Unit'.[35] In his work with the GPO Britten was involved not only in the musical aspects: for his second collaboration, *Coal Face*, he was involved from the very first stages, participating at the script conferences. He was deeply involved in all the aspects of the film. His diaries record how for days he and Coldstream researched 'Daily Herald offices, libraries and bookshops for words'.[36] The literary sketches for *Coal Face* are documentary evidence of how intimately Britten influenced the shape and content of the script.[37] It was probably in these early days that he developed the method of team-work that he was going to apply almost constantly in his operatic projects, especially in relation to his direct involvement in the writing of the libretto. Another person who contributed to the script of *Coal Face* was W. H. Auden, who wrote verses to be sung and/or spoken as part of the soundtrack. The beginning of the collaboration between Britten and Auden was marked by 'a truly extraordinary *musique-concrete* inspired soundtrack (the mechanised world) contrasted with the warmth of Auden's famous madrigal "O lurcher loving collier" (the human world)'.[38]

The second project on which Auden and Britten were to collaborate was an even more ambitious experiment combining words, sound and images. *Negroes* focused on the introduction of the Slave trade into the Caribbean in the sixteenth century, and the subsequent development of the West Indies, which was shown as still producing goods for Europe by cheap labour methods, with a workforce existing on a low standard of living. In Auden's and Britten's original concept the entire commentary was sung in a recitative-like manner rather than spoken, and in effect they produced a miniature cantata. Unfortunately the project was abandoned for economic reasons, and released only in 1938 in a shorter, revised version entitled *God's Chillun*, long after Auden had lost interest in it.

Maybe the most celebrated product of the GPO studio is *Night Mail* (1936), a documentary about the special postal express train from London to Scotland and its nightly routine:

---

[35] MITCHELL 1981, p.58.
[36] CARPENTER 1992, p.66.
[37] On the creative process of *Coal Face* see REED, PHILIP 1999.
[38] REED, PHILIP 1996, *Britten and Auden...*, p.131.

> *Night Mail*, made by the GPO Film Unit and Workers of the Post Office and the Railways, easily surpasses other documentary films made so far in this country. Basil Wright, who directed it, has contrived to give a dramatic and exciting account of the normal night mail service. The sound recording is excellent and there is very little use made of the 'commentator'– the postal and railway workers speak for themselves. When Pudovkin and Eisenstein announced their theory that actual peasants and workers could achieve better results than trained actors, the general answer was that this might have been all right for the Russians, but that the English could not be expected to rise to it. *Night Mail* has shown that this is far from true. On a smaller scale, this film has some of the quality of reality in which the early Russian silent film excelled. The verse and music of W.H. Auden and Benjamin Britten make an admirable rhythmic accompaniment to the train's journey.[39]

Later in life Britten observed: 'I do not take film music seriously qua music',[40] but in the thirties he certainly believed in the importance of the composer's contribution to the art film:

> I think there are great possibilities for music for the films, but it must be taken seriously by the director and the composer, and used as an integral part of the whole thing - not just as a sound-effect, or to fill up gaps during the talking. The nearest approach to this I've seen has been in the Disney cartoons and a few French films.[41]

And stating his eagerness to have substantial responsibility for the finished product, he insists: 'I should always like to be consulted during the writing of the script'.[42] He certainly had such opportunities with the GPO members. As we have seen, his work on a new project always started with a discussion with the director and the script-writer. The situation was slightly different when the market was involved, and there is no doubt that the composer was dissatisfied during his work on *Love*

---

[39] *Left review*, II/7 (April 1936), p.347. Also Hans Keller comments 'If and when film music embarks on a musical history, *Night Mail* will be found – despite or indeed partly because of its elementary simplicity – among those legitimate points of departure from which so many of its successors have illegitimately departed' (KELLER 1950, p.251).
[40] CARPENTER 1992, p.65.
[41] BRITTEN 1944, p.4.
[42] Questionnaire circulated by the film historian Jay Leda, preserved in the New York Public Library (ca. 1940–41), quoted in REED, PHILIP 1987, p.22.

from a Stranger (1936), the only commercial film for which he wrote the soundtrack, especially because of the director's lack of consultation with him from the very beginning, and the fact that he was allowed little involvement in the production. Britten became sharply critical of the commercial cinema, and declined any further offers in that field, although we know that while in America he was hoping to find work in Hollywood, and had signed a contract with an agent there.[43]

It seems a characteristic trait in Britten, that he never got involved - or at least not further than the initial stages - in projects that did not interest him personally. His own problems as a composer and as an artist always had priority over other considerations. It might therefore be relevant to look not only at his choices but, in some instances, the options he discarded, because they are often quite revealing. When in 1943 Gabriel Pascal and Rank Productions attempted to persuade Britten to compose the incidental music for their adaptation of G.B. Shaw's *Caesar and Cleopatra*, he refused because 'the script did not appeal to him', but mainly because 'in doing it he would accomplish nothing towards the solution of his own problems as a composer.(...) He said that money did not interest him'.[44] Amongst the other offers that cropped up was David Lean's *Lawrence of Arabia* in 1962, but, like the others, it was rejected with an excuse: lack of time, too full a composing schedule.

POLITICAL CONSCIOUSNESS

Britten certainly had his reasons for working amongst the team of intellectuals attached to the GPO. They were attempting 'to use cinema for purposes more important than entertainment',[45] as stated by Paul Rotha, with whom Britten was to collaborate in 1936 on *Peace of Britain*. A politically-minded filmmaker, Rotha believed deeply in the educative potentialities of the documentary film, which he considered the most powerful instrument for social change:

> It is absurd to suggest that cinema, with its power to enlarge the public's social conscience, to create new standards of culture, to stir mental apathies, to build new understandings and, by virtues inherent in its form,

---

[43] See MITCHELL 1991, p.284.
[44] Boosey and Hawkes internal memorandum, quoted in REED, PHILIP 1987, p.174.
[45] ROTHA 1936, p.25.

> to become the most powerful of all modern preachers - it is absurd to suggest that it can be left in the hands of commercial speculators to be used as a vehicle for purposeless fictional stories. There must be a world outside that represented by the entertainment film. There must be sources of production other than those demanding only profit. There must be kinds of cinema and ends to serve other than those which portray an artificial world conceived under mass-production methods at the dictates of the balance-sheet. There is – the world of propaganda and education. Real and creative thought must be about real things (...) Let cinema attemp film interpretations of modern problems and events, of things as they really are today, and by doing so perform a definite function. Let cinema recognise the existence of real men and women, real things and real issues, and by doing so offer to State, Industry, Commerce, to public and private organisations of all kinds, a method of communication and propaganda to project not just personal opinions but arguments for a world of common interests.[46]

It is important to note this idea of 'the most powerful of all modern preachers', because the concept of preaching, sermons and the related notion of 'parable' will come up over and over again. Also this statement by Rotha powerfully illustrates the kind of ideas circulating among those working on documentaries, ideas that were certainly shared by Britten. We know that in those years political consciousness had become a central problem for him, probably because of the 'influence' of Auden. In a letter to Marjorie Fass he writes:

> I know you would like W.H.A. very much. He is a very startling personality – but absolutely sincere and very brilliant. He has a very wide knowledge, not only of course of literature, but of every branch of art, and especially of politics; this last in the direction that I can't help feeling every serious person, and artists especially, must have. Strong opposition in every direction to Fascism, which of course restricts all freedom of thought.[47]

It might have been mainly because of Auden's influence, but political awareness was no doubt also a product of the international political

---

[46] ROTHA 1936, p.69. Also quoted in MITCHELL 1981, p.61.
[47] Letter dated 23 October 1935, in MITCHELL 1991, p.378.

situation. We know that in the summer of 1936 Britten was reading Marx, and his diaries report his preoccupation with the situation in Spain. On 24 July he writes:

> News from Spain still bad, tho'government seems to be gaining ground a bit - it varies with what papers one reads. One thing is certain is that Fascists are executing hundreds (literally) of Popular Front or Communist members - including many boys of 14–16. Marvellous to have opinion of that strength at that age. I can't help feeling that not until that 'political consciousness' is more general that the world will get out of this mess.[48]

The fight against Fascism was a heartfelt everyday subject; Auden himself was going to join the loyalists, as for him the choice between art and action veered towards action. Although his mind was apparently 'entirely clouded by the continued disastrous news from Spain',[49] Britten's strong pacifist convictions prevented him from engaging in action in Spain. Furthermore, he regarded his artistic contribution as socially valid and useful. Paul Rotha remembers:

> You must remember the Spanish Civil War dominated many of our lives, including some of our writers and poets who went out there. We used to discuss this amongst ourselves very much; was it really our duty to give up film-making and go to Spain? [...] But our job was to remain in this country (England) and make films about our own social problems, and sometimes our political problems.[50]

And talking about the origins of *Peace of Britain* Rotha recalls: 'One of us said "What the hell are we making? Let's make a film about what we believe in", which in those days was very much the League of Nations'. The film was commissioned by the T.U.C. (Trades Union Congress) and League of Nations Union, and made by an independent group. The film, a three-minute statistical account of defence spending, which culminated in an appeal to 'Demand peace by reason',[51] caused something of a scandal. Due to problems with censorship, it started a sharp political controversy that soon arrived on the pages of the national press. Britten seemed quite

---

[48] Quoted in MITCHELL 1981, p.46.
[49] Quoted in CARPENTER 1992, p.85.
[50] Interview in Tony Palmer's television film *A Time There Was* (1980).
[51] Quoted in CARPENTER 1992, p.79.

amused by the results of his early steps in peace activism, and records in his diary: 'The fuss caused by the Censor not passing that little Rotha Peace film is colossal. 1/2 centre pages of Herald & News Chronicle, & Manchester Guardian - BBC News twice. Never has a film had such good publicity!'[52]

Britten's pacifism has had quite a lot of attention, in its origins, its consequences, and in the way it influenced his work.[53] Without presuming to add to the discussion, I would like to consider Britten's pacifism simply as one of the beliefs that shaped his thought, although it may be argued that it is the one political belief that had the most practical consequences (because of it for example he had to endure a tribunal during the war). Some commentators recognise it as an element that contributed to his feeling of being an outcast from society. From my point of view, what is most relevant about Britten's pacifism is that the works inspired by it are examples of his 'activism'.

RADIO DAYS

Auden left the GPO Unit in the spring of 1936, but his collaboration with Britten continued until the end of the Second World War. Auden wanted to use every chance of having his voice heard, and not being satisfied with writing articles, publishing poems and working on documentary films, decided to make use of radio and theatre, which he considered important openings for his political activism. His political concerns shaped all his works of this period: when in 1937 he produced a broadcast about Hadrian's Wall, for which Britten was asked to write the incidental music, he explained the general conception of it:

> It stood as a symbol for a certain imperialistic conception of war, for military discipline and an international order. In opposition to the Celt and Germanic tribal loyalties which overwhelmed it, only to be transformed in their turn, into the catholic world picture... the front of History now lies elsewhere, but the same issues, of *order* versus *liberty*; the State versus

---

[52] As quoted in MITCHELL 1981, p.66. The article from the *Manchester Guardian* is also reproduced in MITCHELL 1978, picture 92.
[53] Donald Mitchell has discussed the subject on various occasions, and recently in his essay 'Violent Climates' in COOKE 1999, pp.188–216; Britten's pacifism is also the subject of the introductory chapter in COOKE 1996, pp.1–19.

the individual; the more highly economically developed races versus the less, still remains... So, first and foremost, the wall is shown in this broadcast as an idea, part of an international structure, and a boundary in time.[54]

One should remember that in those years Auden also provided the text for several of Britten's works, amongst which it is relevant to mention *Our Hunting Fathers* op.8, *On This Island* op.11 and (together with Randall Swingler) *Ballad of Heroes* op.14. All these works are influenced by a belief in practical rather than theoretical involvement in social problems. In 1939 Britten left England and spent two years in America. Auden had already moved there, and they both looked upon the new continent as a kind of promised land. Recollecting those days, Britten said: 'It seemed the best idea then... to get on with one's work as best one could. At least in the States I could work, could be of some use to other people. Here again I was enormously influenced by Auden'.[55] In America they collaborated on a number of radio broadcasts,[56] as well as the operetta *Paul Bunyan* (of which more later). But Auden was growing more and more disillusioned about what impact art could effectively have. Having been active in a practical way in Spain, where, although not directly fighting, he provided help by driving an ambulance, he now developed a dry scepticism, and was left with little hope in the effectiveness of art's influence upon society. As Louis MacNeice pointed out, by 1940 Auden 'had repudiated propaganda'.[57]

After the beginning of the war Britten realised that for him the best way of being 'useful to people' was to return to England, and so he did.[58] Here he had to come to terms with a different reality from the one he had left. Because of his pacifist beliefs, he refused to join the army, and had to appear before a tribunal in July 1942; in a statement to the Local Tribunal for the Registration of Conscentious objectors he writes

---

[54] 'Broadcast about a ruin', *Radio Times*, 19 November 1937, p.9.
[55] WARRACK 1964, p.20.
[56] See Table 2.
[57] Quoted in HEWISON 1977, p.8. Hewison presents an excellent picture of the apparent impasse in which British artists found themeselves after the Munich crisis of 1938, a situation made worse by Auden's and Isherwood's departure.
[58] He arrived in Liverpool on 17 April 1942, having waited for a ship back to Europe for almost a year.

> Since I believe that there is in every man the spirit of God, I cannot destroy, and feel it my duty to avoid helping to destroy as far as I am able, human life, however strongly I may disapprove of the individual's actions or thoughts. The whole of my life has been devoted to acts of creation (being by profession a composer), and I cannot take part in acts of destructions. Moreover, I feel that the fascist attitude to life can only be overcome by passive resistance. [...] I believe sincerely that I can help my fellow human beings best, by continuing the work I am most qualified to do by the nature of my gifts and training, i.e. the creation or propagation of music. I have possibilities of writing music for M.O.I.,[59] films, and for B.B.C. productions, and am offering my services to the Committee for the Encouragement of Music and Art. I am however prepared, but feel completely unsuited by nature & training, to undertake other constructive civilian work provided that it is not connected with any of the armed forces.[60]

Britten's appeal was succesful, and amongst the statements of support that helped him to be unconditionally exempted from active service was the following one from the BBC:

> This is to bring to the notice of the Tribunal considering the case of Mr. Benjamin Britten that Mr. Britten has been commissioned by us to write music for a series of important broadcast programmes designed to explain this country to listeners in America, and we hope to be able to use Mr. Britten's services for musical composition in connection with a large number of similar programmes in the immediate future.[61]

The series mentioned were two war-time 'propaganda' broadcasts: *An American in England* and *Britain to America.* Britten's musical services were also used for *The Rescue*, an elaborate musico-dramatic radio feature about Odysseus' return to Ithaca with a text by Edward Sackville-West. Sackville-West conceived the work as a 'radio-opera', and it is interesting to note that when presenting the project to his superior at the

---

[59] The Ministry of Information, that had been formed immediately after the outbreak of the war, and that used films as part of the wartime propaganda. See MITCHELL 1991, p.1047.
[60] Quoted in MITCHELL 1991 (p.1046), which also provides a more detailed account of Britten's return to England and of the process that allowed the exemption from military duties.
[61] From the Britten file of the BBC internal papers at the BBC written archives. Quoted in FOREMAN 1988, p.30.

BBC, he proposed 'a dramatic composition on the return of Odysseus, designed to bring out the parallel between the position of Ithaca then and that in Greece generally now – Penelope (the symbol of Greece) surrounded by Quislings, invading generals etc., Odysseus returning as the leader of a sort of Commando...'.[62] So once more we see Britten involved in a project whose symbolism and metaphorical meaning had political implications. From the start music was to have a relevant part in the project, and the drama was conceived as a melodrama: music plays an integral part in it and the dramatic structure was planned with a view to giving the composer at least as many opportunities as myself... In writing *The Rescue* some of the awkwardness incident to radio-drama were automatically removed for me by the operatic nature of the composition, which was deliberately built upon an hypothetical structure of music... [...] I have sub-titled the piece 'a melodrama' using the word in its original sense, i.e. 'a play, usually romantic and sensational in plot and incident, in which songs are interspersed and in which the action is accompanied by orchestral music appropriate to the situations'.[63]

Amongst other things, Sackville-West describes the effect produced by soliloquies accompanied by an orchestral commentary as 'a new kind of aria'.[64] The first broadcast was a considerable success, and Val Gielgud, producer of several of its revivals, considered it 'one of the most interesting plays ever written especially for broadcasting'.[65] Talking about the music George Bernard Shaw said:

> I was very much struck by a broadcast of a classical play with music by Benjamin Britten. It had style and great refinement. He handled his trumpets beautifully; and his manner was not the lawless post-Wagnerism that now sounds so tiresomely old-fashioned, but in the tradition of Gluck, Berlioz and Chopin. It had the forgotten quality of elegance.[66]

The Rescue was a remarkably visionary project, and one can certainly marvel at the fact that in war-time England the BBC had invested considerable resources in such an experimental work. Before we leave

---

[62] Quoted in FOREMAN 1988, p.30.
[63] SACKVILLE-WEST 1945, pp.8–9.
[64] SACKVILLE-WEST 1945, p.14.
[65] In FOREMAN 1998, p.31.
[66] Quoted in REED, PHILIP 1996, 'Britten and "The Rescue"', p.7.

Broadcasting House it is worth mentioning briefly another radio drama: *The Dark Tower*, by Louis MacNeice. Broadcast in January 1946, it is one of the last pieces of incidental music that Britten wrote; at the end of the war, and after the success of *Grimes*, his career moved in a different direction.

What is interesting about *The Dark Tower* in the present context is the fact that it is called a 'radio parable play':

> It tells how "Childe Roland to the dark tower came" – Roland the last of the family of heroes, questioning by nature where his brothers and forefathers had accepted their crusade, beguiled on the way by many temptations, recalled by his dying mother, and through that call suddenly made aware of his mission's significance.[67]

The story is told in verse, rich in metaphor and symbol. MacNeice dedicated the play to Britten, because 'without his music, *The Dark Tower* lacks a dimension'.[68] In this work we again find themes dear to Britten: the questioning of values, the importance of inner coherence, life as a stage on which everyone has to play a responsible rôle. In particular, it is the concept of parable that keeps occurring through the composer's work, and it is a concept that, even if not directly expressed, had already been present during Britten's involvement in theatrical productions during the thirties.

---

[67] MANN, WILLIAM 1952, p.307. The story has a echo of that of Owen Wingrave.
[68] Quoted in MANN, WILLIAM 1952, p.307.

TABLE 2: INCIDENTAL MUSIC FOR RADIO BROADCAST[69]

TITLE	RADIO	COLLABORATORS	DATE OF BROADCAST
King Arthur	BBC Radio	Geoffrey Bridson	23.iv.1936
The Company of Heaven	BBC Radio	R. Ellis Roberts	29.ix.1937
Hadrian's Wall	BBC Radio	W.H. Auden	25.ix.1937
Lines on the Map	BBC Radio	S. Potter, J.H. Miller, D. Aitken, E. Alway	January to April 1938
The Chartists' March	BBC Radio	J.H. Miller	13.v.1938
The World of the Spirit	BBC Radio	R. Ellis Roberts	5.vi.1938
The Sword in the Stone	BBC Radio	M. Helweg adapted from T.H. White	11.vi.1939
The Dark Valley	CBS New York	W.H. Auden	2.vi.1940
The Dynasts	CBS New York	T. Hardy	24.xi.1940
The Rocking-Horse Winner	CBS New York	D.H. Lawrence adapted by W.H. Auden	6.iv.1941
Appointment	BBC Radio	Norman Corwin	20.vii.1942
An American in England	BBC Radio	Norman Corwin	July to September 1942
The Man Born to be King (episodes 10, 11)	BBC Radio	Dorothy Sayers	23.viii.1942 20.ix.1942
Lumberjacks of America	BBC Radio	Ranald MacDougal	1942
Britain to America	BBC Radio	Louis MacNeice	20.ix.1942 7.xi.1942 3.i.1943
The Four Freedoms: No.1 Pericles	BBC Radio	Louis MacNeice	21.ii.1943
The Rescue of Penelope	BBC Radio	E. Sackville-West	25, 26.xi.1943
A Poet's Christmas	BBC Radio Home Service	Text by W.H. Auden Produced by Edward Sackville-West	24.xii.1944
The Dark Tower	BBC Radio	Louis MacNiece	21.i.1946
Men of Goodwill	BBC Radio	L. Gilliam and L. Cattrell	25.xii.1947

---

[69] Data derived from REED, PHILIP 1987 and EVANS, JOHN 1987, pp.154−164.

POLITICAL THEATRE

Britten was certainly not new to the musico-dramatic dimension of the stage when he wrote *Peter Grimes*. Before *Paul Bunyan,* on a text by W.H. Auden, written for the American stage, during the thirties he had written the incidental music for no fewer than eleven plays.[70] Five of these, including *Easter 1916* (1935) and *Stay Down Miner* (1936) were by Montagu Slater, the librettist of *Grimes*, and were produced by Left Theatre, a theatre company with a strong political commitment.

Indeed, Left Theatre was the expression of a bigger cultural phenomenom, as the arts were one of the ways in which communist ideas entered Britain. Although Alick West states that the final aim 'was not the establishment of a political and economical structure, but the heightening of human life',[71] it is beyond doubt that the main drive of the movement was the concern about the Fascist threat, as well as what was seen as the failure of capitalist economics.[72] Thanks to the influence of a number of foreign refugees who were committed to developing an opposition to Fascism, many intellectuals and artists were attracted to the left in general and to communist politics in particular. Amongst them was Britten, who formed an association with a number of workers' choirs and was an active supporter of the 'Workers Musical Association' (WMA), founded in 1936, whose first president was Alan Bush and which counted amongst its members Hanns Eisler.

The association's ambitious programme included 'the promotion of socialist and communist songs from national and international sources, making performance skills available to all and defending the right of professional musicians'.[73] Bush in 1966 commented on how Britten had long ago moved away from direct participation in the struggle of the working class,[74] but there is little doubt that the concepts expressed in the WMA's mission statement were part of Britten's own manifesto until the end of his life.

---

[70] See Table 3.
[71] CROFT 1998, p.1.
[72] See HANLON 1998, pp.68–88.
[73] PORTER 1998, p.175.
[74] Alan Bush, 'Musicians and the Working Class in Britain', in *Essays in Honour of William Gallacher* (Berlin, 1966), quoted in HANLON 1998, p.84.

One of the principal methods of propaganda was the organizations of pageants:[75] 'The Communist party is learning to speak to the English workers in a language they understand. With new and varied methods of propaganda, based upon the knowledge of history and experience of the English workers [...] is revealing itself as the legitimate heir of generations of great English fighters for freedom and progress'.[76] Pageant-making by the mid-thirties was a familiar and relatively popular pastime, much used in the Co-operative movement, and amongst the prime movers of mass pageants in the late thirties were Randall Swingler and Montagu Slater. Britten collaborated with Slater in a pageant for the Co-operative movement in 1937, and wrote pieces for a number of the most ambitious one-off events aimed at serving progressive causes through music.[77] Slater's pageant scripts expressed concepts like:

> Nations, peoples, men and women
> Children in the glow of morning
> Make a ring around the aggressor
> Dispossess the dispossessor
> Build the warm alliance
> Of humanity for peace [...]
> Only in that unity is there
> Hope for mankind and peace.[78]

Slater was attempting a synthesis between formal experiment and a popular register, which is also reflected in his plays, also deeply politically committed: *Stay Down Miner* for example is about the struggle in a Welsh mining village, while *Easter 1916* is a significant text about the Dublin uprising.[79]

Notwithstanding the importance of the collaboration with Slater, especially in view of *Peter Grimes*, Britten's best-known incidental music for the theatre is for two of the plays that W.H. Auden wrote with

---

[75] These spectacular one-off mass-parades were organized professionally, and involved massive forces: for example, Montagu Slater's pageant *Towards tomorrow* involved 3000 performers and 6000 costumes, and it was performed before an audience of 78,000 at Wembley Stadium on 2 July 1938 (see WALLIS 1998, p.55).
[76] WALLIS 1998, p.49.
[77] HANLON 1998, p.71.
[78] Quoted in WALLIS 1998, p.55.
[79] See NICHOLSON 1996, p.215.

Christopher Isherwood. These plays were produced by the Group Theatre, for which Britten became 'house composer', providing incidental music for five productions between 1935 and 1938. Founded in 1932, and led by Rupert Doone, the Group was one of the many small theatre companies that appeared in the thirties. Some of these companies, such as the Left Theatre, were ideologically committed, and they generated a great amount of activity, introducing to the UK new works and challenging ideas. Although not ideologically committed, the Group Theatre was nonetheless adventurous and outward-looking, and, in the case of the Auden-Isherwood team, dedicated to the encouragement and discovery of new talents.[80] The repertoire of the Group Theatre included classic plays as well as new works.[81]

Talking about their original productions Rupert Doone said: 'The form we envisaged for our plays is analogous to modern musical comedy, or the premedieval Folk-Play'.[82] Probably one could read 'modern musical comedy' in terms of the Brecht-Weill musical theatre, and the German theatre of the twenties and thirties. Auden had spent several months in Berlin at the beginning of the thirties, and had direct experience of Brecht's work with Hanns Eisler and Kurt Weill.

Brecht himself viewed Doone, Auden and Isherwood as sympathizers and allies: their names appear in a list of theatre people that Brecht was planning to approach for the creation of an international 'Diderot Society' to circulate papers on 'theatrical science'.[83] According to Donald Mitchell, it is beyond any doubt that *Die Dreigroschenoper* and *Aufstieg und Fall der Stadt Mahagonny* influenced Auden and Isherwood when they were writing *The Dog Beneath the Skin*, as there are clear similarities in form and in the attention they paid to the music.[84]

---

[80] On the subject of the Group Theatre see SIDNELL 1984.
[81] Britten wrote the incidental music for Shakespeare's *Timon of Athens* and Aeschylus' *Agamemnon* (see Table 3).
[82] Monroe K. Spears, *The poetry of W.H. Auden* (New York: Oxford University Press, 1965), p.92; quoted in JENNINGS 1979, p.27.
[83] See MITCHELL 1981, p.96.
[84] MITCHELL 1981, p.120.

TABLE 3: INCIDENTAL MUSIC FOR THE THEATRE[85]

PLAY	AUTHOR	COMPANY AND VENUE	FIRST NIGHT
Timon of Athens	W. Shakespeare	*Group Theatre* Westminster Theatre, London	19.xi.1935
Easter 1916	Montagu Slater	*Left Theatre* Islington Town Hall, London	4.xii.1935
Stay Down Miner	Montagu Slater	*Left Theatre* Westminster Theatre, London	10.v.1936
The Agamemnon	Louis MacNeice from Aeschylus	*Group Theatre* Westminster Theatre, London	1.xi.1936
The Ascent of F6	W.H. Auden, C. Isherwood	*Group Theatre* Mercury Theatre, London	26.ii.1937
Pageant of Empire	Montagu Slater	*Left Theatre* Collin's Music Hall, London	28.ii.1937
Out of the Picture	Louis MacNeice	*Group Theatre* Westminster Theatre, London	5.xii.1937
Spain	Montagu Slater	Mercury Theatre, London	22.vi.1938
On The Frontier	W.H. Auden, C. Isherwood	*Group Theatre* Arts Theatre, Cambridge	14.xi.1938
They Walk Alone	Max Catto	"Q" Theatre, London	21.xi.1938
Johnson over Jordan	J.B. Priestley	New Theatre, London	22.ii.1939
An Agreement of the People	Montagu Slater	*Co-operative Society* Wembley Stadium, London	1942
This Way to the Tomb	Ronald Duncan	*Pilgrim Players* Mercury Theatre, London	11.x.1945
The Eagle has Two Heads	Ronald Duncan from Jean Cocteau	*Company of Four* Lyric Theatre, Hammersmith,	4.ix.1946
The Duchess of Malfi	John Webster	Metropolitan Theatre Providence, Rhode Island	20.ix.1946
Stratton	Ronald Duncan	Theatre Royal, Brighton	31.x.1949
Am - Stram - Gram	André Roussin	Tonybee Hall, London	4.iii.1954
The Punch Revue	W.H. Auden, W. Plomer	Duke of York's, London	28.ix.1955

[85] Data mainly derived from REED, PHILIP 1987 and EVANS, JOHN 1987, pp.144−153.

Britten's music for *The Ascent of F6* and *On The Frontier* pays homage to cabaret and popular music of the time, and is strongly influenced by jazz: it was exactly the use of a popular idiom that was to serve the drama, in accordance with Brechtian theories of epic theatre. Talking about one of the best-know examples of Britten's incidental music – the Blues from *The Ascent of F6* – Donald Mitchell remarks:

> The choral version from the play, so colourfully and yet economically accompanied by two pianos and percussion, fully reveals Britten's mastery of a popular idiom, which he was able to transform and transcend, and thus lift the blues out of its familiar environment and make it serve as a vehicle for the release of the upsurge of feeling that breaks surface with the death of James Ransom in act II scene v of the play; and yet, at the same time, the blues retains its association with, as it were, the cabaret world, entertainment, life's triviality. For a few timeless and ironic rather than satiric minutes, the feelings proper to the cabaret song and the funeral dirge are experienced *simultaneously* through the unifying agency of the music; and it is the disturbing simultaneity of the experience that is primarily responsible for the powerful impact that the ensemble makes.[86]

It is the intelligent use of irony, more than the angry outlet of satire, that reveals in these plays a subtle attempt to influence the consciousness of their audiences. The message is not a ferocious attack that looks for scandal and reaction, but a contained protest that makes its point by creating psychological unease, in order to cause a deeper inner change.

The most ambitious score Britten produced in the thirties was for J.B. Priestley's three-act 'modern morality' *Johnson over Jordan*. Although intended for the commercial theatre it was a highly experimental play. Priestley was an exponent of the avant-garde in his exploration of the concept of time within plays, and in his fusion of different elements – music, dance, mime, scenery and lighting – in order to create not simply a play, but a global theatrical experience.

> Priestley acknowledged the *Tibetan book of the dead* as the source for *Johnson*, in particular the condition known as *bardo*, a peculiar hallucinatory state somewhere between life and death. The play concerns

---

[86] MITCHELL 1981, p.122.

the recently deceased Robert Johnson – an Everyman figure – whose life history is played out in reverse order. Aspects of his character are explored in a series of scenes taken from a widely dispersed chronological sequence. The climax of the play is reached when he must be released from the state of *bardo,* and peacefully bid farewell to all that has been familiar.[87]

In the light of his later development, it is not difficult to see why Britten might have been interested in working with Priestley: the concept of morality play (a didactic, ritualistic and non-realistic enactment of a story) was very near to the forms envisaged by the manifesto of the Group Theatre, and Britten went back to it not only in the second canticle and in *Noye's Fludde*, but also in the church parables, and less explicitly in many other works. Furthermore, the experimental aspects of the work, the ambiguity of the temporal dimension, and especially the balanced overall structure in which every element – especially the music – had a fundamental part to play towards the achievement of the final impact, must certainly have appealed to him. *Johnson* was the last piece of incidental music Britten wrote before leaving England, although after *Grimes*, in the years between 1945 and 1955, he still wrote music for six plays, of which probably the most interesting were two of Ronald Duncan's plays, as they constituted a precedent for their collaboration on *The Rape of Lucretia*.

AN AMERICAN INTERLUDE

While in the States, Britten and Auden had the opportunity to capitalise on their experience in the theatre with a work written especially for the American stage. The idea of *Paul Bunyan* was first suggested by Hans Heinsheimer, whom Britten had met in Vienna in 1934; having emigrated to America in 1938, he was by now an American citizen and was working there for Boosey & Hawkes. In a letter to Ralph Hawkes, Britten mentions that Heinsheimer had told him about immense opportunities for 'an operetta for children', for which he had ideas and was going to write about to Auden.[88] Britten apparently had been fascinated by Aaron Copland's *The Second Hurricane*, a play-opera[89] designed for high-

---

[87] REED, PHILIP 1994, p.53.
[88] Letter dated 29 June 1939. See MITCHELL 1991, p.675.
[89] *The Second Hurricane*, a play opera for high school performance, libretto by Edward Denby, music by Aaron Copland, was first staged in New York in April 1937, directed by

school performance that the American composer had played through for him during a visit to Snape in 1938, and that Mitchell identifies as a source for *Bunyan*.[90] Britten himself suggests the possibility of Copland's influence in an interview for the *New York Sun*,[91] when he also mentions plans for a first performance in a Broadway theatre.

From Britten's letters of this period it is quite clear that the composer was hoping to find work in Broadway, but even more importantly in Hollywood, not so much out of a real interest in the commercial film as a medium, but because he considered this a quick way to consolidate his financial position: he wanted to be able to take financial care of his family, relatives and friends, whom he was trying to convince to evacuate to the States, away from the war, an idea that he mentions over and over again.[92] For this reason he signed a contract with an agent in Hollywood, Abe Meyer, arranged with the help of Aaron Copland, in the hope of obtaining some film work: in a letter to Meyer[93] he lists his experience in the field of incidental music, but returning the signed contract he also specifies that he was not keen to travel to the West 'unless it be for a really good picture & a good fee'.[94] To have a success on the Broadway stage would surely have increased his chances to land a good contract in California, which had become the ultimate goal for several Europeans artists, including Auden, who also was hoping to use *Bunyan* as a vehicle for Hollywood, as it is made clear by the final telegram 'from Hollywood' received by John Inkslinger, Auden's fictional alter-ego,[95] in the last scene of the work.

Although by the end the best Britten's publishers were able to organize was a premiere on 5 May 1941 at the Brander Matthew Hall of Columbia University,[96] given by the Columbia Theater Associates, a mainly

---

Orson Welles. Vocal score published by Boosey & Hawkes (New York, 1937). See MITCHELL 1991, p.567.

[90] MITCHELL 1991, p.567.

[91] Interview with William G. King, *New York Sun*, 27 April 1949, quoted in MITCHELL 1991, p.709.

[92] For example in a letter to his sister dated 30 June 1940, where he says he could guarantee 'maintanance in this country — & that of any young relations or friends you know who can get away'. See MITCHELL 1991, p.822.

[93] Dated 2 July 1940. In MITCHELL 1991, p.824.

[94] See MITCHELL 1991, p.821.

[95] MITCHELL 1991, p.925.

[96] See CARPENTER 1992, p.147.

amateur group, previous plans had included the possibility of professional Broadway performances by George Balanchine and Lincoln Kirstein's Ballet Caravan, the company that had commissioned Copland's *Billy the Kid*.[97] In a letter to his sister Britten writes that 'Wystan & my opera is settled for Broadway',[98] and this notion opens the way to some considerations about the genre to which *Paul Bunyan* belongs: the work, generally defined an 'operetta', as in the title-page of the published vocal score[99] or of the libretto,[100] it is referred to by both Auden and Britten in several occasions as 'opera', as well as 'choral operetta' or 'high school operetta', and in the critical literature, where it is often referred to as Britten's first opera,[101] the terms 'folk-opera'[102] and 'musical comedy'[103] also appear. Donald Mitchell has pointed out the formal ambiguity of the work ('the show, the operetta – call you what you will – more nearly approaches what we recognise as opera'),[104] and so have Arnold Whittall ('something more than a mere "quasi-musical"')[105] and Michael Kennedy, who would ascribe to the work the generic term 'music theatre' ('It is an hybrid, with Gilbert and Sullivan, John Gay, and Kurt Weill among its ancestry, but it is essentially operatic').[106]

There is no doubt that the work was written with Broadway in mind, as the textual and musical references to American popular idiom make clear: Auden and Britten indulged in their passion for a Cole Porter-like style that they had already imitated in the *Cabaret songs*, but one can also find the shadows of Rogers, Hart and the Gershwins.[107] Also, the term 'choral operetta', used by the authors to define a work 'with many small parts rather than a few star roles',[108] points to a work written for a Broadway 'chorus', as well as for the amateur market. It also refers to the initial

---

[97] See SAMSON 1997, p.12, and MITCHELL 1991, p.646.
[98] Letter to Beth Welford dated 19 October 1939, see MITCHELL 1991, p.707.
[99] *Paul Bunyan: an operetta in two acts and a prologue* op.17 (London: Faber, 1978).
[100] W.H. Auden, *Paul Bunyan: the libretto of the operetta by Benjamin Britten* (London: Faber, 1988). See also Arnold Whittall's article on the work in *The New Grove's Dictionary of Opera* (London: Macmillan, 1992).
[101] See for example REED, PHILIP 1995, p.275, and KILDEA 1999, p.47.
[102] KILDEA 1999, p.49.
[103] NEWILL 1978, p.63, and also HINDLEY 1994, p.42.
[104] See AUDEN 1988, p.104.
[105] WHITTALL 1982, p.69.
[106] KENNEDY 1981, p.159.
[107] See SAMSON 1997, p.14.
[108] In the original programme note, quoted in the publisher's note to the vocal score of the work (London: Faber, 1978), p.ix.

influence on Britten of Copland's *The Second Hurricane*, a work where the musical commentary is mainly entrusted to the choruses commenting on the adventure of a group of children lost in the middle of a hurricane, and whose model was Kurt Weill's school opera *Der Jasager*, with a text by Bertold Brecht.[109] Auden, who apparently had taken as a model for *Bunyan* Dryden's *King Arthur*,[110] claimed that there was no conscious German influence on any of his plays, although later in his life admitted that Brecht was amongst those from whom he had learned most;[111] and as we have seen, his theatrical collaboration with Isherwood was at least coloured by a Brechtian influence.[112]

It could therefore prove fruitful to look at *Bunyan* in the light of Britten and Auden's previous collaboration on the London stage, and of the politically aware theatre of the thirties, when Broadway was not the political awareness-free zone we might have come to think of in the Lloyd Webber era. As David Ewen points out, even in the United States "the thirties were an age interested in social and political problems, in crusades, in the common man",[113] and the Broadway stage reflected this interest:

> The musical theatre often became a sensitive sounding board [...] Social themes, political problems, labor conflicts, the question of war and peace, the menace of Fascism often invaded the musical stage; and the humor and satire of the times often cut deeply into the overriding issues and personalities of this era.[114]

After the Great Depression of 1929 the musical stage had moved away from the frivolous twenties comedies, and challenged its audiences with more serious subjects; its political relevance had been sanctioned in 1932, when for the first time a musical comedy, *Of thee I sing*, with music by George Gershwin and lyrics by Ira Gershwin on a libretto by George S. Kaufman and Morrie Ryskind,[115] was awarded the prestigious Pulitzer

---

[109] See MITCHELL 1991, p.635.
[110] SAMSON 1997, p.13.
[111] See NEWILL 1978, p.13.
[112] MITCHELL 1981, p.120.
[113] EWEN 1961, p.140.
[114] EWEN 1961, p.140.
[115] The work had opened in New York at the Music Box Theatre on 26 December 1931. An ambitious sequel, *Let them eat cakes*, a satire on revolution that drew its plot from the Great

Prize. The same authors had already hit Broadway in 1930 with one of the most provocative and original musicals of all times, *Strike up the Band*,[116] a brilliant anti-war satire, and in both cases the style was the same: a profoundly serious subject reduced to the ridiculous by the kind of paradoxes and absurdities commonly associated with Gilbert and Sullivan. Political awareness and social criticism became a new trend, triggered by the Depression and sustained by the ethics of Roosevelt's government, with its belief in the social function of art: in 1935 it launched through the WPA (Work Progress Administration) a Federal Art Project to sponsor a 'federal art relief' programme contemplating, amongst other initiatives, a nation-wide theatre organisation, the Federal Theatre.[117]

One of the strongest protests against war of the period is to be found in *Johnny Johnson*, which opened on Broadway on November 19th, 1936, with music by Kurt Weill on a libretto by Paul Green: with this work, according to a commentator, 'Fascism, the threat of war and then the war itself cast their shadow over the Broadway musical stage'.[118] Green had described the play as a fable, and it is 'a kind of parable filled with social criticism'.[119] It is the story of Johnny Johnson, an ordinary man who hates war but finds himself in the middle of it, tries to stop it and fails; though he is considered a madman, he never loses his faith in humanity. The story, which now and then touches on parody and satire, is told in terms of vaudeville, fantasy and poetry, and its structure is so innovative that it is unclear whether it is a musical or a play with music,[120] although it fits well into Weill's epic conception of 'new operatic theatre',[121] in a time when his central artistic aim was the 'creation of new forms and concepts of musical theater'.[122]

Depression and the rise of Nazi Germany did not repeat the success of *Of thee I sing*, that ran for 441 performances, and, having opened in New York at the Imperial Theatre on 21 October 1933, closed after only 90 performances.

[116] Premiered in New York at the Times Square Theatre on 14 January 1930. A critic, William Bolitho, wrote: 'Here is a bitter satirical attack on war, genuine propaganda at times, sung and danced on Broadway' (quoted in AYLESWORTH 1985, p.108).

[117] See MITCHELL 1991, pp.635–6, and DREW 1987, p.294.

[118] EWEN 1961, p.140.

[119] EWEN 1961, p.140.

[120] See SANDERS 1980, p.228.

[121] See KOWALKE 1995, p.26.

[122] See SANDERS 1980, p.125.

Weill had arrived in New York in September 1935, rich from the experience of his collaboration with Brecht and admired in artistic circles as the author of *The Threepenny Opera*, which had played in Broadway in 1933; after the success of *Johnson* he and Green received a commission from the Federal Theatre for 'a large-scale musico-dramatic portrayal of the beginnings of the American constitution', which Weill saw as 'a picture of early America, completely different from the one we are used to', [123] to be presented in the form of a pageant (which is near to the non-Aristotelian concept of epic theatre).[124] Another project for the Federal Theatre that Weill never completed was *The Ballad of Davy Crockett*, on a text by Hoffman R. Hays, which was to be a much idealised chronicle of the life of the folk-hero. Weill went on to write *Knickerbocker Holiday*, a musical comedy with book and lyrics by Maxwell Anderson,[125] a satire on the early days of New York in the seventeenth century, when the city still was a Dutch colony called New Amsterdam.

It would seem that on Broadway there was a demand for plays about American mythology, or folklore, about the early days of a nation that under the New Deal was apparently trying to reconquer a sense of identity greatly shaken by the economic crisis of 1929. This would explain the choice of the subject for the Britten-Auden operetta, otherwise quite surprising for a couple of Englishmen, although we know that the subject was also dictated by Boosey & Hawkes's demand for something suitable for high schools.[126] Heather Newill points out that 'the stories of Paul Bunyan are so popular in America that, having so little knowledge of the folk background, their operetta was bound to appear unconvincing'.[127]

---

[123] DREW 1987, p.294.
[124] *The Common Glory*, a musical play with text by Paul Green, never completed.
[125] Opened at the Ethel Barrymore Theatre in New York on 19 October 1938. The score features one of Weill's most famous numbers, 'September song'.
[126] See the publisher's note to the vocal score of the work (London: Faber, 1978), p.ix. Indeed, the choice of an American subject and the nationality of the authors was object of criticism: a review on *Time Magazine* describes the work as 'an anaemic operetta put up by two British expatriates' (quoted in NEWILL 1978, p.3).
[127] NEWILL 1978, p.4.

Although not so well known in Europe as other 'heroes' from the American Olympus, the figure of Paul Bunyan, the giant lumberjack, was and still is extremely popular amongst American children.[128] Bunyan is not an historical character, and indeed some of the claims of the legend are quite extreme: apart from his size, that of an American Gargantua who stood as tall as the Empire State Building, Paul would have cut the Grand Canyon by dragging his pick behind him, and the 10.000 lakes around Minneapolis would have been originated by the tracks made by Paul and his pet blue ox, Babe.[129] Like other American heroes, he seems to have born out of America's demand for 'larger than life characters, giant symbols representing America's success in conquering her enemies and cultivating her wilderness'.[130] Apparently Auden did not use any of the original tale, *The marvellous exploits of Paul Bunyan*, issued in 1922 by W.B. Laughead, which first introduced the hero to the American public,[131] and that would probably have provided him with a more 'fantastic' tale, more apt for a work written for children, or even for teenagers. But it is quite clear that he was writing with an adult audience in mind, and that both authors were looking at it as something more than mere entertainment for kids: in an interview Britten expresses the hope that the work 'will have an appeal for adult audiences',[132] and writing to his publisher about Auden's libretto he describes it as 'very witty but nevertheless serious in the fundamental idea'.[133] In the original programme note, the authors explain how they conceive of Paul Bunyan, the giant hero of the Lumbermen, and one of the many mythical figures who appeared in American folklore during the Pioneer period, as "…a projection of the collective state of mind of a people whose tasks were primarily the physical mastery of nature. This operetta presents in a compressed fairy-story form the development of the continent from a virgin forest before the

---

[128] The figure of Bunyan is still very much part of the American folklore: in Brainerd, Minnesota, there is a theme park dedicated to Bunyan's adventures, and Bemidji, a town further north, has well known attractions with prominent Bunyan themes. A giant statue of the mighty logger stands in both towns. Anybody who has seen the movie *Fargo*, by the Cohen brothers, might have noticed the constant background presence of the lumberjack's figure, who, together with his blue ox, has become a symbol for that area of the United States, north of Minneapolis.

[129] Also, he had seven giant axmen, all called Elmer, a magical reindeer, Hoofer, and some giant ants which he trained and could do each the work of 50 men. John Inkslinger is also reputed to have invented book-keeping and the pen.

[130] NEWILL 1978, p.4.

[131] NEWILL 1978, p.8.

[132] See MITCHELL 1991, p.709.

[133] Letter to Ralph Hawkes, dated 7 December 1939, in MITCHELL 1991, p.740.

birth of Paul Bunyan to settlement and cultivation when Paul Bunyan says goodbye because he is no longer needed, i.e., the human task is now a different one, of how to live well in a country that the pioneers have made it possible to live in".[134]

Rather than a musical divertissement about a jolly giant and his two- and four-legged companions, *Paul Bunyan* is thus a 'parable on the theme of man conquering nature, symbolised by the progression in America from the jungle-hacking society of Bunyan to contemporary civilisation, and the struggle to maintain it'.[135] In an interesting article written for the New York Times on 4 May 1941,[136] the day before the first performance, Auden explains how his interest in Bunyan was dictated by the fact that this legend is a myth, a poetical view of history, that is unique in its genre because it was created 'after the occurrence of the industrial revolution'. He also describes the characters associated with the hero as 'eternal human types':

> Helson, the man of brawn but no brains, invaluable as long as he has somebody to give him orders whom he trusts, but dangerous when his consciousness of lacking intelligence turns into suspicion and hatred of those who possess it; and Inkslinger, the man of speculative and critical intelligence, whose temptation is to despise those who do the manual work that makes the life of thought possible.[137]

The didactic intent of the piece is evident in Auden's comment that 'both of them learn a lesson in their relations with Paul Bunyan; Helson through a physical fight in which he is the loser, Inkslinger through his stomach'.[138] What we might be dealing with, then, is a didactic piece whose dramatic structure responds to the demands of epic theatre, thus constituting a logical continuation of the previous Britten and Auden's collaborations in England.[139] *Bunyan* is a moral tale with a didactic quality, which brings us back to the work of Weill and Brecht, and to a work that, although in a different way, also looks upon America as a mythical land, *The Rise and Fall of Mahagonny*: both work use America

---

[134] Quoted in the publisher's note to the vocal score of the work (London: Faber, 1978), p.ix.
[135] HINDLEY 1994, p.45.
[136] In AUDEN 1988, pp.1–4.
[137] AUDEN 1988, p.2.
[138] AUDEN 1988, p.2.
[139] This idea is also suggested in WHITE 1983, p.116.

as a pretext to present universal problems, and their characters are everyman-like figures acting out the moral tale.[140]

It is interesting to note that Britten met Kurt Weill in Maine on August 1940, while working on *Bunyan*, and according to a letter to Elizabeth Mayer they spent quite a lot of time together.[141] The two men had several friends in common, amongst them Hans Heinsheimer, who had suggested the idea of a school operetta to Britten, and who had been Weill's publisher in Europe in the thirties;[142] we have no records of their conversations, but it is quite clear that both composers shared artistic interests, including that for a socially conscious didactic music theatre. Donald Mitchell points out a fact that can be considered a coincidence, but that is nonetheless very interesting from our point of view: although at the time of the meeting Weill was already working at *Lady in the Dark*, which was to be his first successful musical, [143] we know that in his draft for the unfinished *Davy Crockett* he had contemplated 'four so-called "Interscenes", which comprised a hillybilly narrative song', a feature similar to the narrative ballads in *Paul Bunyan* (even more striking is the fact that in both cases the second ballad talks about the hero's marriage).[144] Mitchell suggests there might be a chance that the two composers might have discussed the subject, in terms of 'exploiting an authentically American idiom',[145] but whether those discussions happened, in whatever terms, or not, there is no doubt that the ballad, or narrative song, brings us back to the forms of epic theatre. What we know is that according to Mordecai Baumann, the original ballad singer, these interludes were 'a last-minute improvisation', brought in 'because nothing was happening on stage except ideas'.[146] Baumann's remark is particularly interesting, and indeed, if we look at *Paul Bunyan* from a dramaturgical point of view, there are some observations to be made. We can quite safely say that it is a non–Aristotelian work: although most of the action on stage takes place in the lumberjacks' camp (although the

---

[140] See NEWILL 1978, p.13. A detailed study and comparison of the two works would certainly prouve very interesting, but it is beyond the scope of the present study.
[141] Letter dated 22 August 1940, in MITCHELL 1991, p.845.
[142] Heinsheimer was therefore well acquainted to Weill's school-opera *Der Jasager* when he suggested to Britten a work for children.
[143] *Lady in the Dark*, a musical play by Moss Hart, with lyrics by Ira Gershwin, opened in New York on 23 January 1941.
[144] See AUDEN 1988, p.112–113.
[145] AUDEN 1988, p.113.
[146] See AUDEN 1988, pp.114–15.

dream-like sequence of the 'Blues' is ambiguous in its location), thus providing a sort of unity of space, it does not respect the principle of unity of time, and the unity of action is lacking. We can certainly trace a main line of narration, from Paul's birth to his farewell, but in its nature the work does not have the dramatic urgency of a tightly integrated plot, and it is rather episodic: it is indeed a numbers show, a "company" piece where everybody gets the spot at least once.

Some of the numbers, like the 'Blues', the 'Cats's creed' or indeed 'Inkslinger's song', are on the whole self-sufficient, although not out of the context of a narrative, as they would be in a revue. The action is mainly carried through in the form of narration, in the ballads or in Paul's monologues: what happens on stage is mostly an excuse for entertainment. If we look at the dramatic development of the story, what we have in the whole of the first act is simply the setting up of the camp, with the arrival of the lumberjacks (nos.3a to 5), of Hel Helson (following the King of Sweden's telegram, no. 6), of the cooks followed by Inkslinger (no.7), and of the animals (no.8). By the end of the scene, with Bunyan's goodnight, nothing has really happened: the lumberjack's entry is a big danced choral number in the best Broadway tradition, we know that the animals were introduced as a pretext for using female voices,[147] and the cooks's number, together with the food chorus in the second scene (which indeed provides another choral number), seems a pretext for the introduction here of Inkslinger, and in the second scene of Slim, whom together with Tiny is to provide the love interest, indispensable in a musical.

Similar considerations apply to the following 'Second ballad', which is necessary to introduce the character of Tiny, and also reinforces the perception that Bunyan is not, after all, our protagonist, because we could have otherwise expected his own 'love story' to have greater relevance in the economy of the piece. As Auden (who almost admits of having no interest whatsoever in Paul's romantic life) points out, Paul is not a human character, which is why he is presented as a speaking role, and as a consequence the chief dramatic role is played by Inkslinger, thus 'satisfying' according to the librettist, 'Henry James' plea for a fine lucid intelligence as a compositional centre'.[148] But even with Inkslinger as our leading man, in a story that

---

[147] As explained by Auden himself, see AUDEN 1988, p.3.
[148] AUDEN 1988, p.2.

according to Auden[149] has thus become Inkslinger's own process of discovery of Paul's mythical nature (a fact that surely undermines the concept of unity of action), by the end of the first act not much has really happened in the camp, if we overlook the importance of the changing of the guard in the kitchen.

Act II does not begin with a ballad, as one would have expected, but still with a narration, in which Paul reports on the lumberjacks' achievements, and on the developments of a new impulse 'towards settlement and cultivation'.[150] With the farmers' song (no.18a) we have another big choral number, and after Paul's patronising warning, we are left to witness the discontent in the camp, where the men incite Hel Helson to rebel; the following scene, 'The mocking of Hel Helson' (no.20), again provides an opportunity for a choral number, and it is difficult to sustain the argument that 'Fido's sympathy' (no.21) and the 'Cat's creed' (no.22), where the opposite nature of dogs and cats are compared as respectively Platonic and Aristotelian, are crucial to the development of the story, rather than a literary divertissement. When Paul, who had been away escorting the farmers to their destination, comes back to the camp, he is challenged by Hel, and it is during the ensuing fight (no.23) that we have one of the most striking moments in the work, because in the height of the fight, which of course happens off-stage, we have the insertion of the love duet between Slim and Tiny. Talking of this number Donald Mitchell has commented on the 'bold juxtaposition' of the 'highly dramatic (and operatic!) choral commentary on the fight' and the 'popular style of the love-duet, whose accents (text and music) are unmistakably those of the musical', as of a 'precise example of the mix of idioms that the first audience of *Paul Bunyan* perhaps found puzzling';[151] but maybe we could also look at the stylistic contrast, and even more at the irony of the lovers' comments about the noise of the fight, about which they do not care (although they probably should), as a device to detach the audience from the emotions involved both in the fight and in the romantic interlude, thus avoiding, in the best Brechtian traditon, any sentimental involvement.

---

[149] AUDEN 1988, p.2.
[150] See AUDEN 1988, p.50.
[151] See AUDEN 1988, p.105.

The seriousness of the fight, the only real dramatic occurrence in the play, is further undermined by the 'Mock Funeral March'; and after another of Paul's didactic interventions in the Hymn ('Often thoughts of hate conceal / Love we are ashamed to feel / In the climax of a fight / Lost affection comes to light'),[152] we are back to epic narration with the third and last ballad, where we partake of Paul and Hel's reconciliation, of all the great adventures and developments that followed, and of the progress of civilisation to the point where Paul's help is no longer necessary. The final scene, the Christmas party, is again a choral 'grand finale' where epic narration, rather than dramatic action, is predominant: Slim becomes a chef in New York, where he moves to with Tiny, now his wife; Hel Helson joins the administration in Washington, Inkslinger is summoned by Hollywood, and Paul says goodbye. In her analysis of the work dramaturgy, Heather Newill notices that Auden's satire frequently contradicts and destabilizes his telling of the story. This lack of continuity of thought and action is not entirely due to the pseudo-lore material with which he was working, but owes a great deal to his conception of the work as a whole. The characters he uses are all strongly enough portrayed to have formed the basis of an integrated story and successful operetta, but, somehow, Auden does not seem sure of exactly what kind of play he set out to write. It is by turns an epic, a romance and a satire, and the total effect produced is one of great confusion.[153]

There is no doubt that *Paul Bunyan* goes well beyond the limits of its stated *genre*, and is far away from the idea we could have of a Broadway operetta or musical comedy, if we think of it in the terms of, for example, the likes of Youmans' *No no Nanette*. But what could be seen as lack of stylistic consistency is not necessary a flaw of the work, and rather reinforces the impression that precisely because of its structure - that of a non-Aristotelian narration which develops through mostly self-contained numbers - as well for its didactic content, *Paul Bunyan* can be considered an example of epic theatre. I am not claiming that Britten and Auden set out to write a piece of Brechtian epic theatre, but that they had similar aims, and as Newill has pointed out the work indeed shares many similarities with *Mahagonny*, in terms of mixture of styles, use of strophic and popular songs, parody, and also in the use of an intermediary

---

[152] AUDEN 1988, p.62.
[153] NEWILL 1978, p.33.

figure, a narrator 'that brings the action up to date by filling in the unstaged historic details and sets the scene for the following action';[154] it is therefore possible that their intent was very near to the aesthetic of the German playwright, and even more of Weill's latest efforts towards a form of opera that reflected the spirit of the times, the *Zeitgeist*, both in form and content. It is probably for this reason that Auden did not write an opera libretto, but constructed his text as a quite innovative and experimental play for music,[155] with techniques derived from English ballad-opera, music-hall and musical comedy, Gilbert and Sullivan, Brecht and Weill, and even Greek tragedy (he looked at the ballad as a kind of 'solo Greek chorus').[156]

Paul Bunyan is not dramatically or musically weak, but its dramaturgy needs to be clarified to the light of his creators' intentions. As many audiences have had the pleasure of discovering in recent years, it is in its own terms a strong piece of theatre, with a score blessed with memorable tunes, a testimony to Britten's gift of melodic invention. We are unsure of what input Britten might have had in the planning of the libretto, but it would seems possible that musical considerations, rather than dramatical ones, were at the basis of the structure, thought out in terms of musical numbers linked by speech. This is not necessary a consequence of the fact that the piece was written for Broadway, but a sign of precise aesthetic intention, which probably also contemplated the eclectic use of popular musical forms; and is interesting to note that, while writing *Mahagonny*, Weill had commented on how the piece was being shaped according to purely musical considerations, a fact which for him was opening up entirely new perspectives;[157] indeed, to Weill the epic theatre concept did imply a dramatic structure delineated by its musical form - a form that required and emphasized musical simplicity (simplicity that is associated with the 'epic' attitude) in setting the text.[158]

---

[154] NEWILL 1978, p.14.

[155] The innovative nature of the work is recognised by Michael Kennedy, who even suggests that *Paul Bunyan* could claim to be the historical watershed for the renovation of the idiomatic American musical, traditionally associated with the first production of Rogers and Hammerstein's *Oklahoma!* in 1943 (KENNEDY 1981, p.161).

[156] AUDEN 1988, p.3.

[157] 'I am working with Brecht everyday on the libretto, which is being shaped entirely according to my instructions. This kind of collaboration, in which a libretto is actually formed according to purely musical considerations, opens up entirely new prospects' (letter to Universal Edition dated 18 November 1927, quoted in KOWALKE 1995, p.17).

[158] See BORWICK 1982, p.48.

Britten's eclectic score does respond to this demand for immediacy, and indeed the composer himself, talking of the his stylistic choice for the piece, refers to the *Cabaret Songs* when he defines some of the songs for *Bunyan* 'a little bit more serious than the Hedli tunes but very direct and simple, which is the kind of style I propose to use throughout the work',[159] a comment that once more brings us back to his collaboration with Auden in the Group Theatre. *Paul Bunyan* is more sophisticated than any of his incidental scores, and while keeping the tunes simple, often strophic, Britten makes use of a wider musical palette:[160] through parody and pastiche, extending back from Baroque idioms to the popular songs of the thirties, he creates strong characterizations, and the lack of 'any real, cohesive voice of authorship'[161] actually heightens the puppet-like aspect of the characters, again a characteristic of epic theatre, where stylistic consistency is not a required aesthetic parameter. Particularly interesting is the introduction of the folk-style for the ballads, accompanied on stage by a guitar and double-bass, which must have sounded quite extraordinary at the time ('Nobody knew about folk-style at the time')[162] and certainly unusual even on a Broadway stage, thus providing something similar to the alienation effect advocated by Brecht and Weill; and the use of jazz *formulae*, especially in the Blues, a number that is not necessary to the economy of the story (it is introduced as a dream sequence, and sung by a 'quartet of defeated') and that brings us back to the cynical cabaret-like world of *Mahagonny*.[163] Although Britten might fail to create 'the ironic tension characteristic of Weill',[164] this number betrays the didactic intent of the piece, an intent that is never more obvious than in the final 'Litany', where the chorus' refrain, 'Save animals and men', even brings an echo of *Our Hunting Fathers*.

In a review of the original production Virgil Thompson recognised the piece as 'an allegory or a morality', but he also commented that he found it 'utterly obscure and tenuous', and he could never 'figure out the

---

[159] Letter to Ralph Hawkes dated 7 December 1939, in MITCHELL 1991, p.740. The *Cabaret Songs* had been written for Hedli Anderson.
[160] For a more detailed musical analysis see for example EVANS 1989, pp.95−103, and KENNEDY pp.158−161.
[161] See KILDEA 1999, p.49.
[162] AUDEN 1988, p.119.
[163] The impression that the characters belong to the same world of Brecht's fictional town is reinforced by the mention of the Gold rush and of Alabama in the text of the 'Blues'.
[164] See EVANS 1989, p.97.

theme'.[165] Beyond the narrative presented by the authors in their explanation of the mythical implications of the legend, some commentators see in *Bunyan* Auden's own attempt to 'define America',[166] an impression which might be justified by Paul's final comments:

> Every day America' destroyed and re-created
> America is what you do
> America is I and you
> America is what you choose to make it

Auden certainly used the libretto to express his view on America, and this was probably one of the reasons for the lack of succes; but as he points out in his introduction to the work, 'the implications of the Bunyan legend are not only American, but universal',[167] and 'to define America' seems to be only a pretext to carry on preaching in his usual way, this time to a new audience:

> Until the advent of the machine the conquest of nature was still incomplete, and as users of the machine all countries share a common history. All countries are now faced at the same and for the first time with the same problem. Now that, in a material sense, we can do anything almost that we like, how are we to know what is the right thing to do and what is the wrong thing to avoid, for nature is no longer a nurse with her swift punishments and rewards? Of what happens when men refuse to accept this necessity of choosing, and are terrified of or careless about their freedom, we have now only too clear a proof.[168]

Auden was not very successful in his attempt to become the new voice of America's consciousness. Overall the work did not receive positive reviews, and ran for only a week. It is to be noted that the criticism was directed more to Auden's libretto than to Britten's music: 'the libretto […] seems to wander from one to another idea, without conviction or cohesion. In the plot, as in the score, is a little of everything, a little of symbolism and uplift, a bit of socialism and of modern satire, and gags

---

[165] Review in the *New York Herald Tribune*, 6 May 1941, in MITCHELL 1991, p.916.
[166] See Donald Mitchell in AUDEN 1988, p.96, and REED, PHILIP 1997, p.21.
[167] AUDEN 1988, p.3.
[168] AUDEN 1988, p.3.

and jokes of a Hollywood sort'.[169] Virgil Thompson, again, was not very generous with Auden and with his consciously literary libretto:

> What any composer thinks he can do with a text like 'Paul Bunyan' is beyond me. It offers no characters and no plot. [...] In addition, its language is not the direct speech of dramatic poetry. It is a deliberate parody, for the most part, of the attempts at intensity on the part of our least dramatic poets. Its subject, consequently, is not Paul Bunyan at all, nor even the loggers and farmers of the Northwest that it purports to depict. Its subject is literature itself, as is most of Mr Auden's work.[170]

Britten's music received a generally better welcome, including an almost prophetic comment made by Olin Downes, who noticed that 'what is done by Mr Britten shows more clearly than ever that opera written for a small stage, with relatively modest forces for the presentation, in the English language, and in ways pleasantly free from the stiff tradition of either grand or light opera of the past, is not only a possibility but a development nearly upon us'.[171]

As it is, unlike Inkslinger, Auden and Britten were never to receive a telegram from Hollywood. After the first production there were plans to rethink the work, that in the final stages of rehearsal had received considerable cuts and revisions, and to make it simpler and suitable for school's productions,[172] but due to Britten's return to England, and more probably to lack of motivation, it was withdrawn by the composer and 'forgotten' until 1974, when after Auden's death Britten was finally convinced by his collaborators to have a look at it, and with few amendments and a new orchestral introduction made it into the work we now know.[173]

Paul Bunyan saw the end of the Britten–Auden collaboration on the stage, and with *Peter Grimes* the composer returned to more traditional

---

[169] Olin Downes, review in the *New York Times*, 6 May 1941, in MITCHELL 1991, p.915.
[170] Review in the *New York Herald Tribune*, 6 May 1941, in MITCHELL 1991, p.916.
[171] In MITCHELL 1991, p.916.
[172] See MITCHELL 1991, p.924.
[173] For a detailed account of the revisions see Donald Mitchell 'The Origins, Evolution and Metamorphoses of *Paul Bunyan*, Auden's and Britten's "American" opera', in AUDEN 1988, pp.83–148, and the publisher's note to the vocal score of the work (London: Faber, 1978), pp.ix–x.

forms of music theatre. But the lessons learned during the thirties would bear much fruit, and Britten was to return to the idea of theatre as a didactic medium, and to experiment with more innovative forms of music theatre.

On this matter I would like to mention here two works that we could suspect were significant in Britten's later development. As we have seen, he had been positively impressed by a school opera by Aaron Copland, *The Second Hurricane*;[174] apart from the obvious considerations to be made about his works for children, what is most interesting is that Copland's work, with his contemporary edifying subject, spare staging, choral involvement for pupils and their parents (who are requested to sing in the adult choir), and simple musical requirements, represents an American example of *Gebrauchmusik*, and indeed its inspiration was apparently Kurt Weill's *Der Jasager*, a *Lehrstuck* on a text by Brecht written for the 1930 Chamber Music Festival in Berlin. Interestingly enough, the source of this piece was a fifteenth century Japanese Nô play, *Taniko* by Zenchiku,[175] a choice that might have been influenced by the fact that 'oriental' parables had become a favourite genre in Germany,[176] although there is little doubt that the subject responded to some of Brecht's social concerns. The play is the story of a boy whose father is dead and whose mother is very ill, and who decides to join a trip into the mountains to a nearby town where he hopes to find help for the mother's recovery, although he knows that because of an ancient customs, should he not to be able to climb the mountain, he would have to be sacrificed, so that he is not a burden for the other travellers. The journey proves too hard for the child, who accepts his death ('he says yes') as a consequence for his choice, and shows a social behaviour responsible even to extreme consequences. The resulting piece, a two-act miniature opera of about forty minutes in length, is a development of the *Lehrstuck* genre in the direction of the *Gebrauchmusik* idea: since the main character is a child, Brecht and Weill decided to write a 'school-opera', that could be

---

[174] Particularly striking is a similarity between the 'choral overture' of *The Second Hurricane*, where the chorus introduces the adventure to follow by stating that 'Once in a while something happens, something exceptional', and the prologue of *Paul Bunyan*, where the chorus, in a similar style, introduces Paul's birth by noticing that 'Once in a while the odd things happen'.

[175] Brecht's libretto was adapted from Arthur Waley's English translation published in *The Nô-Plays of Japan*, (London: George Allen & Urwin, 1921).

[176] See SANDERS 1980, pp.159–160.

produced in schools and performed entirely by students. It calls for simple means of presentations, few props and a small orchestra that can vary according to what is available, six characters and a chorus, and the music is written in a very approachable style, although there are no songs or arias in it: the separate sections into which the work is divided are dramatic scenes where expressive recitative is interspersed with choruses and ensembles.

We do not know whether Britten had direct experience of this work, which he might have discussed with Heinsheimer, Copland or even Weill himself, but he certainly knew another of Brecht's *Lehrstuck*, *Die Massnahme*, with music by Hanns Eisler, which he saw on 8 March 1936, when the work was performed in London in a concert that also saw the first performance of Britten's *Russian Funeral*, a march for band.[177] *Die Massnahme*[178] is another oriental fable by Brecht, written in the same year as *Der Jasager*, and whose subject, quite similar in its ethic content, is completely original. Set in modern China, it deals with the decision of a group of Communist agitators from Moscow to put to death a romantic young Chinese revolutionary whose undisciplined ardour leads him to many mistakes that become obstacles to the purpose of the revolution: therefore they persuade him that for a higher good he must be shot and buried without trace. The piece, a critique of false revolutionary attitude, is organised as a trial, where a 'Control Chorus', representing the conscience of the Party, asks the agitators to defend themselves. The formal model of reference is the Christian oratorio, whose religious function is transformed in a political one, in a development of Eisler's use of the form of the cantata for political purposes. The piece is written for a tenor, male chorus and mixed chorus, and an instrumental group consisting of only brass and percussion; different levels of recitative (spoken, sung and *Sprechgesang*) link the choruses, whose homophonic writing, and 'almost exclusively modal diatonicism' create an archaic atmosphere that increases the sense of detachment produced by the performance style requested by the composer: 'What should be aimed at is extremely taut, rhythmical and precise singing, as expressionless as possible, that is, one must not feel one's way into the music... but should

---

[177] See MITCHELL 1981, p.96.
[178] Hanns Eisler, *Die Massnahme*, Lehrstuck von Bert Brecht op.20. Klavierauszung von Erwin Ratz (Wien: Universal Edition, 1931).

present one's notes as if reading a report'.[179] *Die Massnahme*, written specifically as a vehicle for the worker's choruses, is an extreme expression of didactic theatre, 'the most advanced outpost of political art of the late Weimar Republic',[180] and for Eisler it meant a 'transformation of the concert into a political meeting', where the new types of music which had already come into existence, the monodic militant songs, the speaking choruses and aggressive chansons, were given an appropriate function.[181] Its particular dramaturgy, with its stylised delivery, its use of the choruses and its obvious didacticism, might have been an influence on the conception of Britten's first chamber opera, *The Rape of Lucretia*, where the Christian commentary also refers to the oratorio as a model. Britten's formal search in the field of music theatre would continue to develop on the strength of his experiences with the politically committed theatre of the thirties, although we will have to wait until *Curlew River* to see him directly involved, like the Brechtian model, with Japanese theatre.

FINDING THE FORM BEST-SUITED

From this brief account of Britten's dramatic and 'almost-dramatic' output in the thirties there are some interesting observations to be made. First of all, he was constantly involved in projects which were experimental and in some way also propaganda. Secondly, his participation in a project was often a sign of ideological involvement. The concept of parable, of morality, and the idea of preaching, of educating the audience are ever present. He expressed many times his belief in the power of art, and especially of music, of influencing people and therefore of being an agent of social and political change. Not to be underestimated was also his political commitment. The title of an interview published during his American visit in a Canadian newspaper reads: 'Composer would knock out fascists by mighty songs'. According to the writer the young composer's entire energies are being reserved for the fascists. He hates fascists like poison, and he is ready to prove that the song is mightier than the sword. 'Music is becoming more and more political (...) It can't speak directly, but a good song can certainly incite people to do things. Look at the French national anthem, *La Marseillaise,* and what it did during the French revolution. One of the Spanish loyalists best weapons in

---

[179] See BETZ 1982, p.97.
[180] BETZ 1982, p.93.
[181] BETZ 1982, p.94.

their hopeless fight was their magnificent marching song. Nobody knows where it came from, but it certainly helped to unite those people. (...) Composers must become more and more politically minded.' Britten suggests 'Music has an incredible positive force politically'.[182] The tone may be not quite Britten's own, but certainly the ideas presented are recurring themes in his writings of that period, and very much in accordance with the ideas that he seems to have shared in his collaborations during the thirties.[183]

Another element that often attracts the attention of commentators is the amount of music that Britten produced in these years. The conditions he had to face working for the film industry, the radio and the theatre – limited resources, great pressure and very limited time – are known to have contributed to his developing an amazing expertise in writing to order, fulfilling his commissions in the minimum of time. Some of his incidental music is extremely interesting, and some of the soundtracks reveal great creativity in dealing with unusual resources. Although some of the projects he was involved with were experimental, the musical language never was. We have seen that in theatre he often used a pseudo-popular language; in general, he never went beyond the boundaries of tonal language, and often used traditional forms. Britten himself discussed the reasons motivating his choices in an interview: talking about the *Sinfonia da Requiem,* he explained:

> I am making it just as anti-war as possible... I don't believe you can express social or economic theories in music, but by coupling new music with well-known musical phrases, I think it is possible to get over certain ideas... and since it's a kind of Requiem, I'm quoting from the Dies Irae of the Requiem Mass. One's apt to get muddled discussing such things - all I am sure of is my own anti-war conviction as I write it.[184]

In its aesthetic consequences, this implies that his work could not simply describe or express, but had somehow to act on people's minds. The expedient of referring to a well-known tune in order to create an

---

[182] *Toronto Daily Star,* 21 June 1939 (press-cutting in the Britten–Pears Library, Aldeburgh).
[183] In particular the idea of political and militant songs, which was fundamental for the Left and for composers like Hanns Eisler.
[184] W.G. King, 'Constant Composer', *New York Sun,* 27 April 1940 (press-cutting in the Britten–Pears Library, Aldeburgh).

association is just one example. Especially where theatre was concerned, Britten was always keen on involving the audience in an active way, in some kind of participation, not simply in a passive act of enjoyment. Awareness, political to start with and, after the war, ethical and philosophical, was always his end. In this context, I believe we need to differentiate between those works which are the lyrical expression of personal feelings and those that respond to a more public and social 'activism',[185] and his theatrical output to me belongs undoubtedly to the second category.

In the thirties, the core aim of the documentary idea and of political theatre was the development of political awareness. The war brought with it a vast sense of desolation and hopelessness: many artists, including Auden, felt their inability to influence political and economical interests. Britten made good use of lessons learnt in the thirties, and continued what he believed were his responsibilities as an artist. The idea that 'All a poet can do today is warn' is always present, but it also becomes a moral imperative: to warn is a poet's duty. The composer seemed to have always believed that through his work he could somehow influence other people's beliefs and therefore their actions It is an idea that is central to Britten's aesthetic, and deeply influenced not simply the subjects and ideological - or philosophical - content of his work, but their formal structure as well: not necessarily their musical structure in the first instance, but their textual - and dramatic - organisation, and therefore the overall design. And not only in the theatre, as testified by the *War Requiem*. Its innovative structure, alternating Latin text and English poems, reflects Britten's need to find a form that at the same time conveyed a particular meaning and achieved a desired effect. By developing an original solution to the problem of saying new things in an approachable way, he used the same device outlined in his comment about the *Sinfonia da Requiem*, although this time he applied it to the text. The poems by Owen offer a commentary to the text of the Requiem Mass, that set it in a specific context, that of war, altering its meaning and thus proposing a different view, one that we know to be very personal for Britten.

---

[185] The purely instrumental works and some of the commissioned works belong to a different category.

The work again reflects his need to use tradition in order to make his own 'new' voice heard and understood in a broader context: this is probably what he meant in saying that he was 'given strenght by tradition'.[186] With such a solution, he is confident of a deeper impact and therefore of a stronger response from his audience. The theologian François Vouga in his commentary on the *War Requiem* writes:

> Britten's personal engagements is the opposite of Stravinsky's almost monastic seclusion, and of his disdain for public taste. What is to be found here is a completely different conception of Christianity, immersed in the world, with its injustice and its sufferings. The relationship with the times is very new: we are no longer in the eternity of the present, as with Bach, nor in the revolutionary hope for a new age to come, as with Beethoven, but we are in the times when Judgement has fallen on the whole of history. Humanity itself has given rise to the Day of Wrath, and the Apocalyptic symbolism of the *Dies Irae* is embodied within Christianity. Faith is compelled to justify itself, and the artist cannot avoid questioning radically all the values of civilisation. From there derives his necessary alliance with the community in which he lives, and his rôle in making clear its responsibilities.[187]

The artist's vocation is to clarify the community's responsibilities: Britten desperately wanted to be an active and productive part of society, of his own community. One could speculate about the psychological reasons for such a need, but what we know for sure is Britten's own perception of the situation of the composer as an artist in times of modernity, how he expressed it in an article from the American period:

> Those circumstances which prompted the whole movement of Nationalism in England have been not above suspicion. Any cultural "movement" (especially if it

---

[186] MITCHELL 1984, p.96.

[187] 'L'engagement personel de Britten prend le contre-pied de la retraite presque monastique de Stravinsky et de son dédain pour le goût du public. C'est qu'il en va ici d'un tout autre christianisme, immergé dans le monde, dans ses injustices et ses souffrances. Les rapport au temps est très neuf. On ne se trouve plus dans l'éternité d'un présent, comme chez Bach, ni dans l'espérance révolutionnaire d'un âge à naître, comme chez Beethoven, mais sous le Jugement qui est tombé dans l'histoire. L'humanité elle-même a engendré le Jour de la colère et le symbolisme apocalyptique du *Dies Irae* a pris corps dans la chrétienté. La foi est mise en demeure de rendre compte d'elle-même et l'artiste ne peut tout simplement plus rester à l'abri de la mise en question radicale des valeurs d'une civilisation. D'où sa solidarité nécessaire avec la communauté dans laquelle il vit et sa vocation d'en éclairer les responsabilités' (VOUGA 1983, p.96. The translation is mine).

ends in "ism") is more often than not a cover for inefficiency or lack of artistic direction. [...] The attempt to create a national music is only one symptom of a serious and universal malaise of our time – the refusal to accept the destruction of "community" by the machine.

However we decide to Act
Decision to accept the fact
That machine has now destroyed
The local customs we enjoyed,
....
And publicized among the crowd
The secret that was always true
But known once only to the few,
Compelling all to the admission
Aloneness is man's real condition,
That each must travel forth alone
In search of the Essential Stone,
"The Nowhere - without – no" that is
The justice of Societies.
(W.H. Auden)

The English composers of today have consciously or unconsciously seen the danger-signals ahead. They are avoiding the pitfalls that some of their musical fathers and uncles have dug for them. It is only those who accept their loneliness and refuse all the refuges, whether of tribal nationalism or airtight intellectual systems, who will carry on the human heritage.[188]

The refusal to flee to a refuge, and the responsibility towards 'human heritage', were for Britten constant preoccupations in his works. The consequences of these concerns would shape the structure and the musical language of most of his work. The moral imperative is the artist's responsibility towards his fellow men. I think it is very important to have this clear in our minds when we approach critically Britten's dramatic works, especially those that constitute the focus of this study, *The Rape of Lucretia* and *Death in Venice*.

---

[188] BRITTEN 1941, p.74–75.

CHAPTER 2
THE POET'S MIND

> *There are only two things in art:*
> *humanity or its lack.*
> *(Alvar Aalto)*[189]

In the preface to his recent biography of the composer Michael Oliver comments that Britten did not talk much about his work: 'He seldom wrote programme-notes on it, rarely agreed to be interviewed, and his only considered aesthetic statement is a brief pamphlet'.[190] He therefore concludes that the biographer, or the exegete, should resist the temptation to conclude from such meagre evidence what Britten 'must have thought'.[191] Such a statement seems to reflect a quite generalised perception that still today characterises the composer's reception: Britten, the highly gifted technician, the craftsman who wrote music with immense facility and obviously was not thinking too deeply about it, or about anything else. The critical literature does not reflect an interest in what might have been the 'thought' at the root of his phenomenal creative output: monographs tend to build an image of the man relying more on outside perspectives than on self-declared evidence, and give us only hints of the composer's artistic self-image and philosophy. There has not been a study of Benjamin Britten's own writings, and the edition of the letters and diaries is still in progress.[192] Even in the most recently

---

[189] Alvar Aalto, 'The Architectural Struggle', p.144 (speech given to the Royal Institute of British Architects, 1957), in: Alvar Aalto *Sketches*, edited by Göran Schildt (London: The MIT Press, 1978), pp.144−156.

[190] OLIVER 1996, p.9. The pamphlet he refers to is the speech *On receiving the First Aspen Award* (London: Faber, 1964).

[191] OLIVER 1996, p.9.

[192] Only the first two volumes, covering the period 1913−45, have been published (MITCHELL 1991).

published collection of essays on the composer[193] there is no space dedicated to a discussion of his 'aesthetic vision', although its editor, Mervyn Cooke, recognizes that 'a vast amount of primary source material relating to the composer has yet to be studied in the detail it deserves'.[194] As a consequence, the composer's own ideas have not been favoured as an interpretative tool in approaching his works, with perhaps the exception of his longstanding pacifist beliefs. A reason for this might be that enquiring about the composer's intentions has lost relevance within the musicological arena, on the assumption that any interpretation reflects the exegete's ideas and no-one else's. But one would hope that within the scope of criticism there could still be room to investigate and discuss the ideas that support an artistic vision. These ideas might have social or political implications, or simply aesthetic or religious connotations, but often they reveal a pattern within an artist's oeuvre, a focus: we are not talking merely of 'hidden agendas', but of something more radical, a system of beliefs that constitute the philosophical landscape in which the artist moves. I believe that only after we have tried to understand the philosophical background from which a work originates can we approach it in its own terms; this seems particularly fruitful in the case of Britten.

I would like to attempt in the present chapter an analysis of Britten's own writings relating to his ideas about music and art, in an effort to define a personal *poietic* which will form the basis of a discussion of his artistic development. I am certainly not trying to write the 'intellectual biography' advocated by Robin Holloway in his review of the published letters and diaries of Britten,[195] but I will nonetheless try to draw a picture of 'the poet's mind'.[196] I believe that Britten's aesthetic thinking is reflected in the structure and status of his works and that by approaching the works from an inner perspective we might gain a new understanding of the works themselves. This will provide a background for the discussion in the chapters to follow.

---

[193] *The Cambridge Companion to Benjamin Britten*, ed. by Mervyn Cooke (Cambridge: Cambridge University Press, 1999).
[194] COOKE 1999, p.7.
[195] *Letters from a life: the selected letters of Benjamin Britten 1913-1976*, edited by Donald Mitchell and Philip Reed (London: Faber, 1991).
[196] See HOLLOWAY 1992.

'A USEFUL PART OF THE BOROUGH'

Benjamin Britten was generally diffident about expressing his opinions and views on musical and other subjects through the medium of language and the printed page. In a speech made on the occasion of an honorary degree at Hull University, he states:

> I am all for listening to music, looking at pictures, reading novels - rather than talking about them [...] I do not easily think in words, because words are not my medium [...] I also have a very real dread of becoming one of those artists who *talk*. I believe so strongly that it is dangerous for artists to *talk* [...] the artist's job is to *do*, not to talk about what he does. *That* is the job of other people (critics, for instance, but I'm not always so sure about this).[197]

Notwithstanding this declared shyness to confide in the written word, we have a considerable amount of writings, speeches and interviews that give us an interesting profile of 'Britten the thinker', the man behind Britten the composer, Britten the performer, Britten the entrepreneur. The fact that his activities were not limited to 'writing music' is extremely relevant: as a performer and organizer he was more than anything else a facilitator, and what he did in such a capacity not only for English opera, but for English musical life on the whole is perhaps yet to be recognised in full. The Aldeburgh Festival, the English Chamber Orchestra, the English Opera Group (and the English Music Theatre Company which, in a way, followed) are only the principal by-products of his beliefs, and their achievement constitutes a concrete realisation of his aesthetic vision as much as do his works. He certainly did much to provide opportunities for the performance and composition of works, not necessarily his own.

A reason for this 'musical activism' was a belief that artists are and must be an integral part of society: 'Artists are not only artists, they are men, members of society, and must take their place in society - indeed insist on doing so';[198] in all his statements there is always an underlying desire to be 'of use', and he constantly expresses his deep conviction that there is a 'use' for art: 'I believe in roots, in associations, in backgrounds, in personal relationships. I want my music to be of use to people, to please

---

[197] BRITTEN 1963, p.89 (italics in the original).
[198] BRITTEN 1963, p.89.

them, to "enhance their lives" (to use Berenson's phrase)'.[199] Britten believed that there is space in any social context for an artist to be a part of community life, as long as the artist is willing to be part of it. In the speech on receiving the Freedom of Lowestoft, his native town, Britten sets out what 'he thinks and believes his duty to be':

> I am first and foremost an *artist* - and as an artist I want to serve the community. In other days, artists were the servants of institutions like the Church, or of society in the sense of private patrons... Today it is the community, or all of us in our own small ways, that orders the artist about. And I do not think that is such a bad thing either. It is not a bad thing for an artist to try to serve all sorts of different people... [and] to have to work to order. Any artist worth his salt has always ideas knocking about in his head, and an invitation to write something can often direct these ideas into a concrete form and shape. Of course, it can sometimes be difficult when one doesn't feel in the mood, but perhaps that's good for one too! - anyhow, composers (like other people) can be horribly lazy, and often this is the only way that they can be made to produce something![200]

Again, in the speech given at the presentation of the Aspen Award, Britten says:

> At many times in history the artist has made a conscious effort to speak with the voice of the people. Beethoven certainly tried, in works as different as the *Battle of Victoria* and the Ninth Symphony, to utter the sentiments of a whole community. From the beginning of Christianity there have been musicians who have wanted and tried to be servants of the church, and to express the devotion and convictions of Christians, as such. Recently, we have had the example of Shostakovich, who set out in his 'Leningrad' Symphony to present a monument to his fellow citizens, an explicit expression for them of their own endurance and heroism. At a very different level, one finds composers such as Johann Strauss and George Gershwin aiming at providing people - the people - with the best dance music and songs which they were capable of making. And I can find nothing wrong with the objectives - declared or implicit - of these men; nothing wrong with offering to my fellow-men music which may

---

[199] BRITTEN 1964, pp.21−22.
[200] BRITTEN 1951, p.4 (italics in the original).

inspire them or comfort them, which may touch them or entertain them, even educate them - directly and with intention. On the contrary, it is a composer's duty, as a member of society, to speak to or for his fellow human beings.[201]

When receiving the Freedom of Aldeburgh, Britten stresses the fact that the honour is given to him as an active member of the community, a 'useful part of the borough':

> I am proud because this honour comes from people who know me, many of whom have known me for quite a long time too, because although I didn't have the luck to be born here in Aldeburgh, I have in fact lived all my life within thirty miles of it. As I understand it, this honour is not given because of a reputation, because of a chance acquaintance; it is - dare I say it - because you really know me, and accept me as one of yourselves, as a useful part of the borough; and this is, I think, the highest possible compliment for an artist. I believe that an artist should be part of his community, should work for it, with it, and be used by it. Over the last hundred years this has become rarer and rarer and the artist and the community have both suffered as a result. The artist has suffered in many cases because without an audience, or with only a highbrow one - without, therefore, direct contact with his public - his work tends to become 'ivory tower', without focus. This has made a great deal of modern works obscure and impractical: only usable by highly skilled performers and only understandable by the most erudite. Don't please think that I am against all new and strange ideas; new ideas have a way of seeming odd and surprising when heard for the first time. But I am against experiment for experiment's sake, originality at all costs. It's necessary to say this because there are audiences who are not discriminating about it. They think that everything new is good; that if it is shocking it must be important. There is all the difference in the world between Picasso, the great, humble artist, or Henry Moore, and the chap who slings paint on canvas; between Stravinsky and electronic experimenters...[202]

---

[201] BRITTEN 1964, pp.11–12.
[202] Quoted in HOLST 1966, pp.71–72.

Although society might not respond in an ideal way to the needs of the creative artist, this cannot be an excuse for renouncing his duties, shying away and living outside the community:

> The *ideal* conditions for an artist or musician will never be found outside the *ideal* society, and when shall we see that? But I think I can tell you some of the things which any artist demands from any society. He demands that his art shall be accepted as an essential part of human activity, and human expression; and that he shall be accepted as a genuine practitioner of that art and consequently of value to the community.[203]

This is the minimum requirement. It is, of course, a two-way relationship: 'Artists cannot work in a vacuum - they need society, and society needs them [...] artists occasionally forget this, or refuse to admit it, and as a result art has got itself into a bit of a jam today'.[204] While striving to be recognized as a valuable element of society, the artist finds his duty is the creation of a better society, if not an ideal one, an idea that Britten actively cultivated after leaving college, as we have seen in the previous chapter.

PARABLE-ART

The intellectual and artistic experiences of the years 1935–39 were extremely important for Britten's development.[205] Contact with a reality that was not only artistically vibrant, but also concerned with social and political implications shaped his beliefs in a crucial way. It is likely that the emphasis Britten placed all through his life on the role of the creative artist within society might have his roots in the experiences of this period. As we have already discussed, at that time Auden was a strong influence on Britten, and it is likely that he shared Auden's ideas about the function of the artist in society. For Auden the artist was a sort of preacher - he used to call himself 'a mad clergyman'[206] - and his main task is to save civilization: the poet, or more generally the artist, speaks from a pulpit to encourage the development of society's self-awareness, and to spread the hope that a better world can and must be created.

---

[203] BRITTEN 1964, pp.15–16 (italics in the original).
[204] BRITTEN 1963, p.90.
[205] On the subject see MITCHELL 1981.
[206] MCDIARMID 1984, p.1.

In the period between the two world wars, when the survival of civilization was at stake, it was necessary to express these ideas in a political context; but in the context of Auden's theory of art it is the spiritual sphere of men that deserves principal attention. Political activism is only a consequence of the fact that spiritual ideas find their pragmatical expression in society. In 1935 Auden wrote: 'There must always be two kinds of art, "escape-art", for man needs escape as he needs food and sleep, and "parable-art", that art which shall teach man to unlearn hatred and to learn love':[207] the products of creative work are 'parables', and through these the artist tries to influence everyday life in order to make changes that will produce a better society. The oppressive shadow of the Second World War changed Auden's attitude, and he developed a sort of scepticism based on historical pragmatism: 'Art is a product of history, not a cause. Unlike some other products, as technical inventions, for example, it does not re-enter history as an effective agent, so that the question of whether art should or should not be propaganda is unreal';[208] years later he bitterly commented 'No words men write can stop the war'.[209] But while Auden was disappointed by the ultimate failure of his activist efforts before the war, Britten seems to have been willing to preserve and defend his beliefs in the power of art to move people and influence events. The concept of 'parable-art', and the implied idea that the artistic creation is in itself a 'parable', a 'narrative of imagined events used to illustrate a moral or spiritual lesson'[210] which uses allegory and metaphor, is fundamental in his work.

A few years after the composer's death Peter Pears declared in an interview: 'What you have to realise is that much of Britten's music takes a moral point of view, indeed, that's probably the key to understanding him and the music he wrote throughout his life'.[211] The philosophical convictions that in the thirties had found expression in left-wing political activism found a different arena after the war, going back to what was also in origin Auden's main concern, the spiritual sphere of men.

---

[207] Quoted in MITCHELL 1981, p.25.
[208] AUDEN 1939, p.47.
[209] Quoted in MCDIARMID 1984, p.ix.
[210] *The Concise Oxford Dictionary of Current English*, 8th edition (Oxford: Clarendon Press, 1990).
[211] Peter Pears interviewed in Tony Palmer's television film *A Time There Was...* (1980). A copy of the script is at the Britten–Pears Library.

PORTRAIT OF THE ARTIST AS A GAY MAN

> The hypothesis which I wish to test is this: that Britten's moral concern with social issues expressed in his early association with the political left, did not (as has been sometimes supposed) melt away as he became an increasingly successful establishment figure, but was to a large extent transmuted into an attempt to deal in opera with the problems of the homosexual in society, and (though less prominently), to affirm the positive potential of love between men.[212]

After Britten's death, the public acknowledgement of the real nature of his life-long partnership with Peter Pears has been a rich source of studies and a key theme in the critical reading of his works, in particular the operas. The struggle of the outsider against social conventions is a predominant theme, and it is read as a reflection of the composer's struggle with his own sexual identity within a homophobic society which decreed that homosexual acts were illegal and a punishable offence. From this starting point a new strand of Britten studies has flourished, and the consequences of the inner tensions created by the composer's sexual identity has been examined in many contexts. Adding to this the exposure in recent biographical studies of Britten's paedophile tendencies, we are left in even more doubt about this complex character. It is difficult to assess the relationship between artistic creativity and sexual identity, and the extent to which the latter consciously influenced Britten's artistic aims, especially if we take the view that in Britten's case the assertion of such sexual identity never seemed to be a priority, quite the opposite;[213] the presumed sense of guilt arising from his sexual tendencies is also debatable, if we can rely on Peter Pears's statement that Britten was perfectly at ease with his own sexuality;[214] after all, he lived a life-long fruitful relationship with Pears, acknowledged by most people, if never openly declared. One could argue that the issues relating to the composer's sexual identity reflect more the agendas of his exegetes, for

---

[212] HINDLEY 1995, p.68.
[213] The concept of 'gay pride' seems to have been foreign to Britten. Pears points out that 'the word "gay" was not in his vocabulary [...] There was a streak of the puritan in Ben [...] But the gay life, he resented that, I think'. (*A Time there was...*).
[214] DEAN 1992, p.537.

whom 'closet-concerns' are more an actual and contemporary phenomenon than they ever were for Britten.[215]

Britten's desire to be an active part of society might have originated in the perception, whether conscious or unconscious, that such a privilege was forever denied to him on the basis of his sexual orientation. There were nonetheless other elements that concurred to form a personality in many ways at odds with society and the world. The feeling of being an outsider certainly had deep roots in the composer's childhood years, and indeed in his 'vocation' as a creative artist within a society that looked upon art in all its manifestations as a leisure activity, not to be taken too seriously. There is a well-known anecdote concerning the young composer being asked by a family friend about his future:

> He was sixteen-and-a-half when he left school with an open scholarship for composition at the Royal College of Music in London. During that August, while he was waiting for the new term to begin, he happened to be at a tennis party in Lowestoft where one of the guests asked him what career he intended to choose. Britten said he intended to be a composer. The tennis player was astonished. 'Oh!' he said , 'but what else?' It was impossible to try to explain that composing was not just a hobby. The casual, devastating remark came as a warning of what to expect in the future.[216]

Britten was so struck by this episode that he mentioned it again in the Aspen speech, complaining that 'semi-Socialist Britain, and Conservative Britain before it, has for years treated the musician as a curiosity to be barely tolerated [...] the average Briton thought, and still thinks, of the Arts as suspect and expensive luxuries'.[217] It is not difficult to see how the conflict between belief in doing a job, music, that is of service to the community, and the general perception that such activity is a superfluous and unnecessary extravagance might have fed a neurosis.

---

[215] In his article on the *War Requiem* (ELLIS 1997) Jim Ellis also argues that the 'repression hypothesis', related to Britten's homosexuality, may have directed attention away from more politicized readings of the operas.
[216] HOLST 1966, p.24.
[217] BRITTEN 1964, p.15.

Another obvious element of disturbance is that Britten had been a conscientious objector during the war, a choice that was the source of many antipathies in post-war Britain. Donald Mitchell, talking about the operas, points out that

> it is not Britten's sexual constitution that we have dramatized or musicalized before us, but the dramatization in an extraordinary variety of forms of one of the great human topics which is under perpetual debate: the pressure and persuasion to conform on those who assert different values and attitudes from those held by society at large.[218]

There is a further element which does not seem to have been considered much, that would reinforce Britten's own perception of himself as an outcast. Providing a variation on the accepted perception of *Peter Grimes* as 'a parable of the self-oppression of a homosexual man and his victimisation by society',[219] Peter Pears has commented that 'Peter Grimes is an outcast rejected by his community, by the Borough, not just because his apprentice has died in mysterious circumstances, but because he is a *visionary*, a *dreamer*, in a society that cannot tolerate such people'.[220] For Britten, the gift of vision seems to be the source of artistic creation:

> Artists are artists because they have an extra sensitivity - a skin less, perhaps, than other people; and the great ones have an uncomfortable habit of being right about many things, long before their time...Think of the observations on life of Goethe, Milton, Leonardo, or Blake - the wonderful truths that are in the letters of Verdi, or Keats - or Fitzgerald, for instance. Someone once called artists the 'antennae' of society - and I think they were right. So when you hear an artist saying or doing something strange or unpopular, think of this extra-sensitivity - that skin less; consider a moment whether he may not after all be seeing a little more clearly than ourselves, whether he is really as irresponsible as he seems, before you condemn him. Remember for a moment Mozart in his pauper's grave; Dostoievsky sent to Siberia; Blake ridiculed as a madman, Lorca shot by the Fascists in Spain. It is a proud privilege to be a creative artist, but it can also be painful. Great artists have been destroyed by their consciences.[221]

---

[218] MITCHELL 1995, p.312.
[219] HINDLEY 1995, p.66.
[220] Interview in *A Time There Was...* (italics are mine).
[221] BRITTEN 1951, p.5.

There is a hint of evidence that Britten believed in his own ability to see things that ordinary people could not see; he certainly had a considerable faith in the power of sleep and of dreams, and in his works he touched on the subject of the paranormal. Of course it is not relevant for our discussion to assess the reality of such a perception, but it is important to note that he believed in it, and that he considered it a priority to communicate what he saw. I believe that for Britten the pain caused by the conflict between everyday reality and his own perception of the world, filtered through a sensibility characterized by this artistic 'extra-sensitivity', together with the struggle to communicate his vision, constituted a more fundamental trait than the presumed struggle with his own sexuality, and I think that shifting the focus of Britten's unease with reality towards this issue can be quite revealing.

THE CHILD'S LOST POWER OF SIGHT

Britten had apparently been conscious of a particular 'extra-sensitivity' since his childhood. In the documentary *A Time There Was...* Elsie Hockey, Britten's cousin, comments about an episode that happened during Britten's childhood:

> One day Ben said 'something dreadful is going to happen. Not just to us, but I can feel it, something dreadful is coming to the whole world'. And I think that in the family there was that funny knowledge of the occult, and Britten was fascinated by it, by the dark side. [...] Do you think that Ben was perhaps brave enough to dive into that nowadays and express it in his music, to arouse our sympathy? Because there are these tortured souls.[222]

There is little doubt that Britten was a tortured soul. Leonard Bernstein once commented:

> Ben Britten was a man at odds with the world. It is strange, because on the surface, Britten's music would seem to be decorative, positive, charming, but it's so much more than that. [...] There are gears that are grinding and not quite meshing, and they make a great pain [...] when you hear

---

[222] Interview in *A Time There Was...*

> Britten's music, if you really hear it, not just listen to it, you become aware of something very dark.[223]

The dark side of Britten's music and character has mainly been read as originating in unconscious sexual tensions, even in a repressed sado-masochism, but it could also have its roots in the anger and frustration of a constant fight with the world. According to Pears, a fundamental constituent of Britten's personality was 'this idea of the disappointment he felt that the world was not like he had believed during his own marvellous childhood':

> The point is, everything seemed so simple when he was a boy... simple and delightful for the most part. But as he grew up, he began to be increasingly disillusioned - in man - I suppose. So this idea of a lost child, lost childhood, lost innocence, and the search for that innocence, became of fundamental importance to him.[224]

At the core of Britten's creative output is the vision of a better world, of a lost world, the world he had known in his childhood. It would be nonetheless misleading to reduce the issue to the experience of a spoiled child unable to cope with the reality of life. It is as an adult that Britten maintained the capacity of returning to that lost paradise, which would explain his ability to relate to children and their experiences: they still shared the same world. Peter Porter has clarified what seems to be one of the characteristics of Britten's vision, in a comparison with Schubert: 'For both Schubert and Britten the world in which music grows is a poetical place - i.e. is human, speculative, dramatic, aphoristic and spontaneous [...] For Britten, poetry is what the world is, and not what is made in and by music - though music can add to it'.[225]

The disappointment Britten felt seemed to arise from people's inability to perceive that same poetic world: I believe that this was the essence of the concept of 'lost innocence' that was such a concern for Britten, how grown-up men lose their ability to see, and as a consequence live in a world full of violence, where there is no space for poetry and beauty. One could suggest that maybe Britten was not so much concerned with his

---
[223] Interview in *A Time There Was...*
[224] Interview in *A Time There Was...*
[225] PALMER 1984, pp.272–273.

own lost innocence, but rather with everybody else's: we are faced with what Arnold Whittall defines as 'perhaps the most profound image in all Britten's work: the sense of the adult as betrayed, or destroyed, child'.[226]

'ONLY IN PEACE I CAN BE FREE'
Britten made it his life's work to make real for other people the world that he was able to see thanks to his particular sensibility. For this poetic world to flourish there was one obvious preliminary condition, and that was the establishment of peace, and I believe that this was the root of Britten's longstanding commitment to pacifism. In a programme note for a concert held in December 1949 Britten and Pears wrote: 'The governments of the world have declared in the Charter of Unesco "Since war begins in the minds of men, it is in the minds of men that defences of peace must be constructed"'.[227] There is little doubt that Britten committed himself to this very principle, and the extent to which his pacifist beliefs have influenced his work has been extensively discussed. His preoccupation with violence was consistent and persistent, as Donald Mitchell has demonstrated, to the point that Mitchell believes that 'the wealth of music touching directly or indirectly on acts of violence constitutes the creation of a genre *without parallel elsewhere in the history of twentieth-century music*'.[228]

Of course the *War Requiem* is the most outstanding expression of this concern, but it is an idea that in one form or another is substantial in many other works. These express not only a rebellion against violence in its every expression, or a 'prolonged cry of desperate compassion',[229] but also a pro-active attempt to influence people's minds and consciences towards the creation of a peaceful world in which people can find fulfilment: 'however tragic his texts may be, his music will always convey, in Rostropovich's words, "the joy of life and the hope for happiness"'.[230]

---

[226] Arnold Whittall, review of *Britten & Auden in the Thirties: the Year 1936* by Donald Mitchell, *Music and Letters* 62 (1982), p.430.
[227] Programme note for a charity concert on Thursday 8 December 1949, in the Britten–Pears Library collection.
[228] MITCHELL 1999, p.205 (italics in the original).
[229] OSBORNE 1963, p.96.
[230] HOLST 1966, p.80.

In the sixties, when asked in an interview whether his political persuasion had changed after the war, Britten replied:

> Politicians are so ghastly, aren't they? After all, the job of politics is to organize the world and resolve its tensions. What we really need is more international technicians, artists, doctors. Political institutions ought to have shown signs of withering away by now. My social feelings are the same as they have always been. I disbelieve profoundly in power and violence.[231]

There is the belief that politics as such are only a by-product of social interaction, and that what really matters is practical work: if people dedicate themselves to their own work, with professionalism, aiming at doing their best, there would be little time in which to kill for the sake of ideology, or for the sake of power. What Britten advocated was a celebration of humanity in its universality: 'The side of communism which is violent is abhorrent to me. But when one travels to Iron Curtain countries as I have had occasion to do, one is conscious simply of human beings - how plucky and spirited those people are in Poland and Yugoslavia. That is what interests me'.[232] And again, on the subject of timeless humanity, he says:

> I was reading a play of Euripides in bed this morning - *Ion* - which I had read before, but I hadn't reread for some time. And really, the first chorus of that - written, what, nearly three thousand years ago? - seemed to me as if it was being written about a crowd visiting the Maltings, looking around and making comments: 'What's this?; 'Where do we go here?' I feel that there's no difference except the difference of environment, between Euripides and ourselves today. And we all have that feeling reading the Bible, reading any old sagas from Iceland or India. I cannot understand why one should *want* to reject the past. After all, we sit in this room surrounded by pictures and an amphora from Armenia, a very beautiful thing, which is five thousand years old. I'm given *strength* by that tradition. I know it changes - of course traditions change. But the human being remains curiously the same.[233]

---

[231] SCHAFER 1963, p.117.
[232] SCHAFER 1963, p.117.
[233] MITCHELL 1984, *Mapreading*, p.96.

The human being and his interaction with the world and with life is Britten's main concern, a timeless theme to which he is attempting to provide his individual, personal contribution. This was recognized by the committee that awarded him with the Aspen Award, not an artistic or musical prize, but an award established to honour 'the individual anywhere in the world judged to have made the greatest contribution to the advancement of the humanities'. The citation for the award read: 'To Benjamin Britten, who, as a brilliant composer, performer, and interpreter through music of human feelings, moods, and thoughts, has truly inspired man to understand, clarify and appreciate more fully his own nature, purpose and destiny'.[234]

COMMUNICATION

Because for Britten the aim of the creative work is the sensibilization of audiences, music is never an end in itself, only a means, a means of communication. This also explains the choice of musical language that is approachable and can reach a wide audience. In many instances Britten justifies his choice of a traditional language with his need to communicate a message:

> I sometimes feel that the seeking after a new language has become more important than saying what you mean. I mean, I always believe that language is a means and not an end. [...] After all, language is a matter of experience. When we're talking, we are using symbols which have been used by the past. If we rejected the past we should be just making funny noises.[235]

> The craze for originality, one result of the nineteenth-century cult of personality, has driven many artists into using a language to which very few hold the key, and that is a pity. To use a language which can be understood is an advantage, not a disadvantage. Now, I don't for a moment think that *what* you say will immediately be liked or welcomed, but language should not be an additional difficulty.[236]

---

[234] BRITTEN 1964, p.7.
[235] MITCHELL 1984, *Mapreading*, pp.94–95 (italics in the original).
[236] BRITTEN 1963, p.90.

> The rot (if that isn't too strong a word) began with Beethoven. Before Beethoven music served things greater than itself. For example, the glory of God, or the glory of the State, or the composer's social environment. It had a defined social function. That was the kind of setting in which Mozart and our own Purcell worked. After Beethoven the composer became the centre of his own universe. The romantics became so intensely personal that it looked as though we should reach a point where the composer would be the only man who understood his own music![237]

Commenting on the negative reception of the *War Requiem* in Vienna Britten said: 'It doesn't surprise me, as Vienna has always been *traditional* in its tastes, and the *War Requiem* is certainly not in the *traditional* "avant-garde" language. But new works can be misunderstood not only for how they say something, but for *what* they say'.[238] And he continues: 'Some of my right-wing friends loathed it, "Though the music is superb, of course", they'd say. But that's neither here nor there to me. The message is what counts'.[239]

It is also important that the message is conveyed with all possible clarity: 'I certainly can't imagine making my language more obscure on purpose. When I write for a "wider" audience, I obviously don't want to write very subtle things, and the language is, as a result, simpler'.[240]

> Berg and Schoenberg share common ground in the respect of the complexity of their musical thought. The multiplication of parts in their music is often staggering. But I am at precisely the other end of music. Music for me is clarification; I try to clarify, to refine, to sensitize. Stravinsky once said that one must work perpetually at one's technique. But what is technique? Schoenberg's technique is often a tremendous elaboration. My technique is to tear all the waste away; to achieve perfect clarity of expression, that is my aim.[241]

Clarity of expression is accompanied by consideration for the performers' and listeners' characteristics, their age, culture, background:

---

[237] STUART 1950, p.247.
[238] OSBORNE 1963, p.92 (italics in the original).
[239] OSBORNE 1963, p.96.
[240] OSBORNE 1963, p.93.
[241] SCHAFER 1963, p.118.

> I certainly write music for human beings - directly and deliberately. I consider their voices, the range, the power, the subtlety, and the colour potentialities of them. I consider the instruments they play - their most expressive and suitable individual sonorities, and where I may be said to have invented an instrument (such as the Slung Mugs of *Noye's Fludde*) I have borne in mind the pleasure the young performer will have in playing it. I also take note of the *human* circumstances of music, of its environment and conventions; for instance, I try to write dramatically effective music for the theatre - I certainly don't think opera is better for not being effective on the stage (some people think that effectiveness *must* be superficial). And then the best music to listen to in a great Gothic church is the polyphony which was written for it, and was calculated for its resonance: this was my approach in the *War Requiem* - I calculated it for a big, reverberant acoustic and that is where it sounds best.[242]

This attention to the listener, and to the effectiveness of communication, has many practical consequences, amongst which are also stylistic choices: 'It doesn't matter what style a composer chooses to write in, as long as he has something definite to say and says it clearly'.[243] Whatever Britten had to say, he certainly managed to speak directly to a wide public maintaining a balance between simplicity and intellectual appeal in a style that, in Robin Holloway's words,

> has the power to connect the avant-garde with the lost paradise of tonality; it conserves and renovates in the boldest and simplest manner; it shows how old usages can be refreshed and remade, and how the new can be saved from mere rootlessness, etiolation, lack of connection and communication.[244]

THE HOLY STAGE
There is a further idea that deserves attention, and that is Britten's particular conception of the moment of performance, or as he calls it, 'musical experience', a moment of privileged interaction between human beings, in which communication can happen very intensely:

---

[242] BRITTEN 1964, p.10-11.
[243] Quoted in HOLST 1966, p.35.
[244] HOLLOWAY 1977, p.6.

> A musical experience needs three human beings at least. It requires a composer, a performer and a listener; and unless these three take part together there is no musical experience. The experience will be that much more intense and rewarding if the circumstances correspond to what the composer intended: if the *St. Matthew Passion* is performed on Good Friday in a church, to a congregation of Christians; if the *Winterreise* is performed in a room, or in a small hall of truly intimate character to a circle of friends; if *Don Giovanni* is played to an audience which understands the text and appreciates the musical allusions. The further one departs from these circumstances, the less true and more diluted is the experience likely to be.[245]

The creation of ideal circumstances becomes therefore a priority for someone interested in achieving the greatest degree of communication; when these circumstances are fulfilled, a musical experience has the ability to transcend the everyday, and to project us, the performers and the listeners, in a different dimension:

> what is important in the Arts is *not* the scientific part, the analysable part of music, but the something which emerges from it but transcends it, which cannot be analysed because is not *in* it, but *of* it. It is the quality which cannot be acquired by simply the exercise of a technique or a system: it is something to do with personality, with gift, with spirit. I quite simply call it - magic: a quality which would appear to be by no means unacknowledged by scientists, and which I value more than any other part of music.[246]

> [...] This magic comes only with the sounding of the music, with the turning of the written note into sound - and it only comes (or comes most intensely) when the listener is one with the composer, either as a performer himself, or as a listener in active sympathy. Simply to read a score in one's armchair is not enough for evoking this quality. Indeed, this magic can be said to consist of just the music which is *not* in the score.[247]

The listener has to contribute to the experience in an active way:

---

[245] BRITTEN 1964, p.19.
[246] BRITTEN 1964, p.17 (italics in the original).
[247] BRITTEN 1964, p.18 (italics in the original).

> Music demands more from a listener than simply the possession of a tape-machine or a transistor radio. It demands some preparation, some effort, a journey to a special place, saving up for a ticket, some homework on the programme perhaps, some clarification of the ears and sharpening of the instincts. It demands as much effort on the listener's part as the other two corners of the triangle, this holy triangle of composer, performer and listener.[248]

The 'musical experience' acquires here a characteristic of sacredness: it is a ceremony, for which one has to prepare, in order to take part in it in the right frame of mind. There is always a stress on the concept of 'occasion':

> Bach wrote his *St. Matthew Passion* for performance on one day of the year only - the day which in the Christian church was the culmination of the year, to which the year's worship was leading. It is one of the unhappiest results of the march of science and commerce that this unique work, at the turn of a switch, is at the mercy of any loud roomful of cocktail drinkers - to be listened to or switched off at will, without ceremony or occasion.[249]

The idea that the moment of interaction through music between people and the world that surrounds them is akin to a religious ceremony, a sacred ritual, becomes of great importance in understanding Britten's attitude towards theatre. The dramatic stage seemed to offer him the most favourable conditions to create an experience with the characteristics that he advocated, the ritualistic interaction between performers, composer and listener. It could be argued that theatre in general, and opera in particular, is more an 'occasion' than a simple concert: it can only happen when specific conditions are given, in a specific and dedicated place, it requires theinteraction of more people at different levels, and it is in itself a more absorbing experience, as the visual aspect is as predominant as the aural. It can easily be associated to a ritualistic celebration, indeed this is the origin of theatre itself. Britten pursued this idea to extremes in his search for a dramatic format in which the ritualistic aspect was more prominent than in the traditional operatic stage, through his interest in medieval and oriental drama.

---

[248] BRITTEN 1964, p.20.
[249] BRITTEN 1964, p.17.

To sum up, Britten seemed to believe that through his particular sensitivity he was able to have a clearer insight into 'man's destiny on earth', and he made it his duty to communicate his personal 'truth' like a preacher through his artistic work. In his work the communication of this personal message – as reflected in his ideas, whether philosophical, aesthetic or moral – is more important than matters of style, language and form. This is revealed also in his choice of subjects, and how he dealt with them. He considered music-theatre particularly effective, indeed making it a privileged medium, and finding in it justification for writing operas and for creating conditions in which opera could be performed, an aspect we will examine in the following chapter.

CHAPTER 3
THE COMPOSER AS A DRAMATIST, IMPRESARIO, LIBRETTIST

PETER GRIMES, PETER GRIMES, PETER GRIMES...

During the rehearsal of *Peter Grimes* Britten faced many difficulties with members of the company, and it seemed improbable that the collaboration with Sadler's Wells could survive after the production. Nonetheless he was eager to write more operas, and according to Eric Crozier, the director of *Grimes*, the idea of creating an independent company pre-dated the first night.[250] Britten's keen interest in writing for the stage certainly pre-dated *Grimes*. Talking about *Paul Bunyan* he said: 'The critics damned it unmercifully, but the public seemed to find something enjoyable in the performances. Despite the criticisms, I wanted to write more works for the stage'.[251] It was very shortly after the première of *Paul Bunyan,* during the summer of 1941, that Britten had found a copy of 'The Borough', and together with Pears 'began trying to construct the scenario of an opera'.[252] According to the composer's own testimony, those preliminary sketches even pre-dated Serge Koussevitsky's commission for the opera:

> I was waiting on the East Coast for a passage back to England, when a performance of my *Sinfonia da Requiem* was given in Boston under Serge Koussevitsky. He asked why I had not written an opera. I explained that the construction of a scenario, discussions with a librettist, planning the musical architecture, composing preliminary sketches, and writing nearly a thousand

---

[250] Eric Crozier '*The Rape of Lucretia*' programme note, Dublin Opera Theatre, 1990. Quoted in CARPENTER 1992, p.225.
[251] BRITTEN 1945, p.7.
[252] BRITTEN 1945, p.7.

pages of orchestral score, demanded a freedom from other work which was an economic impossibility for most young composers. Koussevitsky was interested in my project for an opera based on Crabbe, although I did not expect to have the opportunity of writing it for several years. Some weeks later we met again, when he told me he had arranged for the commissioning of the opera, which was to be dedicated to the memory of his wife, who had recently died. On arrival in this country in April 1942 I outlined the rough plan to Montagu Slater, and asked him to undertake the libretto. Discussions, revisions, and corrections took nearly eighteen months. In January 1944 I began composing the music, and the score was completed in February 1945.[253]

It is worth noting Britten's determination to write again for the stage, notwithstanding the criticism that had greeted *Bunyan*, even if it meant postponing the project to a later stage; it is also relevant that Britten himself had been the initiator of the project.

The published facsimile of the opera's draft[254] contains excerpts from the correspondence of Britten and his collaborators, giving us fresh insights into the history that preceded the first night.[255] From these and some other sources it clearly emerges how Britten and Pears had started working in detail on the synopsis and the shaping of the plot; theirs were not simply preliminary discussions, but a concrete work. We cannot be certain what kind of material they gave to Montagu Slater once in England, but since the two did not start their collaboration on *Grimes* until late spring 1942, it is possible to assume that the composer by that stage had already well-defined ideas about what he wanted: it was not just a 'rough plot'. In a letter to Christopher Isherwood, who had declined to be librettist (apparently he had no confidence in the project), Britten wrote 'I know that as it stands, P.G. is no more then a rather bloodthirsty melodrama; but it has the elements of what I want in an opera, and we are slowly but surely getting nearer to a serious plot'.[256] As Peter Pears recalled, 'By the time we came back to London, the whole story of Peter Grimes as set in the opera was already shaped, and it simply remained to call in a librettist

---

[253] BRITTEN 1945, p.7.
[254] BANKS 1996.
[255] In particular, the articles by Philip Reed 'A *Peter Grimes* Chronology, 1941–1945', pp.21–52, and by Philip Brett, 'The Growth of the Libretto', pp.53–78.
[256] Quoted in BANKS 1996, p.24.

to write in the words'.[257] Montagu Slater's input was certainly not limited to 'filling in words', but Britten's constant presence during the working of the libretto reinforces the impression that he was in control of the text for the whole of the process, as testified by the amount of discussion and revision work that characterised the collaboration, which ended with Slater publishing his own version of the libretto. Philip Brett points out that 'when Britten began to compose, the musical ideas, which must have been fomenting over the last eighteen months, began to take over. If the words did not fit them, he ploughed along almost regardless, as can be seen from many places in the composition sketches'.[258]

Britten worked on the *Grimes* project for almost four years, a very long period of time when compared with the working rhythms of the operas that followed. The first opera is rightly considered a masterwork, and there is a common feeling that the composer never quite managed to repeat himself. But it is also possible that Britten consciously never wanted to repeat himself, and this would explain some of *Grimes*'s more traditional features, those features that the public sorely missed in the opera that followed. I believe it is in fact arguable that with this 'traditional' work the composer was trying out his ability of writing for the stage, so challenged by the reception of *Bunyan*.

With *Grimes* Britten wrote a work that respected many conventions of grand opera. We have already assessed his contribution to the shaping of the libretto. Apart from the formal structure – the use of separate numbers linked by recitatives – the opera presents many stereotypes of the romantic tradition: big choruses, a storm, an aria sung against the background of a religious ceremony (as in Massenet's *Werther*, Puccini's *Tosca* and many others), a dance scene and a mad scene. Britten's creative eclecticism had learned the lesson from his models:[259] we know that he carefully studied the score of *Rosenkavalier*, although 'the influence of Mozart and Verdi, of course, is more obvious', he says, 'The wonderful stagecraft and wit and aptness of Mozart, Verdi's trust in melody and his sense of form – both these composers taught me a great deal'.[260] Another point of reference is Berg. The theme of the individual

---

[257] Quoted in BANKS 1996, p.61.
[258] BANKS 1996, p.67.
[259] On the subject see STUART 1950.
[260] BRITTEN 1966, p.5.

in conflict with society makes *Grimes* a worthy successor of *Wozzeck*, a work Britten greatly admired: '*Wozzeck* had, for about ten years, played a great part in my life, not only, I may say musically, but also psychologically and emotionally',[261] although the latter 'obviously has an expressionist quality that is foreign to Britten'.[262] Even so, the first to be sceptical about *Grimes* was apparently the composer himself:

> It never occurred to me that the opera would work. I had no confidence about *Grimes*. Besides, at that time such an offbeat story was hardly thought right for an opera. This, and the quarrels going on in the company, were not very good auguries. At the dress rehearsal I thought the whole thing would be a disaster. Looking back, I think it broke the ice for British opera.[263]

OPERA CONSCIOUSNESS

Britten's first major operatic venture came at a time when Sadler's Wells was trying to build an 'English opera consciousness' in London. The first volume in the Sadler's Wells Opera Books, a series inaugurated in 1945, is dedicated to 'Opera in English'.[264] Edited by Eric Crozier, with contributions by Tyrone Guthrie, Edwin Evans, Joan Cross, Edward J. Dent and Ninette de Valois, it was an attempt to take English opera seriously:

> The time has come when we ought to consider a long-term policy for Sadler's Wells and for English opera in general. Can we honestly say that

---

[261] BRITTEN 1966, p.5.
[262] WHITTALL 1982, p.96. Donald Mitchell has also brought to attention the influence of Shostakovich's *Lady Macbeth of Mtsensk*, that Britten had seen in 1936 (MITCHELL 1995, p.310).
[263] KENNEDY 1981, p.46.
[264] *Opera in English*, edited by Eric Crozier (London: The Bodley Head, 1945). With the exception of the first volume, the series featured 'books completely devoted to one opera, with particular reference to its current production in English by the Sadler's Wells Company, but also with more general reference to the work itself, its history, and the ideas which it suggests or with which it is associated' (front-cover flap). Other volumes in the series included *Peter Grimes*, *Così Fan Tutte* and *Madame Butterfly*. The editor explained that 'There is very little written in our own language about opera as an art-form; and it is hoped that this series will appeal not only to the regular opera audience, which has so vastly increased in the war years, but to a much wider public' (back-cover flap). Also, 'all the royalties from the sale of these books will be employed by the Governor of Sadler's Wells to supplement a special fund for commissioning new operatic works in English.'

we had any policy worthy of the name in the past? Can we indeed discover any such a policy for English opera in the history of the last three centuries? The best we can say of ourselves is that it has been the aim of Sadler's Wells to present to a popular audience, at cheap prices, and in the English language, the operatic works which have become famous on continental stages, many of them composed originally for State-subsidized theatres and for audiences of a mentality and cultural background totally different from those of our own people. Throughout those past centuries it has been much the same thing; English opera, or opera in English, never had the courage to pursue a consistently constructive policy. [...] The future of Sadler's Wells and the future of English opera must depend primarily not on the singers engaged but on the works performed. [...] If our opera is to be really national, it is obvious that it ought to be based on a really large repertory of native works. There is no need indeed to be chauvinistic; nobody would want to exclude foreign operas, and indeed even the most self-consciously national house of the continent finds that they cannot exist without a considerable stock of foreign operas. But opera-going public in England of the present day is still unaccustomed to the idea of native opera. [...] In this country the repertory of native works will have to be built up very gradually and very carefully. [...] Few composers realize, I fancy, the amount of intellectual labour that is required merely for the preliminary planning of an opera, the designing of its purely musical structure; and the poet, of course, can hardly be expected to know the technical side of musical composition. On the top of this there is also the technical problem of play-writing, and then the further problem of modifying the play-form to be set to music and make an opera-form. The natural temptation is to look at some successful old favourites and imitate that; that, in fact, is what composers and librettists have been doing ever since the year 1600. If we are to create a really native type of opera we must strike out in new directions. To do this all at once is impossible, and we must recognize the fact; we are bound to begin by building upon the ruins of ours predecessors. But there is a great difference between blindly imitating whatever has been a box-office success in the past, regardless of whether it is suitable to the English language, the English voice or the English temperament, and analysing the methods of past librettists and composers and picking out just those elements which can be recombined, perhaps in an entirely different way, into a form of musical drama that, without self-conscious attitudinizing, naturally fulfils the aspirations of our own souls. [...] It is no longer considered abnormal and possibly disreputable for a well-educated Englishman to be something of a musician. But both poets and composers need educating to the theatre; they have both neglected it for too long. We must bring them together, as Boito was brought into contact with Verdi, in the hopes that they will mate and collaborate intimately in the creation of English opera. [...] And the theatre must be willing to make experiments. The British public is habitually suspicious of operatic novelties, but it must be trained and encouraged to take a sporting interest in their frequent presentation. We want opera to be no longer what Dr. Johnson called it, 'an exotic and irrational entertainment', but an integral necessity of our own civilisation and culture.[265]

Some of these ideas would be at the core of the English Opera Group policy. Britten himself had expressed his interest in 'the creation of English opera':

I am passionately interested in seeing a successful, permanent, national opera in existence – successful both artistically and materially. And it must be vital and contemporary, too, and depend less on imported 'stars' than on a first-rate, young and fresh, permanent company. Sadler's Wells have made a good beginning.[266]

Unfortunately the climate during the production of *Grimes* was spoiled by several problems. Although many of the people involved believed in the new opera, there were hostilities. Britten's and Pears' pacifism was seen as highly suspicious, but mainly there was great tension over the choice of a new opera by a young English composer for the London re-opening of Sadler's Wells. Many feared a failure, as did, we have seen, the composer himself. Notwithstanding the effort of the Sadler's Wells Company, 'there was indeed no tradition of writing operas; there was no tradition among audiences of wanting to see contemporary operas'.[267] Before the 7 June 1945 premiere, later considered 'a dawn for English opera', Britten had written:

---

[265] DENT 1945, pp.31–41.
[266] BRITTEN 1944, p.5. Also quoted in WHITE 1983, p.48–9.
[267] HEADINGTON 1981, p.9.

> The scarcity of modern British operas is due to the limited opportunities that are offered for their performance. Theatre managers will not present original works without a reasonable hope of recovering their costs of production: composers and writers cannot thrive without the experience of seeing their operas adequately staged and sung: the conservatism of audiences hinders experimental departures from the accepted repertory. In my own case, the existence of Sadler's Wells has been an incentive to complete *Peter Grimes*: the qualities of the Opera Company have considerably influenced both the shape and the characterization of the opera. Whatever its reception may be, it is hoped that the willingness of the Company to undertake the presentation of new operas will encourage other composers to write works in what is, in my opinion, the most exciting of musical forms.[268]

The immense success of the opera reinforced Britten's already strong determination to write for the stage. In 1943 he had written to Ralph Hawkes: 'I have a feeling that I can collaborate with Sadler's Wells opera abit in the future - it would be grand to have a permanent place to produce one's operas (& I mean to write a few in my time!)'.[269] After *Grimes* the option of working again with Sadler's Wells was out of question. To succeed in his determination Britten ideally needed two things: a company and an audience. And it is not too hazardous to say that to these aims he dedicated most of his efforts in the decade following the success of *Grimes*.

A NEW OPERA COMPANY

The formation of the English Opera Group and the reasons for its birth are a fascinating subject,[270] to which unfortunately we cannot dedicate the space it deserves. It is probably enough in this context to reinforce the argument that the main reasons for the creation of the company were connected with Britten's own artistic needs, and that the venture, made possible by the support of a group of dedicated people, also coincided with a trend that in the post-war years found an ideal climate in which to

---

[268] BRITTEN 1945, p.8.
[269] Quoted in BANKS 1996, p.28–29.
[270] A monograph on the history of the EOG is currently being prepared by Jill Burrows (paper read in Aldeburgh on 17 October 1996). An interesting outlook on the daily life of the company in the fifties is presented by Maureen Garnham, secretary and general assistant to Basil Douglas, in her recent book *As I saw it: Basil Douglas, Benjamin Britten and The English Opera Group 1955–57* (London: St. George's Publications, 1998). See also KILDEA 1996, in particular Chapter 5.

blossom, as Edward J. Dent's text suggested.[271] Eric Crozier was an important figure in the birth of the company and its administration:[272] he was one of the artistic directors of the company, together with Britten and John Piper, and also their spokesman. Some of his articles can rightfully be considered the manifesto of the new company, and it is not difficult to see how they voice Britten's beliefs and intentions. As Crozier himself recognised, the composer was the catalyst and the motor of the whole operation:

> The production of *The Rape of Lucretia* in 1946 was an experiment. [...] The experiment aims towards encouraging the creation of a living school of British opera, from the belief that opera is a vital and significant form of theatrical art, as capable of thriving in this country as anywhere else.[..] It has been demonstrated time and time again that England is no place for opera. [...] A large, ready made audience for contemporary opera does not exist. [...] Opera till recently has been in about the same condition as drama in the days of Victorian melodrama: public taste as voracious and as little cultivated as that of the Surrey audiences. But public taste is apt to make quick jumps ahead. [...] There is a long and interesting struggle to be faced before opera can be accepted among us as a serious contemporary art. Prejudices must be overcome, critics educated, artists and technicians discovered and taught the particular limitations and virtues of the operatic form. Above all, composers and poets must be convinced that opera is a vital means of expression, suited to the talent of English performers, and as well able to attract large audiences as the symphony concert or oratorio. The small group of people responsible for the production of *The Rape of Lucretia* was aware of many of the aesthetic, economic, and material problems that bristle along the approaches to British opera. The group centred round the composer Benjamin Britten; it included a poet, a painter, some excellent singers, conductors, and a producer. Among them they shared much energy, unlimited enthusiasm, and various theatrical experiences. Benjamin Britten had a strong and positive belief in the musical possibilities of small-scale operas.[273]

---

[271] See above.
[272] According to his recollection, Crozier was the one to suggest a small company modelled on *La Compagnie des Quinze*, by whom he had been greatly impressed at the beginning of the thirties. It is interesting to note that it was again Crozier, with his love for French literature, who suggested Guy de Maupassant's short story *Le rosier de Madame Husson* as a source for the libretto of *Albert Herring*.
[273] CROZIER 1948, p.55.

One of the principal beliefs of the English Opera Group was that it was possible to educate audiences, to create an awareness and taste for opera, and therefore a demand for contemporary works in the native language. The situation of opera in England at the end of the nineties seems to prove that they were right.[274] Their approach to the problem was very pragmatic, as another of Crozier's articles illustrates:

> *The Rape of Lucretia* [...] has been planned as the first of what may grow to be a succession of operas by contemporary composers, for performance during the annual summer seasons by the newly formed Glyndebourne English Opera Company.[...] It must be said that the aim of the Glyndebourne English Opera Company is to complement, and in no way to rival or replace English performances of classical or modern works, on a larger scale, that are being given, and will continue to be given by existing operatic companies. [...] The staple business of British opera companies has been to provide versions of large-scale operas that were originally composed with all the resources of Continental theatres at their disposal. In England, it has been a struggle to match the cost of staging these works against uncertain box-office takings - a struggle in which quality has suffered at the expenses of quantity.[...] The principal belief that has inspired the creation of the new English Opera Company is that it is possible and desirable to develop a kind of British opera that will explore the vital native qualities of the English voice and language. For this, the clear singing of good English will be essential. This will increase the importance of the librettist, since every word of his text should be heard. Vitality in any art is independent of size.[...] If present hopes are realised, the annual season of the new company will offer a focus for outstanding new work in composition, musical performance, production and design, and our composers will be encouraged to write operas on a scale adapted to contemporary conditions, with the certainty of exact performance.[275]

---

[274] Apart from the major opera companies (Royal Opera, English National Opera, Scottish Opera, Welsh National Opera and Opera North) and seasonal opera Festivals (Glyndebourne, Garsington, Buxton and recently Grange Park), there are numerous touring companies, both professional and semi-professional, and even more numerous small companies that present new productions every year. Many of these companies commission regularly new works in English, in particular ENO, Glyndebourne and Almeida Opera, which is dedicated exclusively to contemporary music theatre.

[275] CROZIER 1946, 'Benjamin Britten's Second Opera', p.11.

In a way, such a statement seems to reinforce the argument that Britten reduced the scale of his works partly for economical reasons. It is true that a smaller cast would have allowed performances with reduced financial risk; nonetheless, it is plausible that after the success of *Grimes* it would not have been too difficult for Britten to be offered the resources for another grand opera. Erwin Stein, a close collaborator of the composer in the late 1940s,[276] enlightens us about his change of direction:

> Some fans of grand opera were disappointed when after *Peter Grimes* Britten unexpectedly turned to a very different type of opera with *The Rape of Lucretia*. Even if they admitted that the classical subject demanded a high degree of stylisation and restraint, they still missed their beloved large orchestra. Yet the reason for the employment of a small ensemble in *Lucretia* and in the subsequent operas was simply that Britten needed a company with which he could work artistically to his heart's desire. He founded a new company, the English Opera Group, because elsewhere the working conditions were not to his satisfaction. If he had then been put in charge of a large opera house, maybe he would have written other large-scale operas. As it was, he had to be contented with restricted means, and this was not much of a sacrifice to him.[277]

As early as 1943 Britten, when discussing with Ralph Hawkes the possibility of writing operas, had contemplated smaller orchestral resources: 'It may mean cutting down means abit (no 4 flutes or 8 horns!) - but that doesn't hurt anyone - look at the Magic Flute or Figaro, with just a tiny orchestra. It's the ideas that count'.[278] And in 1946 he wrote: 'I am keen to develop a new art form (the chamber-opera, or what you will) which will stand beside the grand opera as the quartet stands beside the orchestra. I hope to write many works for it'.[279] To Ronald Duncan, with whom he was collaborating in the mid-1940s, well before *Lucretia*, he expressed his desire to write an opera 'which would return to the limitations and economy of means which, since Mozart, had been lost in the Wagnerian circus'. According to Duncan's report, 'he saw there were advantages in writing for small orchestras and looked forward to tackling the problems of obtaining a full musical effect with fewer instruments. He

---

[276] He was Britten's editor and publisher at Boosey & Hawkes.
[277] STEIN 1950, p.17.
[278] Letter dated 12 March 1943, in MITCHELL 1991, pp.1128–29.
[279] CARPENTER 1992, p.225.

thought it possible that a greater intensity and clarity might be obtained'.[280] Later in an interview he stated: 'I often use small groups to accompany my operas - and not only for economic reasons either'.[281] It is Erwin Stein who again gives us another clue about the composer's 'true' reasons:

> Opera in our times has suffered from heavy scoring, and I believe this to be one of the reasons why the art of singing has declined. Great is the temptation for any composer to exploit the huge forces at his disposal, yet - need it be said? - the singer should remain more than only audible: he should be enabled to employ the whole range of dynamics and inflections at his disposal without being frustrated by the prominence of orchestral colour. [...] The employment of a small group of instruments corresponds with Britten's ideas as to the place of voices and orchestra in opera: it should be the singers and not the instruments that carry the burden of the music. Already in *Grimes* he had used his large orchestra sparingly.[282]

Britten's idea of the place of the voice and orchestra in opera may probably account for that 'supremacy' of the singing voice advocated by Crozier and Stein. His attention to the voice was a reflection of his interest in the role of the text, and as a consequence in the setting of the English language. He discusses his ideas in his introduction to the first opera, and more thoroughly in the preface to the libretto of *Rape of Lucretia*:

> One of my chief aims is to try and restore to the musical setting of the English language a brilliance, freedom, and vitality that have been curiously rare since the death of Purcell. In the past hundred years, English writing for the voice has been dominated by strict subservience to logical speech-rhythms, despite the fact that accentuation according to sense often contradicts the accentuation demanded by emotional content. Good recitative should transform the natural intonations and rhythms of everyday speech into memorable musical phrases (as with Purcell), but in more stylized music, the composer should not deliberately avoid unnatural stresses if the prosody of the poem and the emotional situation demand them, nor be afraid of a high-handed treatment of words, which may need

---

[280] DUNCAN 1981, p.57.
[281] SCHAFER 1963, p.118.
[282] STEIN 1950, p.17.

prolongation far beyond their common speech-length, or a speed of delivery that would be impossible in conversation.[283]

A reduced orchestra allows the voice the prominence necessary to restore the text to a level of vitality and freedom proper to the dramatic situation. The music, expressing the feeling, enhances the text, and therefore the dramatic impact of the ideas the text conveys; through musical setting one can fix exactly the dramatic timing, exercising a greater control on the final result:

> Many people think that composers can set any old kind of poetry to music; that any pattern of words may start his imagination working. In many cases this is true. Some of the greatest composers have found inspiration in very poor verse (see Schubert in many places), although not many have gone as far as Darius Milhaud in his 'Machines Agricoles' - which is a setting of a catalogue. But I believe that if the words of a song match the music in subtlety of thought and clarity of expression it results in a greater amount of artistic satisfaction for the listener. This applies equally to the larger forms - oratorio, cantata and opera. In many oratorios, of course, where the words came from the liturgy or the Bible the composer has the greatest possible inspiration for his music; but with a few exceptions, like Metastasio, Dryden, Da Ponte and Boito, few serious poets have provided libretti for these kinds of work. There may be many reasons for this. Opera composers have a reputation for ruthless disregard for poetic values (in some cases rightly) - and all they need is a hack writer to bully, and serious poets won't stand for that. Besides, it takes a great deal of time to learn the operatic formulae - the recitatives, the arias and the ensembles. The bad enunciation of many singers doesn't seem to provide a suitable show place for a poet's finest thoughts. One of the most powerful reasons for a poet's operatic shyness I suspect to be this. To be suitable to music, poetry must be simple, succinct and crystal clear; for many poets this must be a great effort, and the psychological epic poem to be read (or not read) in the quiet of the study is more attractive. I think they are wrong. Opera makes similar demands of conciseness on the composer. He must be able to paint a mood or an atmosphere in a single phrase and must search unceasingly for the apt one. But this is everlastingly fascinating and stimulating, as it must be to the poet.

---

[283] BRITTEN 1945, p.8.

> Similarly fascinating to him should be the problem of continuity, or degrees of intensity, development of character and situation. Also, if he is working with a sympathetic composer, then the timings and inflections of the dialogue can be fixed exactly and for ever - a thing not possible in any other medium.[284]

In a very interesting analysis of the composer's operatic career, Hans Keller considers how particular was Britten's relationship with his libretti:[285] he does not seem to use the text merely as material at the service of his music; rather, he is committing his music to the text, and to the deeper meaning it conveys. According to Colin Graham, he held the theory that 'what goes on in the orchestra is neither a description nor an accompaniment to the action, but is rather what is going on in the hearts of the characters'.[286]

If it is true that Britten's operas strive to convey a message, of whatever nature, it follows that clarity of expression, in both text and music, becomes a priority, that would allow a more direct communication. To reinforce this, Britten also demands singers who understand that opera is first and foremost theatre, singers that give the text its due priority and that therefore can act:

> Some opera-goers seem to prefer singers who cannot act: there is a curious inverted snobbery current in this country which even prefers operatic acting to be as bad as possible. They do not want opera to be serious at all. They like singers who merely come down to the footlights and yell. For my part, I want singers who can act. Mozart, Gluck and Verdi wanted the same thing. [...] I must say one hoped, after the war, that audiences would revolt at seeing opera performed with bad acting, bad scenery and in a foreign language.[287]

These are very much ideas that might have had their origin in Britten's work in the theatre in the 1930s. They reinforce the impression that one of the great attractions in opera for Britten was that, as theatre, it was an effective and powerful means of reaching people, and that no pulpit could

---

[284] BRITTEN 1948, p.7–8.
[285] Hans Keller, 'Introduction', in HERBERT 1976, p.xxv.
[286] CARPENTER 1992, p.204.
[287] BRITTEN 1984, p.179–180.

ever be as effective as the operatic stage. Such an argument seems to be supported by the abrupt stylistic change that characterises the second opera: distancing himself in many ways from the romantic tradition which can be said to support the conception of *Grimes*, Britten created a work for which the simple definition of chamber opera, that would suit perfectly *The Turn of the Screw*, is somehow insufficient, a work that is at odds with traditional denominations.

THE METHOD OF WORK

Before we discuss *The Rape of Lucretia*, it is important to assess Britten's overall responsibility for his stage works, especially if we want to consider operas not simply as musical pieces but as theatrical actions. It is tempting to discard the fact that the final product is often the result of a collaboration, in which librettist and composer may – or may not – have an equal weight. Certainly in the case of the setting of Metastasio's librettos the composer might not have had much say about the overall dramaturgy of the piece, while in the case of Wagner Joseph Kerman's definition of the 'composer as dramatist'[288] is most appropriate. For Philip Brett this problem derives from the modernist attitude of musical scholarship, 'involved for a long time in exclusive notions of authorship and authority'[289] that lead to focus on the score 'as representing the work'.

> In the field of opera, the difficulty of maintaining such separations as were necessary to promote what one might call the theory of the 'only begetter' called for extreme measures. The many people involved in the construction of an opera - librettist, scenic and lighting designers, stage directors, as well as singers, orchestra and conductors - made especially problematic the elevating of the composer into an exclusive, dominant category. It took the eloquence of the most articulate and racy operatic critic of the post-war era, Joseph Kerman, to inscribe for a whole generation the axiom that 'opera is a type of drama whose integral existence is determined from point to point and on the whole by musical articulation', supported by the assertion that 'not only operatic theory, but also operatic achievement bears this out'.[290]

---

[288] KERMAN 1957.
[289] In BANKS 1996, p.53.
[290] BANKS 1996, p.54.

Brett carries on by using *Peter Grimes* as a case study to demonstrate that opera is

> a social process over a considerable period - a notion that undercuts the validating/denigrating seesaw of conventional criticism in favour of an inquiry into what went into the making of the work, and endeavours to broaden the perspective beyond the composer and his psyche brought even more to the fore in critical accounts, if that were possible, by the disclosure of recent years.[291]

Brett's illuminating detailed analysis of the growth of the *Grimes* libretto should lead us to understand that without the people who collaborated, or just even discussed the work with him, and 'without the extraordinary set of events, political and cultural, that took place between the summer holiday in California in 1941 and the premiere in London in 1945',[292] Britten's own decisions, and therefore the work, would not have been the same. Of course such an argument would easily fit any creative artist, and in large measure any 'creative' situation. It has long been recognised that 'no man is an island', and that external influences - of any kind - shape the individual reaction. Still, it remains an individual reaction, and if we can abandon the 'negative' or anti-social connotations of the concept of authorship, it is possible to attribute a 'creative' product to an individual vision in its interaction with external circumstances. In the case of a collaboration, it is clear that the 'vision' the creative process serves can be common or shared.

It is particularly interesting that Brett should use Britten as an example, because I believe that in his case particularly we have a situation in which the collaboration mainly served the composer's own vision. I am certainly not afraid to be defined a 'traditionalist' when I support the idea that Britten's control is absolute, and his responsibility complete; still, my conviction does not grow out of a 'modernist' view of the opera consisting almost exclusively of its score, as Brett puts it,[293] but from considerations relative to the process not only of the composition, but also of the production of the work.

---

[291] BANKS 1996, p.55.
[292] BANKS 1996, p.77.
[293] BANKS 1996, p.75.

To begin with, the fact that Britten did not write his own librettos could be slightly misleading. He never set a pre-existing libretto, with the possible exception of *A Midsummer Night's Dream*, which he adapted himself together with Peter Pears. He stated his need to be involved in it from the start: 'I couldn't ask anyone to prepare a libretto for me without being in on it myself from the start. [...] I have to [shape the libretto]. I get lots of libretti in the post but I have never accepted one. A few of the ideas are attractive enough, but I have to be in on it from the beginning'.[294] The reason seems to be his need to be in control of the dramatic shape of the piece: 'I always have the greatest say in shaping my operas, and could claim the credit, if that's the word, for their form. But credit for the details of the writing obviously I cannot claim, although I do criticize and demand here too'.[295]

This reflects more than a neurotic need to be in total control: it would seem that Britten had a precise idea of what he wanted to present on stage, not only from a musical point of view, but from a dramatic perspective as well. His are the choices related to subject, text, dramatic structure, theatrical conventions and staging. His contribution is never limited to the musical colouring of an action whose canons have been determined by someone else. He has the responsibility of the piece's dramaturgy, and he can rightfully be considered a co-librettist of his own work: the correspondence relative to his collaboration with his librettists testifies to what extent his contribution in 'shaping the libretto' was part of the writing process. It is therefore possible to ascribe to him the overall responsibility for the aesthetic status of his theatrical works.

If we analyse the modality of his work in his collaborations for the theatre, we can see how the co-ordination of each element that constitutes that complex event called opera was in his hands from the beginning. In his 'Introduction' to the Sadler's Wells Opera Book on *Grimes* Britten defines clearly what are in his opinion the preliminary stages in the creation of an opera:[296]

---

[294] SCHAFER 1963, p.115.
[295] OSBORNE 1963, p.92.
[296] See B. Britten, *Introduction*, p.7, in CROZIER 1946, pp.7-8. Britten discusses these points also in an interview, see BRITTEN 1969, pp.8-11.

- choice of a subject
- construction of a scenario
- discussion with a librettist
- planning the musical architecture
- composing preliminary sketches
- writing of the libretto
- composition of the score

It is only after having been involved in the preliminary discussion and in the process up to the writing of the libretto that the composer can concentrate on his own job, as we have seen in the case of *Grimes*. Later Britten himself stated that he found it dangerous to start writing the music before the libretto was completed, which reinforces the argument that his involvement in the libretto was as a equal partner in the shaping of the same:

> In writing opera, I have always found it very dangerous to start writing the music until the words are more or less fixed. One talks to a possible librettist, and decide together the shape of the subject and its treatment. In my case, when I worked with E.M. Forster or William Plomer, for instance, we blocked the opera out in the way that an artist might block out a picture.[297]

Talking about the relationship with the libretto, and therefore with the librettist, Britten specifies:

> What happens after the actual music is started, as E.M. Forster says in his *Aspects of the Novel*, is that the work itself takes charge. As you set the words, fresh demands on the librettist will come, and you will say I'm sorry, but this line is too long, this line is too short - I need more, I need less, and so you work throughout the composition. It is in a sense a master-servant relationship, but both master and servant have to be experts at their job, and I don't wish to suggest for a moment that is an unrewarding or undignified task for a writer to be a librettist.[298]

---

[297] BRITTEN 1960.
[298] BRITTEN 1969, p.8.

Such a working method, that Britten would systematically apply up to *Death in Venice*, probably derived from his experience at the GPO Film Unit, when he used to be involved from the beginning of each project. Probably this first contact with a world in which music does not only respond to its inner needs, but has to adapt to those of the action and to comment on the visual images shaped the composer's approach to theatre. Whether this is the case or not, Britten seemed to consider this procedure the most apt for the creation of a musico-dramatic organism of unity and inner coherence. For reasons that appear to be of a technical nature Britten took on responsibilities normally associated with the dramatist in terms of defining the dramatic structure.

The problem of fusing drama and music seems to be solved by Britten through the organisation on a large scale of the musical structure, made possible by a very original conception of functional harmony.[299] This structure is modelled on the dramatic structure, to which it is indissolubly linked. The two structures are in a relationship of reciprocal influence, because the formal needs required by the architectural musical structure influence the dramatic subdivision, and at the same time the dramatic content is reflected in the musical choices.[300] The best example, and certainly the chief achievement, of such a formal conception, is *The Turn of the Screw*, where maximum formal coherence is attained through the superimposition of the formal musical structure of theme and variations. The sixteen scenes of the opera are not simply connected to each other through the variations of the opening theme that link them, but they are also unified in the general formal structure.[301]

Nonetheless, this does not seem to be the only reason for Britten to have a direct involvement in the making of the libretto: since *Grimes*, when he actively started his career as an opera composer, Britten managed to have at his disposal a group in which composer, producer, designer and interpreters could work together from the beginning. Eric Crozier's statements about the English Opera Group leave little doubt about Britten's central position inside the group. As Erwin Stein points out, the composer wanted to be

---

[299] See FLYNN 1983, p.44.
[300] Talking about the working process of *The Rape of Lucretia* Ronald Duncan reports how formal considerations in the shaping of the opera preceded any other kind of considerations.
[301] For a detailed study of the musical structure of this opera see HOWARD 1985, in particular pp.71–90.

able to work 'artistically at his heart's desire',[302] and to see his own artistic and aesthetic visions completely supported. From the beginning Britten's ideas determined the final result: his vision influenced not only the musico-dramatic structure, but also the stage design, the costumes and every detail related to the production. So testifies John Piper, designer of many first productions of Britten's operas, in the case of *The Rape of Lucretia*:

> Without commenting on the public or private success or failure of the settings and costumes for *The Rape of Lucretia*, I believe that the way it was set about is the only right way to set about designing – at any rate – a new opera. Composer, librettist, producer and designer discussed the whole production from the start. The general principle, the 'manner' were indicated by Britten in the very beginning.[303]

The composer seemed anxious to realise not only his musical ideas, but also his own dramatic and theatrical vision. In the preliminary discussion the choice of subject and the drafting of a preliminary sketch of the scenes and their content was followed by a detailed definition of the set and of the manner of the production. Usually they would build a model of the set, as Colin Graham, director and designer who worked with Britten from 1958, explains in relation to *Curlew River* :

> I was asked to design the set and to give Britten a model before he started composing, so that he could have it by him at all times when working at the logistic and dynamic balances. He usually wanted to involve the director and the designer at the libretto stage of the conception so that production ideas could be included as he went and he himself could build up a picture at the same time.[304]

Britten himself would nonetheless deny that the reason for such a procedure was of practical nature: 'I don't have to physically create the production for myself when I work'.[305] We can therefore assume that the pre-definition of the dramatic conventions exemplified in the stage design and in performance style does not have simply a practical reason, but is an important aspect of the global conception of the work. This seems to

---

[302] STEIN 1959, p.17.
[303] John Piper, 'The Design of Lucretia', in BRITTEN 1948, p.69.
[304] GRAHAM 1979, p.49.
[305] SCHAFER 1950, p.116.

derive from a vision of the musico-dramatic object in which not only is the music shaped by the text, but it also includes and unifies words, gestures, action and images. The scenic structure is completely integrated with the dramatic and musical structure, and the way they interact is at the root of the creative process of the composer, who is the co-ordinator of these three structures. As such, he is the one who gives to his colleagues the basic instructions related to the various aspects of the creative process. Quite significant in this context is the concern showed by the composer for the scenic conventions he has chosen, as is evident in the case of *Curlew River*: the published score contains almost twenty pages of stage directions, designed to make the performance not 'traditionally operatic'.[306]

We can see how Britten progressively developed this 'team method' of work, refining it opera by opera throughout the whole of his career. It responds to a very precise vision of theatre, which seems to have influenced the choice of collaborators, and I believe it is partly the reason behind his 'rejection' of old partners whenever the collaboration did not seem to be able to support the direction in which he was heading.[307] The choice of subjects is very indicative. Britten's libretti are often transpositions of literary subjects whose content bears a personal interest or relevance for the composer, who chooses them. At the same time, his overall control of the conventions and modality of the theatrical transposition reinforce the concept that what we have in Britten's opera is the composer's own interpretation of a subject dear to him.

It would be difficult on the basis of the evidence here discussed not to hold Britten completely responsible for the final choice. He is the one to get in touch with the librettist, and although we know that texts were often suggested to him, as in the case of *The Turn of the Screw*, the fact that a project was taken to completion is a sign that it matched Britten's need at the time. His correspondence abounds with literary suggestions that were never taken into consideration. There are numerous projects

---

[306] In fact all the church parables have this material. Similar indications were already given in the published score of *Noye's Fludde*, and additional notes for the performance were printed as a separate leaflet (see BRITTEN 1958).

[307] This idea can be supported by the correspondence with Eric Crozier, for example. The projects the librettist-producer was suggesting in the late 1950s responded to a late-romantic vision of opera, and were systematically discarded by the composer (see the Britten-Crozier correspondence at the Britten–Pears Library, Aldeburgh).

which he discarded after an initial phase of interest: among them, an opera based on Abelard and Heloise's letters, *King Lear*, Jane Austen's *Mansfield Park* and Tolstoy's *Anna Karenina*. About this last project, in February 1965 Britten wrote to Colin Graham, who had suggested it:

> It is a fabulous book and I have been over-excited by it and had lots of ideas about the possible opera. But oh, - how *can* one completely compress it into one evening? The main difficulty as I see it is - how to convey the main ideas of the work, of these two couples, the one living only for 'self' (altho' brilliant, beautiful and occasionally touching) and the other, for God or Goodness - viz. the last section (although Levine and Kitty are never pompous or pretentious). Of course, the Anna–Vronsky story is famous, and useful as the impetus for the whole, and one must keep the main features. But can we find a way of doing the two strands side by side? One, one might typify by the city life, and the other by the country, but avoiding, of course, too much over-simplification and, above all, avoiding making the main characters abstractions - the moral, tho' clear, unexpressed. What a task! I hope we can do it, because I can think of nothing more important in one's life than finding another medium (the operatic) for this wonderful story.[308]

Notwithstanding the apparent enthusiasm of his reaction, Britten soon got involved in other projects, and *Karenina* was shelved. It may be because the challenge presented by its operatic transposition was not supported by a personal involvement with the themes expressed in the story. Whenever Britten really wanted to complete a project, he would hold onto it at any cost and for any length of time, as we will see in the case of *Curlew River* and *Death in Venice*. Meanwhile, my next task is to clarify what might have been Britten's personal involvement with the themes presented in his second opera, *The Rape of Lucretia*.

---

[308] HERBERT 1979, p.51.

CHAPTER 4
WHY DOES LUCRETIA DIE?

After the first performance of *The Rape of Lucretia* Ferruccio Bonavia wrote in the *New York Times*: 'Britten's second opera is even more striking, more adventurous and more important than his first. Mr. Britten is a very gifted composer of music and a courageous thinker who faces the problems of opera with a mind that is not tempered by a bias or tradition'.[309] Not many other critics would compare *Lucretia* so favourably with *Grimes*: on the whole the general reception of the first chamber opera was not so warm and insightful, and even Britten's closest collaborators seemed to have expressed doubts about the composer's newly chosen path. After the negative reactions Britten had written to Edward Sackville-West:

> What surprises me a little, my dear, is a rather marked lack of <u>faith</u> that you show in me. Given that you approve of my talent generally, isn't it possible that, if there are some passages that you find confusing and/or inadequate it is because you yourself aren't familiar enough with it to see what I am aiming at? [...] My own feeling about works of artists whom I love & trust, is that when there are passages I don't like or understand, that it's my fault, & that if I work hard enough or love enough then one day I shall see the light![310]

---

[309] BONAVIA 1946.
[310] Letter to Edward Sackville-West, 23 August 1946, in the Britten–Pears Library collection.

It is in the belief that there is light yet to be seen in *The Rape of Lucretia* that I would like to attempt an alternative reading of this work, which I consider to be one of the most challenging in the 20th-century operatic repertoire.

THE LIBRETTO

As Ronald Duncan recalls in his personal memoirs about his collaboration with Britten, the two had known each other since 1935, brought together by their common love for poetry.[311] In the late stages of the composition of *Grimes* Britten, not completely happy with Montagu Slater's libretto, turned to Duncan for help. The latter appeared at first to be a more suitable collaborator, with regard to Britten's need to be in control of the text, for Slater was not very flexible about the alterations to his libretto.[312] While still working on *Grimes* Britten and Duncan were already planning a new opera: '(Britten) said he wanted to write a comedy, or two or three one act comedies, which might somehow be linked together. Eventually we settled on *The Canterbury Tales* and decided to select three, using the pilgrims as a link through an overture, two interludes and an episode. We drafted out a synopsis and later I started to write a libretto'.[313] Eric Crozier made some valid criticism about the already drafted libretto, which he thought would not work as an opera. He suggested instead André Obey's *Le Viol de Lucrèce*,[314] which he had seen performed in Paris. The play had been written in 1931 for La Compagnie des Quinze, an idealistic group that, following the theories of Jacques Coupeau (1879-1949), aimed at reviving the French theatre by bringing back to the French stage 'truth, poetry and beauty'.[315]

Coupeau was a major influence on the development of French theatre at the beginning of the century. A man of letters, who had been active as a

---

[311] DUNCAN 1981.
[312] As already mentioned, Slater published his own version of the libretto. For more details about the collaboration between Britten and Slater, see Donald Mitchell, 'Montagu Slater (1902–1956): Who was he?' in BRETT 1983, pp.22–43, and Philip Brett's studies of the libretto in BRETT 1983, pp.47–87, and in BANKS 1996, pp.53–78
[313] DUNCAN 1981, p.43.
[314] André Obey, *Le Viol de Lucrèce* (Paris: Nouvelles Editions Latin, 1931), first performed by La Compagnie des Quinze, producer Michel Saint-Denis, Paris, Theatre de Vieux-Colombier, on 12 March 1931.
[315] CROZIER 1993, p.21.

theatre critic,[316] he was dissatisfied with the apparent divorce between literature and the stage which had developed during the *belle époque,* the years before the Great War, when theatre had become more and more commercial, and in 1913 founded on the then unfashionable Left Bank an 'art theatre', the Vieux-Colombiers. His aim was to attract an audience of students, writers and artists to a daring combination of classic and new plays, in order to launch a renewal of the theatre. In opposition to the realism then popular on the stage, in itself a reaction to 'theatrical convention', Coupeau wanted to remind his audience that they were at the theatre by way of enhanced stylization in setting and acting. From this new style of staging, strongly influenced by the Nô theatre, the medieval and Elizabethan drama and *commedia dell'arte,* a new school of drama began to emerge, and Copeau even set up a theatre school, in which an all-round training, which included mime and acrobatics, was given, in order to produce 'the complete actor', master of all the means of expression. In 1924, following a religious crisis, Copeau closed the Vieux-Colombiers and moved to Burgundy, in the village of Pernand-Vergelesses, where with few disciples continued what had become not only an artistic but an almost spiritual quest: Les Copiaus, as the group was known, concentrated on the art of improvisation and farce, and performed *divertissements* at harvest and vintage celebrations in Burgundy. As Michel de Saint-Denis recalls,

> every morning, beginning at nine o'clock, in a big open shed, which had been used for making wine, one could see a dozen young people busy at gym, fencing, and acrobatics. An hour later rehearsal began: under the direction of one of the group, the actors prepared a mime on a given theme; for example, inspired by the memories of 1914, they would show a French village, quiet and prosperous, where the daily round of activities would be going on: suddenly comes a noise, followed by an alarm bell, the beating of drums - declaration of war - men at the front - the ups and downs of the battle - women doing men's work - the war nearly lost - the final effort, and victory - the joys of the armistice, then the return of the survivors to their families. This young company, of which I was a member, was trying to find the means of representing dramatically a vast theme of this kind, relying entirely on mime, rhythm, noises and music.[317]

---

[316] He was co-founder with André Gide of the *Nouvelle Revue Française,* which published art and theatre criticism.
[317] OBEY 1967, p.xi.

With no stage or scenery, the actor became the focal point of the action: as Coupeau himself stated, 'there is no scenery, and so you can see the words'.[318] Some of his disciples formed La Compagnie des Quinze in 1929, which under the direction of Coupeau's nephew, Michel de Saint-Denis, aimed at creating a style of theatre at once poetic and acrobatic. In order to exploit at the best the characteristics of the company new texts were commissioned, and amongst them the most successful were probably those by André Obey.

Obey has not received much attention in the context of Britten's criticism, nor he is given a very high place in the French literary pantheon, where he is seen as 'a writer who never had quite the personality to achieve his full potential'.[319] Born in 1892, he studied law and literature, and after the war was active as journalist; his early works for the stage were a couple of quite conventional psychological plays, one of which won an Académie Française prize, and another was produced at the Comédie-Française. It was nonetheless his association with Les Quinze and with Saint-Denis which resulted in his best work; the collaboration started in 1931 and produced six plays, the first of which was *Noé*, a work inspired to the medieval miracle plays.[320] Coupeau, who still was looking over the work of the company, saw in Obey the only French dramatist who had been prepared to adopt his methods, and in return Obey recognised in Coupeau his teacher and in Les Quinze the source of his inspiration. Saint-Denis describes the company for which Obey wrote as

> fifteen actors, whose four years' training and five years' practical experience had moulded to that type of acting which did not lend itself easily to complex psychology, but which was able to animate a broadly-treated general theme. We were actors capable of showing life rather than explaining it, relying more on sound and physical movement than on talking, used to singing and dancing, able to build up from choral work to the invention of simple, clearly defined characters. Admittedly, we had two or three experienced actors with us, but our principal virtue lay in our

---

[318] Quoted in KNOWLES 1967, p.21.
[319] See SMITH 1983, p.72.
[320] *Noé* was staged with great success in London at the New Theatre in 1935, with John Gielguld in the title role, directed by Michel Saint-Denis, who then stayed on to found the London Theatre Studio, and later helped to establish the Old Vic Theatre School. Britten's *Noye's Fludde* bears no direct relationship with Obey's *Noé*.

concerted strength; we were a team whose members were as used to acting together as they were used to living together: we were in fact a chorus, wonderfully united and trained.[321]

Le viol de Lucrèce was the second work written for Les Quinzes, and was inspired by Shakespeare's poem, in an homage to Elizabethan theatre; in his introduction to the plays the author explained that while for *Noé* the formal inspiration was that of the medieval play, for *Lucréce* he had in mind the form of the oratorio. Amongst the other influences on the piece, which was to provide 'a spectacle in which there was greater harmony between conception and execution than in any other performance by the company',[322] Obey acknowledges Cocteau[323] and Claudel, in particular the latter's enthusiasm for Nô play and its techniques, with which the Quinzes were well acquainted: the result was for the most 'a piece of miming supported by the rhetoric of the two narrators',[324] who were stationed in wooden pulpits on either side of the proscenium:

> As Tarquin approached Lucrèce's bed, which was placed on a raised platform towards the back of an otherwise bare stage, he went up and down invisible stairs, along invisible corridors and through invisible doors, sometimes pressing forward with fevered haste, sometimes hesitating at the thought of the deed. He spoke no words, but a vivid picture of his progress through the house was evoked by the narrators.[325]

The work that followed, *Bataille de la Marne*,[326] again written specifically for the company, and inspired to the Great War, is so removed from the dramatic norm that is best described as a spoken oratorio for chorus and soli.[327] These two influences, the oratorio and the medieval theatre, come together in two other plays: *Loire*,[328] an 'allegorical pantomime' representing the struggle of men against the elements and the power of flood waters; and *Le Trompeur de Séville*, a re-

---

[321] OBEY 1967, pp.xii–xiii.
[322] KNOWLES 1967, p.222.
[323] It is therefore possible that Obey might have been influenced by Stravinsky/Cocteau's *Oedipus Rex*, first performed, as an oratorio, by the Russian Ballet in Paris at the Théâtre Sarah Bernard on 30 May 1927.
[324] KNOWLES 1967, p.223.
[325] KNOWLES 1967, p.223.
[326] First performed in Paris, Vieux-Colombier, 5 December 1931.
[327] KNOWLES 1967, p.223.
[328] First performed in Paris, Atelier, 28 April 1933.

working of the Don Juan story, in which Obey does not respect the element of time or space, allowing a production that makes use of simultaneous setting, as in the medieval mystery play.[329]

Apparently Crozier, who was to be the in-house producer, had La Compagnie des Quinze in mind when the English Opera Group was founded, and this made Obey's text even more apt for the new operatic venture. Crozier gave his own translation[330] of Obey's play to Britten, who passed the text on to Duncan. According to Duncan's report of the writing of the libretto, the opera's subject matter was not the most important element; both Duncan and Britten were interested primarily in formal considerations. Duncan, who recognized himself as belonging to the tradition of verse-play, 'always thought that verse should be written within a rigid form';[331] at the same time, Britten wanted to see music return to a greater austerity and clarity of form. He told me of his ambition to write an opera which would return to the limitations and economy of means which, since Mozart, had been lost in the Wagnerian circus. We immediately began to consider the form of a new opera without any subjects in our minds, form being our first consideration.[332]

Britten had already expressed his formal concerns in the 'Introduction' to the Sadler's Wells book on *Peter Grimes*: 'I am especially interested in the architectural and formal problems of opera, and decided to reject the Wagnerian theory of "permanent melody" for the classical practice of separate numbers that crystallize and hold the emotion of a dramatic situation at chosen moments'.[333] Obviously these considerations influenced the shaping of the libretto, a process in which again Britten's ideas had great relevance. In his preface to the published libretto Britten emphasises the importance of the collaboration between poet and composer:

---

[329] Performed in 1937, with incidental music by Darius Milhaud.
[330] The work does not seem to have been published in England. There is an American translation of the play, by Thorton Wilder, *Lucrece* (Boston, 1933), which presents very few alterations from the French original, and was first produced at the Hanna Theatre, Cleveland, Ohio, on 2 November 1932.
[331] DUNCAN 1948, p.61.
[332] DUNCAN 1948, p.61.
[333] BRITTEN 1945, p.8.

> This 'working together' of the poet and composer mentioned above seems to be one of the secrets of writing a good opera. In the general discussion on the shape of the work - the plot, the division into recitatives, arias, ensembles and so on - the musician will have many ideas that may stimulate and influence the poet. Similarly when the libretto is written and the composer is working on the music, possible alterations may be suggested by the flow of the music, and the libretto altered accordingly. In rehearsals, as the work becomes realised aurally and visually, other changes are often seen to be necessary. The composer and poet should at all stages be working in the closest contact, from the most preliminary stages right up to the first night.[334]

A close reading of this statement reveals how the alterations are always to be suggested by the composer to the librettist, and not vice versa. This seems to emphasise once again Britten's wish to have the main responsibility for the genesis of the work. In the case of *Lucretia*, this is not only borne out by the correspondence, but also by the fact that the librettist himself held Britten responsible for the inclusion of the Christian commentary, one of the most problematic aspects of the opera.[335]

Duncan described in detail the method of work on the libretto, and also the general principles that were at the basis of the collaboration, which mainly concerned the limitations of the form:

> I soon discovered that a libretto is a distinct literary form. It should not therefore be judged by ordinary literary or dramatic standards. For a libretto is not a mere drama that is then set to music. It should be a drama which is written *for* music. That distinction describes the form itself. A libretto is a vehicle for music, for song. An opera is not music spread over drama. An opera is a marriage between words and music, an organic growth and not a compound.[336]

He also revealed his views on the relationship between music and words and his notion of the 'dramatic' in music-theatre:

---

[334] BRITTEN 1948, p.8.
[335] See also ELLIOTT 1985, p.iv.
[336] DUNCAN 1948, p.61 [italics are Duncan's].

> At the beginning of the work I found I was under-estimating the power of music to express precise emotions and characterisations, but later relied more on its contribution to the actual statement of the drama. The most successful example of this, I think, is Lucretia's unsung aria when she enters to make her confession to Collatinus. Speaking purely as a dramatist, I could not be more satisfied with her silent statement. In such places music can be more coherent and lucid than language.[337]

Britten had advocated for the operatic text poetry 'simple, succinct and crystal-clear'. Duncan agreed with him on a theoretical level:

> Verse that is to be sung to must be written with the capabilities of voice in mind. The poet must drive his metaphor to the point of clarity and contain in one image the condensation of a mood. He must never forget that the audience is listening to both words and music, and that their concentration, thus divided, cannot be imposed upon. It is useless to write a complicated sentence. It is dangerous to write in the passive tense. One must often abandon a happy metaphor which might look well on the page for the sake of obtaining clarity within the song.[338]

It might seem difficult to reconcile lines such as 'With the prodigious liberality Of self-coined obsequious flattery' with these professed views. Indeed, the 'verbosity and affectation'[339] of Duncan's libretto make it one of the weakest elements of the work, and it is possible that Duncan, writing in 1948, after the production of *Lucretia*, was trying to signal to Britten that he now understood better the function of text in opera. These ideas about clarity and simplicity are certainly significant in the light of Britten's further development: the libretti of his operas became more and more refined in terms of simplicity and conciseness, and this may be why the collaboration with Duncan, that on the paper seemed so promising, did not carry on.

Duncan found the subject of Lucretia very suitable for setting, since he thought that audiences might already be familiar with the plot, and he saw this as an advantage. Amongst his sources he quotes not only Obey, but Livy, Shakespeare, Nathaniel Lee, Thomas Heywood and F. Ponsard. In

---

[337] DUNCAN 1948, p.65.
[338] DUNCAN 1948, p.63.
[339] As defined in an early review (DOWNES 1948).

the programme of the original production Duncan acknowledged as inspiration for the libretto numerous plays written on what he calls a 'European legend'.[340] As a result, in the opera the subject of Lucretia's rape is completely reinterpreted, although many aspects of Obey's dramatic adaptation are maintained: 'Having chosen our subject, Britten and I immediately began to mould it to our needs without any other consideration. History is interesting, it may even be true, but it is useful in so far as it can re-create itself through art'.[341]

A comparison between the two texts, Obey's and Duncan's, reveals that the libretto retained little from the original, and that the common features are concerned more with structure and with 'manner' than with anything else.[342] The original play is symmetrically organised in four acts, I and IV having two scenes. The rape takes place at the end of act II, thus occupying a central climactic position in the action, and what follows is a decrease in the dramatic tension. In the Britten-Duncan libretto, while the symmetry is maintained - two acts of two scenes each - such balance is altered, because the rape happens at the end of the first scene of act II, thus shifting the structural weight of the dramatic tension. The dramatic rhythm is increased in the last scene, which condenses Obey's acts III and IV, especially through Lucretia's hysterical reaction, and the tension thus built resolves only after Lucretia's death. In terms of construction and dramatic delivery, it is possible to argue that in the opera the climax of the action is not the rape, but Lucretia's suicide; I will elaborate this point later.

The action is very simple, and takes place in Rome during the war between the Etruscan-led Romans and the Greeks. Everything happens within, we can assume, twelve hours, probably from 10pm to 10am, in two locations: a military camp outside the city walls, and Lucretia's house. The respect for the Aristotelian concept of unity may not be particularly relevant, as it derives from the French original, but it certainly contributes to the focus and unity of the opera. In essence, what happens is that Tarquinius, taking advantage of Collatinus' absence,

---

[340] DUNCAN 1948, p.62.
[341] DUNCAN 1948, p.62.
[342] The derivation of Duncan's libretto from Obey's play was the subject of a legal dispute, won by the French dramatist who was then entitled to a percentage of the royalties. Duncan defended himself from the accusation of plagiarism, and maintained his position that his libretto was original in its conception. For a more detailed account see SMITH 1983.

imposes his presence in the household, rapes the mistress and then runs away. Lucretia is devastated, her world is shattered and she decides to kill herself, which she accomplishes in the presence of her husband.

It is a simple story compared with the average operatic plot, as noted by Humphrey Searle, who in a review of the first production noticed how 'the story itself is not capable of sustaining a full-length opera'.[343] Here instead we have only six characters, strictly speaking, as the Choruses have no real part in the plot, which we could reduce to four, as the secondary female roles, Bianca and Lucia, have also very little impact on the action itself, and their presence seems to originate more from the aesthetic desire for symmetry than from a real dramatic need. What seems to be relevant here is that by keeping the action to a minimum Britten gave himself room for a special experiment in dramaturgy and operatic structure, and this might account for the fact that the plot was not a major consideration in the planning of the opera.[344] It is quite easy to compare it with the minimal dramaturgy of the first church parable, which only requires three main characters, plus the chorus and the child.

Obey's play contains many more *dramatis personae*: five female characters (Lucrèce, Emilie, Sidonie, Julie and Marie), Tarquin, Collatinus, Junius Brutus, a fourth Roman general (Valère), two soldiers, three servants and La Récitante and Le Récitant.[345] Because of the limited resources planned by the newly formed opera company, the number of characters in the opera are reduced from sixteen to eight, four men and four women, thus creating another symmetry which reflects that of the general structure. The story itself is altered considerably, not only in its approach to the characters, but in many other details. For example, in the first scene of the French play, in the Roman camp, the action is described and commented upon by two soldiers who are guarding Collatinus's tent: the men are inside, and they hardly speak at all (Collatinus does not speak until the end of the play). One of the main driving elements of the action in the opera, Junius's challenge, is not present in the original play:

---

[343] SEARLE 1946, p.284. It is worth noticing that Ottorino Respighi, in his operatic rendering of the Obey's play, while expanding considerably the text by going back to Ovid and Shakespeare, and introducing a reference to Dido in Lucretia's narration, still only managed a one act opera (first performed at the Teatro alla Scala on 24 February 1937, one year after the composer's death).
[344] See DUNCAN 1948, p.61.
[345] See OBEY 1931, p.3.

Tarquinius rides to Rome on his own initiative, driven by his own jealousy towards Collatinus.

One of the characteristics of La Compagnie des Quinze was that the actors had been trained to use not merely speech but also movement as a vital part of expression. Taking advantage of this Obey introduced the two roles of La Récitante and Le Récitant, as their presence requires a style of performance that can merge almost imperceptibly from acting into mime. In this way the author created a kind of extra dimension that seemed to transcend the normal limitations of realistic stagecraft. Duncan retains these two characters, which he originally called Male and Female Commentators, and although their function may appear similar to that in Obey's original, because of their attitude and dramatic position, they are substantially different. In the French play their presence might suggest a sort of metatheatrical level, between the stage and the audience, but they are in effect inside the action, and very much part of it; they relate exclusively to Lucretia and Tarquinius, and their main function is to express what the characters are thinking and feeling. Furthermore they appear when the action is already unfolding, at the beginning of Act I, scene ii, so it is not up to them to create the background for the action, as it happens in Duncan's adaptation. In the opera the Choruses are on stage from beginning to end, and they are presented 'reading from books' when the house curtain raises. At the beginning of the first and second acts, and in the two *Interludes*, their narration reveals the opera as an epic drama with moments of lyricism and depiction that appear like images supporting the Choruses' narration. The moments of 'dramatic' action are not continuous, nor self-sufficient, and they do not seem to be the essence of the drama. This is made evident by the intervention of the Choruses in the most crucial moments: even when a character exposes his or her inner thoughts through the conventional means of an almost traditional aria (see for example Junius in Act I, scene i), the presence of the Chorus deprives him of the intimacy that in a traditional operatic context would make the character individual and real. This never happens in the French original, where the Narrators support the dramatic action, but their comments are never a substitute for it.

Apart from the dramatic narrative, in essence the Choruses' interventions deal mainly with two subjects: the political situation in Rome during the

Etruscan oppression, and what has been dubbed the 'Christian commentary'. The most problematic aspect of the opera is the fact that the Choruses are looking at the story, which is allegedly taking place in the 6th Century BC, from a Christian perspective. The references to the Christian faith are made in the three occurrences of the 'Hymn' (at the beginning of Act I, at the beginning of Act II and at the very end), and in the Interlude of Act II, after the rape scene. According to Duncan, this was the composer's idea. Audiences seems to have been not a little puzzled by the presence of the Christian commentary, critics even more: 'The only totally incongruous element here is the Christian doctrine preached by the chorus at the end. It works neither dramatically nor philosophically. Indeed its inexcusability weakens the power of the story, which is that of the grandeur of Lucretia in her chastity and fidelity to her husband in surroundings of decadence and corruption'.[346] And also: 'A larger problem is posed by the final interpretation of the tragedy in terms of Christian Faith. I cannot help thinking it to be an artistic error'.[347]

It is indeed very difficult to reconcile a traditional perception of opera with this didactic presence. I believe that in order to understand the meaning of such a presence we need to look at the opera from a different perspective. In this work the concept of different levels of action is amplified in a very interesting direction, that also deals with the relationship of the characters with the audience, and of the audience with the action. A clarification of the dramatic structure may help us in coming to terms with what Philip Brett defines as 'Lucretia's odd dramaturgy'.[348]

OPERA-ORATORIO

In her analysis of the many narrative levels of the opera Margaret Mertz refers to the critical theories of voice, in particular to T.S.Eliot's distinction between lyrical, epic and dramatic:

> I shall explain at once what I mean by the 'three voices'. The first is the voice of the poet talking to himself - or to nobody. The second is the voice of the poet addressing an audience, whether large or small. The third is the voice of the poet when he attempts to create a dramatic character speaking

---

[346] DOWNES 1948.
[347] TAYLOR 1946.
[348] BRETT 1987, p.360.

in verse; when he is saying, not what he would say in his own person, but only what he can say within the limits of one imaginary character addressing another imaginary character.[349]

Without following up Mertz's own analysis, I would like to use this concept as a starting point, keeping in mind that what I am concerned with is the way those three different modalities of expression interact in the narrative structure of *The Rape of Lucretia*. It can also be useful to keep in mind Pierluigi Petrobelli's distinction of the three systems interacting in music theatre, that is dramatic action or plot, verbal organization and music.[350] If we consider the dramatic action - that is, the opera from beginning to end - as an horizontal or temporal dimension, we could also identify a kind of vertical or spatial dimension that is the scenic space, the fixed environment in which the theatrical experience takes place. In *Lucretia* in this dimension we find three basic levels, defined both physically and conceptually according to their relation to the action: the *stage*, as defined traditionally, which is the level where the representation takes place; the *audience*; and a third level, a *metatheatrical* one, suspended between the audience and the representation. This is the level where we would expect to find the narrators.

As in the horizontal dimension the three modalities of lyrical, dramatic and epic narration interact, at the same time as the focus of the action moves between the three vertical levels, and the characters themselves move within them. It is important to make clear that there is not necessarily a close relationship between the two dimensions: although most dramatic narration happens on stage, the different levels interact freely. The vertical levels cannot simply be defined as corresponding with epic, lyrical and dramatic, but they are determined by their relationship to the representation.

We can consider the plot the essence of the representation, lying beyond, or before, the modalities of representation. The first level, the *stage,* is that of traditional realistic stagecraft, i.e. that space where through suspension of disbelief we can accept a story as a real world of its own.

---

[349] ELIOT 1954, pp.6–7, quoted in MERTZ 1990, p.158. Similar ideas are approached in a different way by Roland Barthes in his 'Introduction to the Structural Analysis of Narratives' in *Image.Music.Text* (London: Fontana, 1977) and by Cesare Segre in *Teatro e romanzo* (Turin: Einaudi, 1984). In musical terms, the application of similar concepts is at the core of E.T.Cone, *The Composer's Voice* (Berkeley, 1974), but in a context that is quite different from the one we are dealing with at present.

[350] PETROBELLI 1994, p.113.

'We' are the *audience*, living in the present, looking upon the enacting of a story but well aware of the difference between us, real people, and the fictional characters living on the stage. It is important to point out how in a realistic dramatic representation the fictional characters are not conscious of their own fictitiousness, but they act and think as if the time/space they are moving in is the real world. In a space between *stage* and *audience* are the narrators, who comment on or describe the action: I would define this level as *metatheatrical* because it is not real or part of the story, but is somehow beyond the theatre, a link between the two more traditional levels. In a way, the narrators are spectators themselves, distanced from the events unfolding on the stage, but still differentiated from the audience, whom they address; although they are part of the dramatic representation, they do not completely belong to it, and sometimes one has the feeling that they almost join the audience, at least ideally.[351]

A characteristic feature of this opera is that the characters cross the boundaries of these three different levels: the narrators occasionally take part in the action on stage, and at times the other characters address the audience directly. This theatrical technique is not unprecedented, the classical examples being the addresses to the audience at the end of Shakespeare's *Midsummer Night's Dream*, or, in the realm of opera, the moralistic ending of Mozart's *Don Giovanni*. Nonetheless with *Lucretia* we have something more complex.

John Piper, the designer of the first production of *The Rape of Lucretia*, describes how the Commentators function in the context of the staging:

> At the very beginning it was decided that there should be a permanent fore-stage, with the two Commentators occupying thrones there, on each side. This permanent fore-stage had several advantages. First, it served to set the visual key and shape and colour around which the rest of the scenery could play, agreeing or contrasting as the action demanded. Secondly, it formed a permanent, timeless structure which, like the Commentators themselves as they have been conceived by the composer and the librettist, could act as an interpretative medium between action

---

[351] I am not aware of a production of the opera in which the Commentators where placed in the audience.

and audience. It was understood that the Commentators should, here and there, themselves take part in or at any rate stand on the edge of the action; so their thrones must not be too high or too far removed from the main stage. Lastly, the fore-stage reduced the width of the main playing space, which was an advantage, especially in larger theatres and opera houses, because the opera was planned as an intimate opera as to its size of cast; and as there was no chorus beyond the two commentators themselves, the playing space should not be too large.[352]

Piper refers to 'commentators', because such was their definition in the first draft of the libretto. It was only later that 'La Récitante' and 'Le Récitant' became the Female and Male Chorus, adding a reference to Greek tragedy. Although I have emphasised how there is no strict connection between the three spatial levels and the modality of narration, it is true that most of the time the Choruses limit themselves to 'epic' mode, as they are only 'narrating' and not 'acting' the story; furthermore, it is specified that they do not belong to a particular time, they are timeless (although in the first production they wore ancient garb). In this way they are as contemporaneous with Lucretia as they are with the audience. Because of the length of their narratives and the way they describe and introduce the action, they seem to relate more to epic than to drama. One could say that what the audience sees on the reduced stage is a dramatisation of the story the Choruses narrate. Nothing similar is present in Obey's text, where the presence of the Choruses enhances the realism of the dramatic action.

A work that bears many similarities with Britten's opera is Stravinsky's *Oedipus Rex*. This connection has been discussed by Arnold Whittall,[353] who notes that both works are contemporary treatments of a classical subject, in which stylisation plays a fundamental role. Britten's enthusiastic reaction to *Oedipus Rex* is recorded in an article from 1936, where he defines it as 'one of the peaks of Stravinsky's output'.[354]

In the Cocteau-Stravinsky revisitation of the Greek mythological tale we can also identify the three different spatial levels, due to the presence of the Narrator, a speaking voice that introduces the audience to some aspects of the myth being represented on stage. In *Oedipus Rex* though,

---

[352] John Piper, 'The design of *Lucretia*', in BRITTEN 1948, p. 70.
[353] WHITTALL 1982, p.113–114.
[354] BRITTEN 1977, p.11.

the three levels are kept well separated. It was one of the aims of the authors to avoid a direct emotional or psychological involvement of the audience in the drama: the Narrator's function is to distance the listeners from the story's dreadful happenings and, since he narrates the events in advance, to prevent a dramatic surprise that could trigger an instinctive emotional reaction. *Oedipus Rex* is defined by its authors an 'opera-oratorio'. Although in the spirit of neo-classicism such a heading was coloured with historical recollections of early eighteenth-century musical theatre, we could attempt another definition in the light of the interaction of the different narrative modalities previously considered. In traditional opera a story is narrated through dramatic action and lyrical moments; on the other hand, oratorio narrates mostly through epic and lyrical episodes.

Furthermore, while in opera the two spatial dimensions of stage and audience are kept separated, in oratorio the audience is somehow involved; it is possible to say that oratorio can at times move over the three spatial levels. In a musical theatre context, where the three modalities of expression interact, it is possible to talk of opera-oratorio, and I am not the first to make such a claim for *The Rape of Lucretia*. Although Britten and Duncan did not use this definition, in an article of 1946 W.H. Haddon Squire warned us that 'to approach the work as an opera in the usual sense of the word is to start with a wrong focus'.[355] He recognised the aesthetic roots of the work in the combination of the two forms, although he cites the use of allegory as an important factor in defining the genre:

> both oratorio and opera were developments of the early form of drama; indeed opera of a kind existed long before the Christian era, and is as old as the drama itself. In England oratorio may be said to be the successor of the Medieval Mystery play, and opera that of Morality. These religious plays, for many hundred years the only form of drama existing in England, were at first interludes in the church services. Later they were given at the church door, or by the church wall and later still, as they became more dramatic in character, on platforms in the market place. They had scenery and were accompanied by music. Their language was that of allegory, symbol and hidden metaphysic.[356]

---

[355] HADDON SQUIRE 1946, p.1.
[356] HADDON SQUIRE 1946, p.1.

Keeping in mind Britten's later interest in English Medieval plays, and the development of the church parables, such an hypothesis is not so unlikely; and as we have seen oratorio was Obey's model. The other obvious connection with the concept of oratorio is the insertion of the Christian commentary, but I would like to deal with this aspect at a later stage. A further point is worth some attention here: in *The Rape of Lucretia* the characters are not confined to a single spatial level. Although in the opera the narrators are always outside the inner action, they often join the other characters on stage, as if they were travelling through time. On other occasions, they seem to invite the audience to join in, for example in the hymn that is repeated at the beginning of each act and at the end of the work ('Whilst we…'): at such moments the audience is somehow transformed into a congregation.

Britten explored this idea further in later works such as *Let's make an opera*, *Saint Nicolas* and *Noye's Fludde*, where the involvement of the audience is not just a notion, but is accomplished through their active participation in the hymns. Even more interesting is the fact that the main characters occasionally join the Choruses in the metatheatrical level between the audience and the action, as in the quartet of act II, scene i, just before the rape. At that moment, the dramatic time is suspended, and Lucretia and Tarquinius join the Choruses in a metaphorical reflection upon the events, detaching themselves from the inner action. In a way, we could say that generally the characters never completely identify with the role they play. We can see this in the way that they often objectivize their experience. They are not individuals on the stage: they are characters acting out a ritualistic drama, and they seem to be aware of it.

I have consciously used the word ritualistic, for I believe it is one of the keys to the opera. Mervyn Cooke has stressed the fact that in *Lucretia* 'conscious stylisation and the element of ritual play an important role';[357] if we consider how for the librettist the story of Lucretia was essentially a myth, and as every myth has a metaphorical and allegorical element, we can read the work as a ritualistic re-enactment of the myth. It is worth noting that in a ritual the audience/congregation and the officiants are all on the same time/space level, that is the present, being differentiated only by their function. That means that effectively the characters, the Choruses

---

[357] COOKE 1987, 'The Prophecy of Lucretia', p.54.

and the audience are really on the same level; they just have different functions within the re-enactment of the myth, and those functions imply moving across different spatial levels to take on different dramatic responsibilities. This idea connects with Britten's notion of what constitutes a 'real musical experience' according to his statements in the Aspen Award Speech, where the experience is coloured with elements of celebration, if not definitely of ritual.[358]

To summarise, we have seen how in *The Rape of Lucretia* the dramatic structure is strictly related to the style of performance and the stage directions; the overall dramaturgy is built into the text, and is relevant to interpretation. Devices such as the stylisation of the acting and the crossing of narrative and spatial levels enhance the sensation that what we are seeing is not a window on a past event recreated for our enjoyment, but a contemporary ritual in which we, the audience, are taking part. The emotional distance that the stylisation creates paradoxically involves us more directly in the action: being timeless, the Choruses are our contemporaries, and the moment the actors on stage join them they reveal themselves not simply as characters but as our contemporaries too: they are members of the community who happen to be the officiants of the ritual. There is no suspension of disbelief here, on the contrary we are requested not to fall into the theatrical illusion.

This element can be very relevant to an interpretation of the work, and we will see how the musical structure enhances those elements which contribute to make of *Lucretia* something of a *Lehrstuck*. In a way such a conception is quite near to a peculiar element of Brechtian theatre:

> although Brecht, like Shaw, Ibsen and other realists, was an ardent crusader for humanity, he despised the realistic form - especially the form of the well-made play. Brecht was a reformer determined to make audiences think, determined to drive home his points by any and every theatrical device at his disposal. He detested romantic and sentimental emotions, demanding that audiences remain awake and critical, not hypnotised by pretty stories. When he called for the elimination of

---

[358] See BRITTEN 1964, p.20.

emotions he was thinking of the sentimental emotions - the romantic mandolin love themes of popular 'well-made' plays and operas.[359]

The Rape of Lucretia certainly does not respond to a traditional idea of 'well-made' opera, and its ambition of being far from realism is emphatically reinforced by the musical architecture of the piece, as I hope to elucidate with a brief discussion of the musical context itself.

HARNESSING SONGS TO HUMAN TRAGEDY

The first essays[360] on the work that provided detailed musico-dramatic analysis focused particularly on the interaction of two main thematic ideas, identified with Lucretia and Tarquinius; they were recognized as a basic element of the opera, as they pervade the musical content, if not the structure. This idea has become commonplace in critical literature. For Eric Walter White, who in 1948 wrote the first monograph on Britten and his operas, these two contrasted musical ideas represent the dramatic conflict at the base of the opera, spirit defiled by fate or Lucretia ravished by Tarquinius. In his view, even if these cells are spoken as of motifs, and their permutations and transformations traced in some detail, the idea that Britten used a comprehensive system of leitmotifs has to be avoided. Peter Evans has given a convincing reading of the significance of the relationship, or maybe we should say of the contrast, between these two motifs, together with a reading of the possible meaning of the tonal plan. Nevertheless, he himself accepts that his discussion of tonal operations can be dismissed as entirely subjective.[361] Even if we accept that 'Britten made unequivocally clear elsewhere how naturally attracted he was towards a fusion of structural functions and symbolic functions in his tonal design',[362] a symbolic reading is still subjected to the association of meanings that precede the musical analysis, and unfortunately Britten was not very open about his own associations. Margaret Mertz has underlined how the musical structure relies heavily on cross references and different levels of allusions:

---

[359] See WHITING 1978, p.163.
[360] KELLER 1947; BOYS 1948; Norman Del Mar, 'The Chamber Operas', in KELLER 1952, pp.132–145.
[361] EVANS 1979, p.141.
[362] EVANS 1979, p.141.

> Many of these cross-references are not as explicit as literal quotations, though explicit quotations do occur at one very important moment in the final scene. More important still are the indirect, less literal references which produce a multi-leveled set of connections across the entire span of the opera. The most pervasive level of allusion consists of the continuous motivic connections within and between the discrete scenes. Within the separate numbers, the musical structures are projected by the set of relations established in the tonal system. [363]

In the present context such elements are not primarily relevant. We can understand motifs as a compositional device, and as a way to achieve organic unity. At the same time, because we cannot be certain about Britten's own perception of tonal symbolism, it may not be necessary to give names to the elements that combine to create the dynamic tension inside the tonal structure. It may be possible to accept a superficial reading of tension against resolution, which may be sufficient to the basic understanding of the dramatic situation. What I find more interesting - and possibly in this context more significant - than problems of overall tonal structure, or harmonic language, are problems of formal representation. The choice of lyrical or narrative moments, with the expansion of time that this implies, and the differentiation of levels of narration and action, which clearly reflects the multi-levelled structure of the libretto and of the action itself, is in my opinion a key to reading *Lucretia*, and to understanding the kind of experiment Britten attempted with this unusual work.

Such an approach can be justified by Britten's method of composition. In an interview he describes how 'First I sit down and conceive the idea of a piece. By "idea" I mean the structural plan - forms, moods, contrast, texture, key system. Then I work out the details, embody the idea in notes'.[364] It looks as if overall structure and formal considerations have more relevance here than motivic connections, and that the system of cross-references and allusion, although functional to the feeling of consistency and unity of the work, may not have been a priority in the planning. Some of the ambiguities in the interpretation of the work do not seem to be resolved by looking at the music, but this might be due to the

---

[363] MERTZ 1990, p.23.
[364] 'Profile: Benjamin Britten', *Observer*, 27 October 1964.

fact that we look at the work as if it were a traditional opera. Defined 'classical in feeling and neo-classical in form', with a 'complete avoidance of everything that could be called romantic',[365] this is a work that in many ways does not belong to the dramatic operatic tradition, not only on the grounds we have discussed until now, of interaction of different narrative modes, but especially when we look at the music and at the use of genres and stylistic conventions.

As we have seen the opera is organised in two acts, each divided into two scenes. These are introduced by narrative sections in which there is no action represented on the inner stage, no dramatic playing: instead we have an historical introduction that reinforces the association with the epic mode of the oratorio. When talking about the general musical structure of the opera Britten explained how early on librettist and composer had decided to divide the narration into a succession of small numbers (arias, recitatives, duets, etc.); nonetheless the work is not divided into small scenes, and the definition of 'scene' is used in its broader sense, indicating the setting where the action takes place more than the number of characters on stage.

---

[365] NEWMAN 1946.

TABLE 4: *THE RAPE OF LUCRETIA*[366]
ACT I

CUE/TEMPO MARKING	text/ stage direction	form
SCENE 1: Prelude *Allegro con fuoco*	[House Curtain rises] 'Rome is now ruled…'	Recitativo accompagnato, with episodes of secco.
[7] *Solenne*	'Whilst we…'	**Hymn**
(Scene 1): Frame i [8] *Lento tranquillo*	[Front Cloth rises] 'Here the thirsty ev'ning…'	Narration: arioso
[10] *Vivace*	[The tent opened from inside] 'Who reaches heaven first…'	'Drinking song', verse 1
[11] *Lento tranquillo*	'They drink…'	Narration: arioso
[12] *Vivace*	'Who reaches heaven last…'	'Drinking song', verse 2
[13] *Lento tranquillo*	'The night is weeping…'	Narration: arioso
[14] *Vivace*	'Who drowns…'	'Drinking song', verse 3
Frame ii [16] *Recitativo*	'Love like wine spills …'	Narration: recitativo secco
[18] *Allegro pesante*	'Peace! Peace!…'	Terzetto
Frame iii [19] *Allegro con fuoco*	[Junius rushes angrily from the tent] 'Lucretia…'	Junius' aria
[22] *Tranquillo*	'Oh, it is plain…'	Narration: arioso
[23] *Animato*	'Tomorrow the city…'	Junius' aria
[24] *Sempre in tempo giusto*	'Collatinus is politically astute…'	Narration: recitativo accompagnato
[25] *Molto più largamente*	'Oh, my God…'	Narration: arioso
Frame iv [26] *Andante con moto*	[Collatinus coming out of tent] 'How bitter of you…'	Dialogue: arioso
[30]	'Those who love…'	Collatinus' aria
Frame v [32] *Vivace come sopra*	'Oh, the only girl…'	Drinking song, then recitativo secco
[33] *Moderato*	'Good night!…'	Dialogue: arioso
[34] *Allegro agitato*	'What makes the Nubian…'	Duet
[37] *Sempre in tempo giusto*	'It seems we agree…'	Dialogue: arioso
[42] *Lento tranquillo*	'Tarquinius does not dare…'	Narration: cantabile

---

[366] Refers to Benjamin Britten, *The Rape of Lucretia*, vocal score (London: Boosey & Hawkes, 1946).

ACT I

INTERLUDE [44] *Allegro con fuoco.*	[Front Cloth] 'Tarquinius does not wait…'	Epic narration with orchestral accompaniment
SCENE 2: Frame i *Molto moderato*	[Front Cloth] 'Their spinning wheel…'	'Spinning song', refrain [Female Chorus' narration]
[58]	'Till in one word…'	'Spinning song', verse 1
[60]	'Their humming...'	'Spinning song', refrain
[62]	'Till like an old ewe…'	'Spinning song', verse 2
[64]	'Their restless wheel…'	'Spinning song', refrain
[66]	'Till somebody loves her…'	'Spinning song', verse 3
[68]	'Their little wheel…'	'Spinning song', refrain
Frame ii *Recitativo agitato*	[Lucretia stops the spinning with a gesture] 'Listen! I heard a knock…'	Dialogue: recitativo secco
[72] *Agitato*	'How cruel men are…'	Lucretia's arietta
Recitativo	'Madam is tired…'	Recitativo secco
Frame iii [74] *Andante tranquillo*	[Lucia and Bianca fold linen] 'Time treads upon the hands…'	Lyrical narration with accompaniment of orchestra and chorus
Frame iv *Recitativo tranquillo*	'How quiet is tonight…'	Recitativo accompagnato
[78] *Lento*	'The oatmeal slippers …'	Narration: arioso
Frame v [85] *Allegro – Recitativo agitato - Allegretto*	[Knocking. In the following scene the characters mime the action described by Male Chorus and Female Chorus] 'None of the women move…'	Recitativo with orchestral accompaniment. The music is very descriptive, as in the Interlude.
[93] *Allegro grazioso*	'Goodnight…' [The characters leave the stage. The Male and Female Choruses pick up their books and continue reading. House Curtain slowly falls]	'Goodnight quartet', with insertion of recitative (i.e., the choruses' description)

ACT II

CUE/TEMPO MARKING	text/ stage direction	FORM
SCENE 1: Prelude *Allegro sostenuto*	[The House Curtain rises] 'The prosperity of the Etruscans was due…'	Recitativo accompagnato
[12] *Solenne*	'Whilst we…'	**Hymn**
(Scene 1):Frame i [13] *Allegretto comodo*	[The front cloth rises] 'She sleeps as a rose…'	Female Chorus' aria
Frame ii [18] *Poco lento e misterioso*	'When Tarquinius desires…'	Narration: *Sprechgesang*, with percussions only
[21] *Allegretto comodo*	[Tarquinius stands at the head of Lucretia's bed] 'Thus sleeps Lucretia…'	End of Female Chorus' aria
[22] *Molto tranquillo*	'Within this frail…'	Tarquinius' aria
[24] *Poco agitato*	'Wake up…'	Duet
Frame iii [26] *Più tranquillo*	[Tarquinius kisses Lucretia] 'Her lips receive Tarquinius…'	Narration: recitativo accompagnato
[27] *Allegro agitato*	[Lucretia wakes] 'Lucretia!…'	Dialogue: arioso
[31] *Molto animato*	'How could I give Taquinius…'	Duet
[35]	[She turns away from him] 'Oh, my belov'd Collatinus..'	Lucretia's arioso
[36] (*furioso*)	'Easier stem the Tiber's flood…'	Tarquinius' arioso
[37] (*largamente*)	'Is this the Prince of Rome?…'	Dialogue: arioso
Frame iv [38] *Grave*	'Go, Tarquinius…'	Quartet
[41] *Poco più moto*	[He pulls the coverlet from the bed and threatens her with his sword] 'Poised like a dart…'	Quartet
[42] *Più largamente e molto sostenuto*	[Tarquinius mounts Lucretia's bed] 'See how the rampant centaur…'	Quartet: a cappella
INTERLUDE [43] *Presto*	[Tarquinius beats out the candle with his sword. Front cloth quickly falls] 'Here in this scene…'	Chorale figurato

ACT II

SCENE 2: Frame i [53] *Allegro molto*	[The 2nd Curtain rises showing the hall of Lucretia's home] 'Oh what a lovely day…'	Duet
[61] *Vivace*	'Oh Lucia, please help me…'	Flowers' duet
[after 67] *Recitativo*	'Bianca, how long...'	Recitativo secco
Allegretto semplice	'I often wonder…'	Lucia's arietta
Frame ii *Recitativo*	[Enter Lucretia] 'Good morning my Lady…'	Dialogue: recitativo secco
[68] *Allegro agitato*	'How hideous!…'	Recitativo accompagnato
[71] *Un poco più largamente*	[Lucretia seizes an orchid] 'Give him this orchid…'	'Orchid song'
[74] *A tempo*	'Shall I throw the rest away…'	Recitativo accompagnato
[75] *Andante lento*	[Lucretia sits and makes a wreath with the orchids] 'Flowers bring to ev'ry year…'	'Flowers' aria'
[77] *Poco animando*	'My child...'	Recitativo accompagnato
[78] *Allegro molto*	'Yes, I remember'	Bianca's aria
Frame iii *Recitativo agitato*	[Enter Lucia] 'You were right...'	Dialogue: recitativo secco
Frame iv [81] *Poco adagio e dolente*	[Lucretia is seen slowly walking to Collatinus]	Oboe solo
[82]	'Lucretia…'	Duet
[84]	'Now, there is no sea..'	Recitativo accompagnato
[91] *Moderato*	'O my love…'	Cantabile
[92] *Andante sostenuto*	'If spirit's not given…'	Arioso
[93] *Più mosso ed agitato*	'Even great love…'	Recitativo accompagnato
Frame v [95] *Alla marcia grave*	[Collatinus kneels over the body of Lucretia] 'This dead hand…'	Vocal passacaglia
FINALE/POSTLUDE [102] *A tempo*	'Is it all…'	Recitativo accompagnato
[104] *Sempre in tempo giusto lento*	'It is not all…'	Arioso
[107] *Poco più' lento*	'Since time...'	**Hymn**

The score does not indicate separate numbers, as in *opera seria*, but it is quite easy to recognise within each scene the smaller units, and it is possible to divide each scene into what we can, with a cinematographical reference, define as 'frames'. Within each scene, we have a sequence of smaller units: songs, arias, ariosos, different degrees of recitative.[367] We can then see the musical structure responds to the poetic structure of the libretto, and this is the level Britten was referring to in his introduction to the opera, when talking about the preliminary planning stages of the work.[368]

What is most significant though, is Britten's choice of musical styles, with the reference to genre that this may imply. On the whole, we do have quite a number of what might seem traditional 'operatic' ensembles, for example the 'drinking' or 'spinning' songs.[369] The only occurrence of what could be properly defined an aria is Lucretia's 'flower song',[370] and Peter Evans points out that 'extended solos of aria-like balance are far less common than are elaborated ensembles'.[371] The most noticeable feature is the predominance of narration, most of the time expressed through different types of recitative, from *secco* to the 'most lavish *cantabile*'.[372] As we have already mentioned, the narration is not confined exclusively to the Male and Female Choruses, but there are instances when they are joined by the characters: for example after orchestral number 16 in act I, scene i, where Tarquinius and Junius take over from the narration of the Male Chorus (although in this case the separation between levels is still well defined). A particularly relevant instance is the *a cappella* quartet that precedes the rape. The text

> See how the rampant centaur mounts the sky
> And serves the sun with all its seed of stars
> Now the great river underneath the ground
> Flows through Lucretia and Tarquinius is drowned

---

[367] See Table 4.
[368] BRITTEN 1948, p.8.
[369] Act I, scene i and scene ii.
[370] The 'Flower song' was published separately, together with 'The ride' and the 'Slumber song', under the title 'Three arias from *The Rape of Lucretia*' (London: Boosy & Hawkes, 1946).
[371] EVANS 1989, p.129.
[372] EVANS 1989, p.129.

is sung by Tarquinius and Lucretia, who cease to be the characters and become narrators themselves. The 'static tableau'[373] that has started with an accompanied quartet at the line 'Go Tarquinius!' is one of the most unusual moments of the whole work: exactly when the tension reaches its climax Britten and his librettist abruptly hold the action still, in the most unrealistic of manners, and force the 'characters' on stage, as well as the audience, to distance themselves from the emotional content of the scene. The musical structure goes from accompanied vocal quartet ('Go Tarquinius') through accompanied recitative ('Poised like a dart') to the contrapuntal stillness of an unaccompanied quartet only to plunge into the Chorale of the interlude. A reviewer at the original production was particularly puzzled by Britten's musical solution, when he commented on the

> curious failure to make a great musical climax of the central episode of the story - a failure which is part of the price paid for the introduction of the Christian motif. One does not, of course, demand a crude Straussian representation of the lustful crime, but the violence of rape must surely be matched by some sort of musical violence, and I cannot think that this was the moment to launch the two commentators on a figured chorale.[374]

It would be probably naive to talk of the composer's 'inability' to achieve an effective dramatic impact, considering the degree of musico-dramatic prowess displayed in *Peter Grimes*. It seems to be more likely that Britten was consciously attempting something very different, as is implied by the unexpected use of a chorale, a form more typical of sacred music than of opera, in the interlude. It is true that the music in the interlude might easily suggest 'aggression', or that it could even be read as a rhythmic description of intercourse, as pointed out by Ernest Ansermet, conductor of the first production, who defined the orchestral passage a 'depiction of the rhythm of copulation'.[375] Ansermet goes on to say that such a depiction would contradict the pious hymn sung by the Choruses, although this is not necessarily true, as the musical representation of the 'violence' in the background could be seen to reinforce the Choruses' plea. The point is that the context in which the Chorale is heard does not seem to require a Chorale, and I would therefore suggest that it is used

---

[373] MERTZ 1990, p.93.
[374] TAYLOR 1946.
[375] In DUNCAN 1981, p.83.

not only to suggest religious association but structurally, as part of the overall conception of the work, thus creating a decisive ambiguity in the genre definition of the work. This impression is reinforced by considering the other episodes in which there is a strong reference to a genre proper to sacred music, the three occurrences of the hymn sung in unison by the Choruses ('Whilst we…').

Although not indicated as such in the score or in the libretto, the initial section of the first scene in each act is a sort of prelude: in both cases we have an historical introduction narrated by the Choruses. The inner curtain (or front cloth) that encloses the dramatic action is still closed, and it is quite relevant that there is no specified division in the score or the dramatic layout between the Choruses's narration and the beginning of what we would consider the 'real' action. Musically, in these initial sections, we are presented with two long portions of *recitativo secco* - although the orchestra is involved in the accompaniment, it never supports the vocal line as such.

The narration leads into a hymn, and only after the hymn does the front cloth rise and we are presented with the action. We find the hymn also at the end of the opera, and this structural position enhances the importance of the hymn itself. After Lucretia stabs herself, all the characters on stage (basically all the characters in the opera, excluding the dead Lucretia and Tarquinius, who does not appear on stage after the rape) sing a long passacaglia which sets a series of individual epitaphs over Lucretia's death. This should have been the end of the piece, but apparently Britten requested of the librettist a coda, because his sense of structural balance was not satisfied. According to Duncan's own report of the events, Britten felt that the piece was 'musically…not finished', and he wanted to 'write a final piece beyond the curtain, as it were to frame the entire work'.[376] Britten specified he wanted a vocal piece for the Male and Female Choruses, saying: 'At the moment, the piece ends with your line "Is this all? It is all! It is all!", but for me it isn't'.[377] This might suggest that although Britten felt the piece was not finished musically, he was really considering a text-related problem; as it were, Britten asked Duncan to write 'One big piece. The biggest of the opera'. Duncan describes the final

---

[376] DUNCAN 1981, p. 75.
[377] DUNCAN 1981, p. 75.

canzone as a 'universal comment on the entire tragedy', stating Lucretia's rape as a 'violation of humanity'. Musically it is a succession of two long arioso sections sung first by the Female Chorus and then by the Male Chorus, which leads again to a final statement of the hymn, in the same key as its first occurrence, but with different words.

The whole final section is very similar to the two introductory sections of each act, and in this way the final hymn, while nicely rounding off the musical structure,[378] also becomes one of the most relevant features of the whole work. The structure of the hymn can easily be likened to a chorale (four verses, the first two similar, the third slightly varied, the fourth harmonically resolving). We are therefore left with a work that starts and ends with a chorale-like melody, sung in unison by the Choruses, and that has a chorale at what seems the dramatic climax of the action. This is enough to make us wonder whether we are looking at an opera at all. By framing the work with chorale sequences, i.e. the chorale itself, the hymns and the sections of 'epic narration' that precede them, Britten made these sections very important, if not the most important elements of the work, shifting the focus of the work onto the commentary rather than on the story itself. Of course this reinforces the connection with the oratorio tradition, and even with Bach's great passions, as the two narrators could be easily likened to the function of the evangelists.[379]

By using references to genres other than opera, Britten created a work in which stylization predominates not only in the text and in the staging, but also in the music. Through stylisation and distance the emotions in the opera are crystallised not so much in their essence or intensity, but in the modality of expression. The audience is not allowed to subside into empathetic impersonation, but is forced to look at the drama in a critical way. There is not a final resolution, an emotional catharsis. Once the re-enactment is over, the audience should not be able simply to discard it, but in theory they should leave the theatre thinking about it. What we can wonder, in the case of *The Rape of Lucretia*, is the substance of what they should be thinking about.

---

[378] For a tonal plan of the opera see EVANS 1979, pp.137-141.
[379] Recent stagings of Bach's Passions might support this connection.

LUCRETIA

In the critical literature the figure of Lucretia is usually seen as the centre of the drama, and interpretations of the opera deal mainly with her character. In Arnold Whittall's view, 'the attempt to place feminine psychology at the centre of the action tells us more about the librettist than composer';[380] a similar view is supported by many who see Britten's work as an expression of his own psychological struggle to deal with his own homosexuality, and with his own position inside - or maybe outside - society. In the context of such an approach it appears sometimes difficult to come to terms with works like *Lucretia* or *A Midsummer Night's Dream*; similar problems are presented by the church parables (with the possible exception of *The Prodigal Son*). Nonetheless, I believe it is possible to present a reading of the opera in which the focus of the drama is not Lucretia's psychology.[381]

From what we have so far discussed about the genesis and structure of the work one could get the impression that psychology was not really a matter of great interest for either the librettist or the composer. What seemed important for them was to represent a myth, a parable, in which the characters' inner life is not as relevant as the metaphor they stand for: their role is simply to move the action. We are not so much concerned about what they feel, but rather about what they represent and what they do. On the whole, the description of the characters - for example in the linen scene (act I, scene ii, frame iii) - is so general as to deprive them of individuality; Duncan's universal statements, whose function is probably to reinforce the sensation that they are outside time and space, makes them even more unreal. This could derive from Obey, whose play is essentially concerned with action: there is little psychological working out of the characters, as physical action is what for him constituted the drama.[382] Mime - a discipline that uses physical expression while

---

[380] WHITTALL 1982, p.118. The same could also be said of *Gloriana*, *The Turn of the Screw* and *Phaedra*.

[381] Germaine Greer notices that on the general subject of the Lucretia's myth 'what happens to Lucretia is not the issue; damage done to the victim is never the point in masculine account of rape. The woman does not stand for herself, but for a galaxy of notions, some of which can be described as political' (GREER 2001); and Jill Burrows also points out that 'Lucretia is not her own creature. She is, even after marriage, a function of her father. She is also the possession of her husband' (BURROWS 2001). This notion has not been questioned in any of the versions of the story, making it problematic to consider Lucretia's psychology the focus of the events.

[382] See KNOWLES 1967, pp.222–223.

completely disregarding words - has great relevance, and as a consequence there is not much space for the exploration of inner thoughts and self-aware psychological processes. I am not trying to deny that Lucretia plays a central part in the drama, but I would like to suggest that maybe her psychology is not the main focus of Britten's operatic treatment of the 'Lucretia myth'.

A main problem in the interpretation is what has been considered Lucretia's ambiguity; the myth itself has always caused interpretative problems, and we will later examine on what grounds. As a starting point, it may be helpful to look at how the main character is presented in the two plays. In Obey's play, Lucretia is depicted as a happy young lady, proud of her house ('the best ordered house in Rome'), and of her condition, a steady Roman gentlewoman in every sense: amongst other things she is described by the narrator as a gourmet, and with a sensitive nose. In the first scene in which she appears, while at the spinning-wheel in the evening, she does not talk at all, therefore not revealing anything about her inner thoughts. When Tarquinius arrives, she behaves as the perfect hostess her social status requires of her, and her cordiality suggests that she feels nothing to fear from Tarquinius' presence, as it is described by the narrator:

> She is remembering all that Roman hospitality comprises of courtesy and thoughtfulness [...] She is wondering if the steward is aware of all that must be done for a royal guest [...] She is hoping that his room will be warm enough and not too warm; that it will not have the air of a room too long shut up; that the sheets will be cool and dry.[383]

In the following scene, the rape scene, she suddenly awakens when Tarquinius, who has entered her room, kisses her breast: she tries to resist, she cries, she shouts, she asks for help, causing a great deal of amusement to the Etruscan Prince, who never more than on this occasion appears as a total sadist:

---

[383] 'Elle se rapelle tous les égards. Les soins, les prévenances de l'hospitalité romaine [...] Elle se demande si le majordome sait bien tout ce que l'on doit à un hôte royal [...] Elle espère que la chambre est tiède, qu'elle ne sent pas le renfermé, que le draps du lit sont bien secs'. (OBEY 1931, p.138; English translation by Thornton Wilder, in WILDER 1933, pp.28–29).

> How beautiful you are in your tears; your sobs shake me from head to feet. Weep! Weep![384]

In the play Lucretia has to submit voluntarily, for Tarquinius threatens to kill her and a slave as if he had found them together:

> Be still! [*Drawing his sword*] Listen! If you refuse me – I shall slay you in your bed. Then I shall cut the throat of one of your meanest, lowest slaves. I shall throw his body into your dead arms, and I shall swear before the immortal gods that it was in his embrace I slew you.[385]

The morning after, when she gets up, she resolves to die, and she stabs herself alone in the bedroom, before sending for Collatinus, to whom she wants to confess in order to save him from Tarquinius' derision:

> Collatine! If it is true that your honour is deposited in my hands, know that it has been snatched from me by violence. The blame is not mine. It was for your honour that I received him into the house. It was from you he came. How could I sent him from the door? He complained of his fatigue...he, he talked of courage and virtue...[...] I bequeath my honour to the blade of a knife. I bequeath my blood to Tarquin. My blood stained by him, soiled by him, shall be poured out for him. Let my testament be drawn up, and let that be his portion in it. And you, my dear lord and husband, what shall I bequeath to you? My resolution, oh, my beloved. My soul to heaven! My body to earth; and my good name, let it be left without fear to those that come after me.[386]

---

[384] 'Que tu est belle en larmes!...Ah! tes sanglots m'émbralent de la tête aux pieds... Pleure! Pleure!' (OBEY 1931, p.153; WILDER 1933, p.49).

[385] 'Tais-toi! (*Il tire son glaive.*) Si tu me repousses, écoute! Je te tue dans ton lit, puis j'égorge quelqu'un de tes plus vils esclaves. Je jette son corps dans tes bras morts et je jure les dieux que je vous ai tués en te voyant l'embrasser!' (OBEY 1931, p.154; WILDER 1933, p.50).

[386] 'Collatin! s'il est vrai que je sois responsable de ton honneur, il m'a été arraché par un assaut violent. Je ne suis pas coupable. C'est en ton honneur que j'ai accueilli cet homme. Il venait de ta part. Pouvais-je le renvoyer?... Et puis, il se plaignait d'être las... Et il parlait de vertu...[...] Je lègue mon honneur au couteau. Je lègue mon sang à Tarquin. Mon sang impur, souillé par lui, sera versé pour lui. Qu'on l'inscrive comme son dû dans mon testament. Cher Seigneur, que te léguerai-je, à toi?... Ma résolution, mon bien-aimé! Mon âme, au ciel; mon corps, à la terre; et quant à ma réputation, qu'elle soit livrée sans crainte à ceux qui viendront après moi. (OBEY 1931, pp.162, 166; WILDER 1933, pp.62, 67).

While she is waiting for her husband she dresses up, she reassures the maidens and makes plans for the future of the household. Her confession is never spoken, and she dies when Collatinus angrily realises what has happened.

Duncan's and Britten's Lucretia is quite a different character. We are introduced to her in the first scene, when the men are drinking to her, and she is described as chaste and lovely, represented not as an individual, but as a symbol: a symbol of political power in the eyes of Junius, a symbol of personal gratification in the eyes of Tarquinius. For the latter she represents something he cannot have: when talking about his 'barren bevy of listless whores' he specifies: 'Oh, I am tired of willing women! / It's all habit with no difficulty or achievement to it'.[387] Certainly Lucretia represents a challenge, and it looks as if Tarquinius' desire is excited by Lucretia's chastity (i.e. her unattainability) as much as by her beauty, two elements that in his mind are equal: 'Lucretia's chaste as she is beautiful'.

Not to be underestimated is the fact that Tarquinius has been challenged by Junius: his delirious ride to Rome tells us a lot about the impetuous anger and outrageous pride of the 'Prince of Rome'. As we have seen this is a detail that was not present in the French version, where Tarquinius rides to Rome on his own initiative. When Lucretia finally appears, her first words are a statement of her longing for her husband: the dramatic reason for the whole scene seems to be the representation of her passionate nature. As Arnold Whittall points out, 'it is made abundantly clear that Lucretia is a woman of experience, but of experience "within the law"'.[388] It is also made very clear that she is a passionate woman, who yearns for her husband:

> Collatinus! Collatinus!
> Whenever we are made to part
> We live within each other's heart
> Both waiting, each wanting.

And later

---

[387] All quotations from the libretto are from HERBERT 1979.
[388] WHITTALL 1982, p.114.

> How cruel men are
> To teach us love!
> They wake us from
> The sleep of youth
> Into the dream of passion
> Then ride away
> While we still yearn.

These brief statements are essentially the only insights we get into Lucretia's inner life, and although they help to contextualize most of what happens after, I believe that they are not sufficient to make 'feminine psychology' the centre of the drama. Lucretia is in no way a rounded character like Carmen or Vitellia, or to remain within the limits of Britten's operatic characters Peter Grimes or even Ellen Orford. She seems to lack individuality: she does not have characteristic traits, unlike her French equivalent. All the time she is a symbol, the chaste Lucretia, the perfect Roman *matrona*. In the rape scene the highly allegorical and sententious dialogue does not leave much space for the expression of feelings; the morning after she is represented in a highly emotional state, but even then her statements are on a universal level. Duncan, in his attempt to construct a universal myth, has made the three female characters archetypes, limiting their individuality, and it is interesting to note how this does not happen to the male counterparts. While Bianca and Lucia represent two different ages of 'woman', caring motherly middle age and naive inexperienced youth, Tarquinius, Collatinus and Junius remain individuals with their own personalities: they do not seem to merely represent the abstract ideas of 'tyrant', 'envious manipulator' and 'trusting citizen' or whatever. Somehow their personalities are better defined:[389] if we look at the text we can see that while the two scenes in the first act are supposed to mirror each other, in effect their content is very different. The men are indeed presented as individuals, probably because the three of them are equals, while Lucia and Bianca are but subsidiary characters to Lucretia. The women express themselves in general terms, talking about 'broadly feminine characteristics' during their spinning and linen-folding songs, while the Female Chorus presents what demands to be perceived as a universal condition of women.

---

[389] See also EVANS 1989, p.127.

Somehow Lucretia is not given the chance to present herself as a real character, at least not in the first scene: even when she expresses her yearning she still does it in general terms using the plural, 'while we still yearn'.

The main reason to consider 'feminine psychology' the focus of the drama seems the fact that the main character is a woman who is raped and as a consequence is driven to such a level of despair that she kills herself. Critical literature seems quite divided about the reasons for Lucretia's suicide. The story as presented in the opera is ambiguous: when Tarquinius approaches her bed and kisses her, she returns his kiss, a detail not present in the Obey version. We are informed that she was 'dreaming of Collatinus', and we know that she was yearning for his physical presence. But is Lucretia merely a victim, or is she not also, however reluctantly, a willing participant?

The arrival of the Etruscan Prince in the middle of the night creates a tense situation: yet when Tarquinius awakens her she does not seem surprised by his intrusion, as if she was somehow expecting it. That she has always been suspicious of Tarquinius is revealed in her statement: 'In the forest of my dreams/ You have always been the Tiger'. This statement does not need to be read as a confession of Lucretia's attraction to Tarquinius. According to Peter Evans, who supports his reading with a group of other references, the tiger is here a symbol of the 'powerful fascination that Tarquinius has exercised in Lucretia's dreams'.[390] But as Evans himself recognises, alternative explanations are possible, and in this specific case the tiger can also be seen as a symbol of blind cruelty and lustful voracity. Furthermore, the image of the tiger was already present in Shakespeare, where it is dangerous rather than erotically charged: "the tiger that doth live by slaughter"'.[391] Such an alternative reading would also accord with the crude description of the Etruscans given in the Choruses's introduction to the second act: 'passion for creation and lust to kill'.

The dialogue between Tarquinius and Lucretia in the rape scene has been considered one of the main sources of ambiguity. The context we are

---

[390] EVANS 1989, p.141.
[391] BURROWS 1996, p.13.

presented with is not wide enough to allow an interpretation of the personal relationship that existed between Lucretia and Tarquinius, but one could suspect that there was not one. It is made quite obvious from the introduction to act II that the Etruscans are seen as oppressors:

> And Tarquinius Superbus ruled in Rome
> Relentless as a torrid sun.
> And the whole city sulked in discontent
> Hating the foreign aristocrats.

There is nonetheless some basis for the argument that Lucretia in the opera is actually represented as guilty, and the real accusation seems to come from the Female Chorus, when she implores Tarquinius to retreat:

> Go Tarquinius,
> before your nearness
> tempts Lucretia to yield
> to your strong maleness.

At the same time, Tarquinius has accused Lucretia over and over again of being attracted to him:

> Yet the linnet your eyes
> lift with desire
> and the cherries of your lips
> are wet with wanting.

Indeed, Duncan's erotically charged text appears quite unambiguous, and Lucretia's denials unconvincing. In the first drafts of the libretto Duncan assigned to the Choruses a commentary in which the sexual imagery was even more direct. The most interesting change between the first draft and the final version relates to Lucretia's evocation of Collatinus's love:

> The pity is Collatinus
> You have loved too well
> and have coaxed my body
> from lively pleasure
> to the little death of ecstasy

> and thus you have taught my blood
> a different measure
> to my mind's true constancy
> Oh go Tarquinius.[392]

This statement seems to be self-accusatory. We would be led to believe that Lucretia's physical reaction threatens to overcome her better judgement, also because Tarquinius has just challenged her commenting about her physical excitement: 'Can you deny your blood's dumb pleading?/.../Can you refuse your blood's desiring?'. In the final version this statement was changed:

> Oh, my beloved Collatinus
> You have loved so well
> You have tuned my body
> To the chaste note of a silver lute
> And thus you have made my blood
> Keep the same measure
> As your love's own purity
> For pity's sake, please go!

In this version, Lucretia is clearly denying Tarquinius' accusation, and it looks like the definitive version changed the perspective of the interpretation; it would seems that Duncan's interpretation of the story changed or was changed during the working process, possibly due to Britten's intervention. What follows is an increasingly angry reaction from Tarquinius, that turns to violence: 'Easier stem the Tiber's flood / Than to calm my angry blood'.

Patricia Howard, in her study of the opera,[393] notices how in the Britten-Duncan rendering of this classical subject there is no apparent reason for Lucretia's submission. In Shakespeare and in Obey Tarquinius threatens to kill her and a slave, and to pretend to Collatinus that he had found them in illicit intimacy. Howard assumes that, without this reason, the 'seduction of Lucretia becomes a real alternative'.[394] Furthermore, there is a textural ground in the last scene for suspecting that Lucretia was ultimately a willing victim, as during the 'confession' scene the orchestra

---

[392] From Ronald Duncan's working notes. Quoted in MERTZ 1990, p.91.
[393] HOWARD 1969.
[394] HOWARD 1969, p.39.

recalls Tarquinius' accusation: 'Yet the linnet of your eyes lifts with desire'. This was certainly not the interpretation that informed the first production. Nancy Evans, who shared the role of Lucretia with Kathleen Ferrier, explains that 'something which is essential to the role is the pure nobility of her character: her passionate and unalloyed love for Collatinus, and her capacity for an ideal love that distinguished her from many other noblewomen',[395] and she insists that the notion of Lucretia secretly longing to be raped by Tarquinius destroys the essence of the drama.

Other commentators have underlined how Lucretia had no real reason to give in, apart from the fact of being physically overwhelmed by Tarquinius; it is nonetheless true that Tarquinius approaches her bed holding a sword, as it is clear not only from pictures of the first production but also from the stage instruction at the end of the scene: 'Tarquinius beats out the candle with his sword'. It is not very plausible that he would have carried the sword with him had he ever imagined he would be somehow welcome. In a way, the absence of Tarquinius' threat emphasises the violence of his action: I believe there are reasons to state that in the opera Lucretia does not submit, she is raped by strength against her will. The musical commentary is not very supportive of either reading, however, because Britten does not write a 'traditional' scene of aggression, revealing the inner feelings of the characters in the music.

THE SUICIDE

A major source of ambiguity in the interpretation of the piece is that Lucretia kills herself; this is a problem pertinent not only to the opera, but to all the literature about the subject.[396] Lucretia's suicide has become a myth in classical literature, being read as the ultimate act of virtue and resistance to oppression. In the Roman pagan culture shame was seen as the ultimate disgrace, and curiously enough there was no distinction between rape and adultery. To kill herself was the only way for Lucretia to prove her innocence, and she was therefore seen as a heroine because of

---

[395] CROZIER 1993, pp.25–26.
[396] On this subject, I am greatly indebted to a lecture given by Stephen Arthur Allen at *The Rape of Lucretia Study Day* on 13 October 1996 (Britten–Pears School of Advanced Musical Studies, Snape Maltings), which presented ideas from his work on Britten's relationship with the Christian faith. See also BURROWS 1996, pp.12–13.

her brave action. Amongst the writers that praise her are Livy, Valerius Maximus, Dio Cassius and Ovid, who describes her as *animi matrona virilis*. The troubles arise when we are introduced to the Christian culture, where suicide is a greater sin than adultery: if she were innocent, she should not have killed herself. Augustine is the first to deal with the subject in *The City of God* (413AD), where he questions: 'If she is adulterous, why is she praised? If chaste, why was she put to death?'.[397] In the later literature, Lucretia is generally condemned for her suicide, which according to Church teachings cannot be seen as an act of virtue. Shakespeare was apparently the first to make an attempt to reconcile the two arguments: as Jill Burrows has noted,[398] in his early epic poems he prefigures many of his later themes, particularly the relationship between virtue/honesty and beauty. In the opera, the situation is complicated as the pagan action is set against a Christian commentary.

Britten and Duncan are not clear about where their interpretation stands. On one hand, Duncan gives us his own reading of the Etruscan legend: 'Just as fertility or life is devoured by death, so is Spirit defiled by Fate. Lucretia is, to my mind, the symbol of the former, Tarquinius the embodiment of the latter'.[399] The concept of Fate puts the interpretation in a pagan context, but at the same time the Christian commentary during the rape scene talks of 'virtue assailed by sin'. Patricia Howard has underlined how, once we recognise that the seduction of Lucretia is a real alternative, we are dealing with Lucretia's own sin. This would introduce the concept of guilt, which constitutes the ground on which Lucretia kills herself. Such a reading is not completely at odds with the final meditation of the Male Chorus, which is about sin and the power of Christian forgiveness:

> He bears our sin and does not fall
> And He, carrying all turns round
> Stoned with our doubt and then forgives us all.

Nonetheless this comment does not necessarily relate to Lucretia's presumed sin, as it can equally be referred to Tarquinius' violence.

---

[397] *The City of God*, I, 19; quoted in ALLARD 1996, p.12.
[398] BURROWS 1996, p.13.
[399] DUNCAN 1948, p.62.

In Peter Evans' view the insertion of the Christian framework, considered unnecessary, is a major problem in the interpretation. Using Howard's remark that 'once we are introduced to the Christian doctrine we are not concerned any longer with Fate but with sin'[400] as a starting point, he tries to justify the epilogue on grounds other than the rightness of its musical function. In his view

> much incidental detail builds up to a view of Lucretia as at once revolted by Tarquinius' assault and horrifyingly attracted towards the realisation of a nightmare. Her struggles are real enough and, in this sense, she could be said physically to have defended her innocence, but her mental torture after the event suggests a recognition that revulsion and attraction can co-exist, that some part of her has shared the guilt.[401]

Such a reading, that Evans supports with a series of textual references, strengthens Howard's observations that Lucretia's character is a demonstration of how self-destructive is the combination of virtue and passion in the same person. Philip Brett recognises that *The Rape of Lucretia* is among the most problematic of Britten's stage works, because of its 'odd dramaturgy'. In his view the oddness can be illuminated by a comparison with *Peter Grimes*. Both Grimes and Lucretia are victims, victims of the society in which they live: Lucretia symbolises the fertility of life devoured by death, which is symbolised by Tarquinius, the Etruscan prince who embodies the worst features of a corrupt and oppressive society. For Brett, the Christian frame emphasises the fact that Lucretia is a victim; Christianity is a religion that celebrates the victim, therefore offering an 'universally understood context for the Lucretia story as well as a personal and spiritual way of interpreting it'.[402] He adds: 'In Lucretia we are asked to divorce the moral and spiritual values of Christianity from their institutional connotations as a means not only of seeing the universal significance of the tragedy, but also of finding a path out of the dilemma with which the opera ends'.[403] Brett confesses he finds it difficult to overcome revulsion at the view of rape that shifts the onus of responsibility on to the victim, and argues that we could clarify Lucretia's position again with a comparison with Grimes:

---

[400] EVANS 1989, p.141.
[401] EVANS 1989, p.141.
[402] BRETT 1987, p.360.
[403] BRETT 1987, p.360.

> what lies behind the exploration of the outsider's condition in the earlier opera [...] is Britten's realisation that those who are oppressed in one way or the other tend to internalise their oppression. Grimes is a classic case, an unclubbable man who can think of nothing better than joining the club while doing everything to ensure that he could never be accepted. Similarly Lucretia in the second scene of Act 2 dramatizes the shame and guilt involuntarily experienced by rape victims even if they are totally innocent and have been wronged in a particularly horrible manner.[404]

In this interpretation the suicide is seen as a gesture of despair, more than an attempt at rehabilitating herself, as it was in the French original and indeed in the perceived historical reality. Brett accepts that Lucretia is represented as partially guilty, 'a passionate person whose natural desire is turned into the material out of which her guilt is fabricated. By raping her Tarquinius manages to make his desire her crime'.[405] But is it really true that once we introduce the Christian framework we are dealing with the problem of sin, and therefore need to identify it in Lucretia's ambiguous behaviour? I think it is possible to convincingly support the idea that in Britten's interpretation Lucretia is passively - and I would like to emphasise this word - a victim of Tarquinius's lust: and his is ultimately a lust for power, not simply for Lucretia, but for all she represents. Tarquinius' lust expresses itself through violence and destruction:

> For violence is the fear within us all,
> And tragedy the measurement of man
> And hope his brief view of God.
> Oh Christ, heal our blindness which we mistake for sight
> And show us your day for ours is endless night.

These words are 'spoken' by the chorus at the end of the introduction to the second act. The passage that precedes in the introduction has a strong political connotation, which was not present in the French version. Why would Britten and Duncan put so much emphasis on the fact that the Etruscan were oppressors? And how do these statements account for the

---

[404] BRETT 1987, p.363.
[405] BRETT 1987, p.364.

view of Lucretia as the potential sinner torn between an immoral passion and her virtue?

It is not too difficult to understand how the experience of rape was in itself a good enough reason for Lucretia to kill herself. The psychological burden was simply too heavy for her to carry - and the burden does not necessarily need to be identified with a guilt complex, but more simply and logically with the emotional pain following the abuse: she had been subjected to brutal violation. Her psychological and emotional stability has been violently shaken, as we learn from the hysterical reaction at the beginning of act II, scene ii, which is very different from the one portrayed in the French original, where Lucretia takes her decision rationally. In the opera Lucretia's reaction portrays all the symptoms of what is clinically defined as 'post-traumatic stress disorder',[406] one of the few mental illnesses that is triggered by events and not by disposition. It features the development of characteristic symptoms following a psychologically distressing event that is outside the range of usual human experience.[407] Amongst these symptoms, which begin immediately after the event, are intense fear, terror, helplessness, numbing of general responsiveness, venting of anger over a symbol, breakdown of communication, increase of manic arousal.

We can recognise some of these symptoms in Lucretia's reactions the morning after the rape: her numbed conversation with the maids, her anger at the orchid, symbol of her love for Collatinus, her over-excitement after she asks to send the messenger, her shouting. According to statistical studies suicide attempts, concurrent with post-traumatic stress disorder, are very common after sexual assault.[408] From a clinical point of view it is also relevant that she plans her suicide:[409] she carries the lethal weapon with her, she dresses in purple mourning and she waits for Collatinus before taking her life in what can be recognised as a 'ritualistic' way (another difference from the French play, where she stabs herself in the intimacy of her bedroom, to die later in front of Collatinus). The ritualistic suicide,

---

[406] I am grateful to Ian Noonan RMN for his help with this section.
[407] American Psychiatric Association, *Diagnostic and Statistical Manual of Mental Disorders*, 3rd rev. edition (Washington, 1987), p.247.
[408] J. Davidson, D. Hughes, L. George and D. Blazer, 'The association of sexual assault and attempted suicide within the community', *Archives of General Psychiatry* 53 (1996), pp.550–5.
[409] Donna C. Aguilera, *Crisis intervention. Theory and Methodology*, 7th edition (St. Louis, 1998), pp.184–85.

incidentally, seems to be the only element after the rape that reconciles Lucretia with the image of a Roman matron, whose 'decorum' surely would not have allowed the emotional outburst that precedes Collatinus's arrival.

In the opera therefore the question seems to be: 'Why should Lucretia not kill herself?'. She has been raped in her own house, in her own bed, with no-one being able to protect her. She is well aware that the violence was carried out partly on account of her being a symbol (she refers to herself as 'the chaste Lucretia'), the symbol of what the Etruscans could not have: her chastity was the essence of Roman virtue and character. As such, she was the ultimate target of the attempt to exercise power, a political power that wants to be also psychological, and that is perpetrated through violence.

> Her house is sacked, her quiet interrupted,
> Her mansion battered by the enemy;
> Her sacred temple spotted, spoiled, corrupted,
> Grossly engirt with daring infamy;
> Then let it not be called impiety
> If in this blemished fort I make some hole
> Through which I may convey this troubled soul.[410]

Thus Shakespeare explains the reasons for the suicide, and although we can consider the rich imagery a poetic metaphor, the comparison to a sack is nonetheless extremely apt in this context. In a more contemporary background, as the timeless representation of the opera aims to be - since it is out of time, it belongs to all times - what we can see is that Lucretia has been raped and depersonalized: she has been abused both physically and psychologically...why should she carry on living?

In his parallel with *Oedipus Rex*, considered a study of the consequences of guilt, Arnold Whittall sees *Lucretia* as a study about virtue. For him, it is exactly the loss of that virtue that destroys Lucretia, who cannot decide between restraint and passion. I would suggest that the opera could also be read as a study about the consequences of violence. If we look at the action from this point of view, the ethical problem is not pertinent to

---

[410] W. Shakespeare, *The Rape of Lucretia*, vv.1170–76.

Lucretia any longer. Because of the abuse, her life, symbolised by her psychological stability, is destroyed. Tarquinius's violence causes her death by triggering a mental illness that leads to her self-mutilation. The focus of the moral drama therefore is not Lucretia any longer, although she is the object of it. The problem becomes gratuitous violence over helplessness, life and beauty, a blind violence driven by insane and insatiably rapacious greed for power. It is not difficult to see how the opera becomes a metaphor for 'man raping the world', man's inhumanity to man.

THE FIRST PARABLE

While maintaining that interpretation is often a matter of subjectivity, I think it might be interesting in the case of *The Rape of Lucretia* to change the perspective on the story in a way that allows us to see what the composer might have perceived as its universality and its relevance to the present: the Christian commentary does not address the action of the opera, but the metaphor it represents. Possibly the two Choruses represent the reality and contemporaneity of the violence, as perpetrated in the war. It is important to note that both Duncan and Britten were pacifists, and that their work had been politically engaged since the thirties. Furthermore, a few weeks before starting work on *Lucretia*, Britten, who had been a conscientious objector during the war, had a first hand experience of what the conflict had really meant on the continent. In late July 1945, a few weeks after the opening of *Grimes,* Britten went to Germany with Yehudi Menuhin. The two had been introduced at a Boosey and Hawkes party, and on hearing that the violinist was about to visit Germany and give recitals to the survivors of the concentration camps, the composer urged Menuhin to take him as an accompanist, instead of Gerald Moore. They gave two or three recitals a day, and Britten wrote to Pears that 'under the circumstances the music was as good as it could be'. In the letter he says about the trip:

> We travelled in small cars over bad roads ... saw heavenly little German villages ... & ... completely destroyed towns....And....millions of D[isplaced] P[erson]s in, some of them, appalling states, who could scarcely sit still & listen, & yet were thrilled to be played to. We stayed

the night in Belsen & saw over the hospital - & I needn't describe *that* to you. [411]

Apparently, Britten never talked to Menuhin about his reactions to Belsen. Later Peter Pears said that Britten would not speak about it until near the end of his life, when he said 'how shocking it was, and that the experience had coloured everything he had written subsequently'.[412] In an interview in the sixties Britten said

> I wrote my *John Donne Sonnets* in a week while in bed with high fever, a delayed reaction from an inoculation. The inoculation had been in order to go on a tour of concentration camps with Yehudi Menuhin in 1945. We gave two or three short recitals a day - they couldn't take more. It was in many ways a terrifying experience. The theme of the *Donne Sonnets* is death, as you know. I think the connexion between personal experience and my feelings about the poetry was a strong one. It certainly characterized the music.[413]

During the whole of his life, Britten seemed to favour the lyricism of song with piano accompaniment for the direct expression of personal feelings. Although the practical reasons for these settings can indeed be recognized in his busy professional partnership with Pears, and in his desire to increase the repertoire - along with his love for Schubert - it is quite striking to see how the choice of text seems to be a direct expression of his sentiments. The *Donne Sonnets* are not the only work in which we recognize a 'strong connection' between the composer's personal experience and the feelings expressed in the poetry, the most obvious case being the *Seven Sonnets of Michelangelo*, written at the beginning of his relationship with Peter Pears. Indeed, it looks as if we could gain some insight into the stage works by comparing them with to some of the concepts expressed in the song-cycle. Britten often chose to express his own mind through the words of poets who moved him. If part of him looked upon the operatic stage as if it were a pulpit dedicated to the enhancement of public consciousness, as we have argued, then it is especially with *Lucretia* that the stage seems to become a space in which a didactic artistic exercise takes place, and the direct expression of more

---

[411] CARPENTER 1992, p.226.
[412] CARPENTER 1992, p.228.
[413] SCHAFER 1963, p.122.

personal feelings seems to be reserved for the intimacy of a chamber recital. There are striking connections between the first chamber opera and the *Donne Sonnets*, for example the images used in the Christian commentary in *The Rape of Lucretia* have very strong echoes of Donne's text, as we can see from a section of the *Interlude* from act II:

> Nothing impure survives
> All passion perishes
> Virtue has one desire
> To let his blood flow
> Back to the wounds of Christ. [414]

Blood and tears, blindness and night, sin as sorrow, hope which is not defied by death are concepts already tackled by Britten in the song-cycle:

> Marke in my heart,
> O Soule, where thou dost well,
> The picture of Christ crucified, and tell
> Whether that countenance can thee affright,
> Teares in his eyes quench the amazing light. [415]

At the first performance of the opera in July 1946 many members of the audience were perplexed and, as Imogen Holst reports, 'acutely embarrassed' by the introduction of the Christian commentators:

> They were aware that beautiful music was going on, but they felt so uncomfortable they could hardly listen to it. 'Why couldn't he be contented with what happened in history in 500 B.C.?' they asked. 'Why drag in Christianity?' But in Britten's mind there was no question of 'dragging in Christianity': it had been there all the time. He would never have set a cruel subject to music without linking the cruelty to the hope of redemption.[416]

This testimony is quite significant, as Imogen Holst was not simply Britten's personal assistant, but also a close friend. In her biography Holst has preceded the brief discussion of the first chamber opera with the

---

[414] *The Rape of Lucretia*, act II, 'Interlude'.
[415] B. Britten, *The Holy Sonnets of John Donne* (London: Boosey and Hawkes, 1948), no.5: 'What if this present'.
[416] HOLST 1970, p.43.

mention of the tour to Germany and of the Donne settings, which she described as Britten's own way to 'defy the nightmare horror': 'passionate settings of passionate poems in which death is triumphantly defeated'. Holst goes on to quote a letter Britten had sent to a friend a few days after 'this somewhat bewildering first performance' of the opera:

> Your understanding of my work, of Lucretia especially, gives me great encouragement. Especially the manner in which you approach the Christian idea delighted me. I used to think that the day when one could shock people was over - but now, I've discovered that being simple and considering things of spiritual importance, produces violent reaction.[417]

In a letter to the composer dated 15 July 1946 Holst herself had written: 'No one who has listened to the "It is all" scene will ever be quite the same person [...] It is a 1946 B Minor Mass, and it is what we have all been wanting and waiting for, whether we realized it or not'.[418] This comment would be in tune with a reading of the musical architecture of the work that moves it from a purely operatic context into the genre of sacred theatre. In such a context it might be limiting to read the spiritual importance of the work simply as Lucretia's moral struggle. And after the experience of the war, is it really plausible that a 'politically aware' Britten would concern himself simply with a matter of guilt due to infidelity? I believe his concern was of much wider relevance.

The readings that put Lucretia's psychology at the centre of the drama might be influenced by comparison with later works, in which a psychological moral dilemma, and indeed ambiguity, are the focus of the drama. But *The Rape of Lucretia* does not belong with that kind of work; *Lucretia* is in itself an experiment that would bear fruit much later, with the church parables. *The Rape of Lucretia* can rightfully be considered the first parable, as Mervyn Cooke points out,[419] and not only for the presence of ritual and stylization, but also for the didactic extra-dramatic commentary tinged with Christian faith. In the church parables the commentary is introduced by the Abbot, who also points out the moral at

---
[417] HOLST 1970, p.44.
[418] Imogen Holst letter to Benjamin Britten in the Britten–Pears Library, Aldeburgh. Recently in the review of a performance of *The Rape of Lucretia* at the Edinburgh Festival 1999 the work was likened to Bach's Great Passion (MONELLE 1999).
[419] COOKE 1987, 'The Prophecy of Lucretia'.

the end. In *Curlew River* (1964) Britten once again Christianized a 'pagan' story, in this case a Japanese Nô play, but he had waited almost twenty years, before attempting something similar to the 'patently didactic' dimension of the first chamber opera, and he had worked on the idea of the church parable for almost ten years, which implies that 'he took the criticism of *Lucretia* to heart'.[420]

Philip Brett relates the significance of the drama to 'Britten's lifelong preoccupation with the senseless violence of man'.[421] I believe we can justifiably read in it an attempt to express the composer's own despair at violence that, born out of greed, leads ultimately to the destruction of what is noble and venerable: life. The story of Lucretia, a European legend with strong political connotations, was perfect material for a parable about war, and the Female Chorus's *Epilogue* seems very much a recollection of the tragedy of the war:

> Is it all? Is all this suffering and pain
> Is this in vain?
> Does this old world grow old
> In sin alone?
> Can we attain nothing
> But wider oceans of our own tears?

In the *Donne Sonnets* the last sentence was an attempt to discard the nightmarish experience of Belsen through the denial of the power of death: 'Death, thou shalt die'. The final meditation of the Male Chorus in *Lucretia* seems to communicate Britten's own attempt to believe that 'It is not all'. At the end of his discussion of *The Rape of Lucretia* Peter Evans, expressing his discomfort with the whole conception of the work, points out 'two questions which any writer on this opera has to face: is the Christian framework necessary, and does it in fact provide a logical commentary on the action'.[422] I hope I have provided an alternative reading that convincingly shows how the Christian commentary becomes not simply a frame added to the action, but an essential part of the concept of the work, a reading supported by both musical considerations and critical interpretation.

---

[420] COOKE 1987, 'The Prophecy of Lucretia', p.55.
[421] COOKE 1987, 'The Prophecy of Lucretia', p.55.
[422] EVANS 1979, p.141.

The *Rape of Lucretia* is Britten's first significant experiment in musico-dramatic form: as in his other works, most obviously in the *War Requiem*, he moulds a traditional form to fit his own need to express his beliefs and to communicate a message in the most effective way, 'without being tempered by bias or tradition'.[423] This is a journey that, starting with *The Rape of Lucretia*, continued throughout his career and found a final apotheosis with *Death in Venice*, as we will see in the following chapters.

---

[423] BONAVIA 1946.

CHAPTER 5
SACRED AND PROFANE

> With *Noye's Fludde*, but even more strikingly with the three church parables, Britten resorted to the medieval Mystery Play and succeeded in unifying what in music history ad been so often arbitrarily separated, oratorio and opera, the sacred and the profane.[424]

Most commentators seem to identify *Noye's Fludde* as the first work in which Britten starts to integrate the different dramatic dimensions of oratorio and opera. Nonetheless, as we have seen in the previous chapter, one of the most interesting features of *The Rape of Lucretia* is exactly the integration of the two different narrative modalities, epic narration and dramatic action, that are associated with oratorio and opera respectively. In *Lucretia*, this association is further emphasized by the use of chorale-like melodies, strongly suggestive of sacred music, sung by the Choruses. As W.H. Haddon Squire had already recognized in an early article,[425] Britten was attempting to create a sacred drama; probably as a consequence of the cold reception and general misunderstanding of the work, he apparently abandoned his idea of integrating oratorio and opera, sacred and profane.

The stage works that follow *Lucretia* still present moral themes, but within a more traditional operatic framework, although they maintain one of the characteristics of the opera, a moral ambiguity that seems to have become a hallmark of Britten's style. Most of these works present a moral dilemma, the need for a choice between good and evil, in a situation where

---

[424] 'De fait, dès *Noye's Fludde*, mais de manière plus nette encore grâce aux trois church parables, Britten recourrait avec le mystère médiéval et parvenait à conjuguer ce qui fut tant de fois arbitrairement séparé dans l'histoire de la musique: l'oratorio et l'opéra, le sacré et le profane'. GAULLE 1996, p.339. (The translation is mine.)
[425] HADDON SQUIRE 1946.

good and evil are confused and where it is not possible, for the characters and often for the audience, to identify a clear-cut division between what is right and what is wrong. This is an element we find in *Billy Budd*, in *Gloriana* and in *The Turn of the Screw*, as well as in *Peter Grimes* and in *The Rape of Lucretia*. But while at the end of *Lucretia* Britten takes a clear position, and offers an answer to the drama with the final Chorus and the Christian commentary, in the other works the ambiguity is unresolved, if not somehow increased by the lack of a defined solution.[426] With these works Britten not only creates psychological dramas, but by leaving them unresolved he creates ethical dramas that cannot fail to involve the audience in moral questioning and self-examination. By not providing an answer, he leaves us trying to find one, and the extent to which audiences are left asking questions is a measure of his success not only as a dramatic composer, but as a preacher. In such works he might not succeed in communicating directly a spiritual truth, but he certainly prepares the ground for it, by provoking moral questions: the work he has created becomes an 'ethical tool'. It is only with the church parables that Britten again patently expresses a spiritual truth, and it is therefore interesting to note many other similarities between the church parables and *The Rape of Lucretia*, for example, the ritualistic stylization, that we find again in *Curlew River*; *Lucretia* itself is a parable, an allegorical tale that expresses a moral or religious teaching.

The filiation of the parables from *Lucretia* has been widely recognized;[427] a recent study sees the church parables as

> probably Britten's most extreme examples of operatic experimentation with the simultaneous presentation and re-enactment of a story. These short musical dramas, intended for performance in a liturgical setting, are strongly influenced by Britten's experience of Japanese Noh plays in the 1950s. The stylized gesture and movement bluntly emphasize the ritualistic nature of the drama; Lucretia's formalized separation of narrative voices, characterizations in terms of symbols and archetype rather than particular individuals, and juxtaposition of different historical eras (pagan Rome, medieval Christianity, and Britain in the twentieth

---

[426] On the subject see for example WHITTALL 1990, in particular p.168.
[427] For example, see COOKE 1987, 'The prophecy of Lucretia', pp. 54–55.

century) may all be precursors of the defining features of these miniature operas.[428]

The passage from opera-oratorio to church parable is not direct, however, and the fusion of the two genres, the simultaneous presence of sacred and profane on the stage, is a path that Britten follows initially not on the operatic stage, but on the concert platform.

CHAMBER DRAMA

In striving to find the best way to deal with the themes that mattered most to him Britten not only re-interpreted traditional form in a modern context, as in the case of *War Requiem*,[429] or developed new forms, but he also created works that challenged the relationship between the audience and the performers, and the perceived nature of the performance itself. At the same time, Britten tried to break, or at least change, the divide between audience and performers, in order to create an experience which is all the more involving for both groups. An early example of this is the form he termed 'canticle', extended settings of a text on a subject of spiritual significance written for chamber performance, often described as 'miniature cantatas'.[430] As Graham Johnson explains, they are 'all to religious texts and all embodying a new approach to a time-honoured means of presenting vocal music in a semi-dramatic context. The texts are much longer than is usual for a song, and Britten sets each as a miniature cantata which is in itself a sort of continuous song-cycle'.[431] The composer wrote five such works, between 1947 and 1974, and although the sources of the texts are strikingly diverse dramatically (from the Chester Miracle Plays to Edith Sitwell and T.S.Eliot), they are in their own way 'of spiritual significance'; mainly lyrical in content, these compositions offer, often very directly, themes for reflection and meditation.

The first of the five canticles was composed in the summer of 1947,[432] written for the Dick Sheppard Memorial concert on 1 November 1947,

---

[428] MERTZ 1990, p.201.
[429] For a detailed study of this work see COOKE 1996.
[430] See for example KENNEDY 1981, p.187.
[431] Graham Johnson, 'Voice and Piano', in PALMER 1984, p.292.
[432] The completion date reads 12 September 1947.

where it was performed by Peter Pears and the composer. According to Britten, the form 'was a new invention in a sense although it certainly was modelled on the Purcell *Divine Hymns*'.[433] By the beginning of the 1940s Britten and Pears had established themselves as performers, and the composer had started to write works regularly for their recital programmes: these include the folksong arrangements and original works such as the *Seven Sonnets of Michelangelo* op.22 and the *Holy Sonnets of John Donne* op.35; for the same purpose during the war Britten had also started to make realizations of works by Purcell, and his own vocal writing was strongly influenced by the melismatic freedom of Purcell's settings. Talking about the Michelangelo settings, Peter Pears remarks how 'this sort of song had never been done by an Englishman before. It was this Sonnet [XXX, the third of the set] and the last one of the set which, in the early performances of these songs, opened the eyes of his audience to what vocal writing could be'.[434]

It was not simply a matter of vocal writing: if with the sonnets Britten had set texts 'of spiritual relevance', with the form of the Canticle he was now attempting to change not only the way songs were written, but also the context in which they were performed. Britten was certainly nurturing with his compositions a style of performance which 'dramatized' the recital. His folksong arrangements are not simply harmonizations of a melody, but through his re-interpretation[435] they are transformed into short dramatic scenes: the piano accompaniment creates (through the use of figurations, harmonic contrast, dissonance, increase in density of texture, for example) a powerful and colourful dramatic background, full of 'positively dramatic gestures',[436] against which the story unfolds.

> His treatment of the folksong 'The Ash Grove' is a famous example of what can happen when a twentieth-century composer, his ear sensitive to every psychological nuance of a text, decides to confront the unvaried strophic structure of the original tune. The result might be deemed a clear case of a composer subverting the simple (folklike) qualities of the original in order to

---

[433] SCHAFER 1963, p.121; for an analysis of the work see WHITTALL 1982, p.123.
[434] Peter Pears, 'The vocal music', in KELLER 1952, p.66.
[435] On the subject see ROSEBERRY 1961 and 1999.
[436] MITCHELL 1995, p.10.

do proper justice – 'proper' in the sense of what psychologically aware music can achieve – to the expressive range of the text.[437]

The 'time honoured' dimension of presenting vocal music in a 'semi-dramatic' context is thus given the potential of a real dramatic experience; when dealing with texts 'of spiritual relevance' the dramatic charge, paired with the spareness of means, raises what is already an uplifting experience on the verge of ritual, to the point that it is no longer solely an entertainment, but can become a powerful 'spiritual experience'. This is quite evident in *Canticle II: Abraham and Isaac* op.51, written in January 1952 for Peter Pears and Kathleen Ferrier, and dedicated to them.[438] The text is taken from a Chester Miracle Play, *The Sacrifice of Isaac*, adapted by Britten himself. His source is a copy of Alfred Pollard's collection of *English Miracle Plays*, which contains Britten's annotations:[439] various verses are crossed out in pencil to reduce the text, and he does not use the last part of it either, ending with the section that begins 'Such obedience grant us Lord'. This section, which has the annotation 'envoi' in Britten's hand, is a final comment sung in imitation by the two singers, now 'out of character', about the episode that they have just presented:

> Such obedience grant us, O Lord!
> Ever to thy most holy word
> That in the same we may accord
> As this Abraham was bayn
> And then altogether shall we
> That worthy king in Heaven see
> And dwell with him in great glorye
> For ever and ever, Amen.

This ending suggests that 'obedience' is the subject of the canticle, and not simply 'the sacrifice of a child', as Michael Oliver has suggested.[440] Whatever its focus, the second canticle is like a church parable *in nuce*;

---

[437] WHITTALL 1995, p.292.
[438] The work was performed that same year at the Fifth Aldeburgh Festival by Ferrier, Pears and Britten, in a very interesting programme which paired it with Frank Martin's *Six Monologues from Everyman* (1943), settings from Hugo von Hofmannsthal's version of the Morality.
[439] POLLARD 1927. Britten's own copy is in the Britten–Pears Library.
[440] OLIVER 1996, p.143. Oliver's interpretation seems to reflect a general view that much of Britten's works are about childhood, innocence and abuse. See also ELLIOTT 1985, p.117.

just as the three church parables are meditations about *fides, spes* and *caritas*, it too is a meditation about a virtue, obedience.

Arnold Whittall describes *Canticle II* as a 'compressed cantata'[441] because of its alternation of recitative and aria sections, and the work is effectively a dramatic scene. This was clearly in the composer's mind, as we find indications of the musical structure, such as 'walking music', 'recitative', 'aria and duet' and 'funeral march' by the text in Britten's working copy of the Pollard volume. G.M. Bennett emphasizes how the work lends itself well to the stage,[442] because 'Britten has outlined some very direct and simple stage directions and gestures that if used by the performers, will make the music and story all the more coherent',[443] and he even goes as far as considering the work a short chamber opera similar to Mozart's *Bastien and Bastienne* and Debussy's *L'enfant prodigue*. Britten had in fact transcribed in the score some stage directions from the original play: for example, after God's initial words the score has the indication 'Abraham riseth and saith', which seems to suggest that at the beginning of the Canticle the two singers are kneeling. Most of these stage directions are quite simple: they ask the singers for a gesture, or a little movement, or to kneel, as for example when Isaac asks for his father's blessing before the sacrifice. These 'dramatic' gestures could easily be understood as embedded in the text Britten was using, and it could be argued that their insertion does not necessarily demand a 'theatrical' performance. Nonetheless Britten had already used a similar device, the introduction of a 'dramatic' gesture in a non-theatrical context, in his 1948 cantata *Saint Nicolas*.

CHURCH DRAMA

Saint Nicolas was commissioned by Lancing College, Peter Pears's old public school. The commissioners knew the *Hymn to St Cecilia* and, according to Humphrey Carpenter, 'suggested "a hymn to St Nicolas", patron saint of children (and co-patron of Lancing itself)'. Britten planned the work for the forces available at Lancing, mainly amateur singers and

---

[441] WHITTALL 1982, p.144.
[442] There has been at least one attempt at staging the five canticles, a co-production of Streetwise Opera and Tête à Tête Productions in November 2001, an effort that underlines the intrinsic dramatic power of these works.
[443] BENNETT 1988, p.50.

players, but with a few professional players (the string quintet leads, the first percussionist and, of course, the tenor); he asked Eric Crozier to write the libretto, and apparently gave him Haydn's *Creation* as a model.[444] For his part, Crozier read volumes of history and legends of the early church, and wrote a libretto in which a strong dramatic structure is interspersed with lyricism: the presence of Nicolas as main character and the interaction between the tenor and the characters represented by the choruses make it a dramatic rather than an epic work. From this point of view, the cantata, more than the canticles, attempts a fusion of different genres, and even more manages to break the barrier between performers and audience – or in this case the congregation: Britten himself refers to the audience as the 'congregation', since the work was originally intended for church performance, and was first performed during the first Aldeburgh Festival in Aldeburgh Parish Church.[445]

The process of fashioning the libretto is not well documented, probably due to the fact that during the work's gestation Crozier spent a considerable amount of time in Aldeburgh, working *vis à vis* with the composer, and it is therefore difficult to assess the degree of Britten's input; we lack the wealth of written testimony that we have for other works, as in the case of Britten's collaborations with William Plomer or Myfawny Piper. It is nonetheless likely that the composer was, as usual, directly involved in the shaping of the text and consequently in the dramatic structure of the work. Apparently the episode of the Pickled Boys, the most interesting in the present context (as I will discuss below), was not in Crozier's original draft, but was added at Britten's request.[446]

The narrative structure of the cantata is particularly interesting because of the way it integrates epic narration and dramatization, and for the way it challenges the relationship between audience and performers, with its alternation between observation (passive) and participation (active). One thing worth noting to begin with is that there are at least three levels of narration just concerning the function of the choir: 1. as **narrator**, taking on its classical function, it narrates episodes from the life of the Saint; 2. as **a dramatis persona** it plays a character, or characters (the mariners,

---

[444] See CARPENTER 1992, p.264
[445] For a discussion of the musical structure of *Saint Nicolas* see EVANS 1989, pp. 258–264, in particular the table on p.264.
[446] CARPENTER 1992, p.266.

the travellers); 3. as part of the **congregation** in the hymns it renews its status as being outside of the historical setting and part of the contemporary audience. It is important to underline how it not only addresses the congregation, it is at times part of it, when the congregation participates in the two hymns. The aim of this device is to achieve a similar effect to the one obtained through the function of the choruses in *The Rape of Lucretia,* and the same idea is used in the church parables through the ceremony of the robing (although the 'robing' in itself separates the performers from the observers, at the same time underlining the fact that before the robing the performers were part of the congregation). When the cantata begins the chorus, now representing a part of the contemporary congregation that has met to perform the ritual of re-enacting the life of Nicolas, is contemplating the appearance of the Saint. In the 'dramatic' fiction he is joining the congregation (both the choir and the audience) to guide them during what could be described as a 'ritual'. Nicolas himself states that he is now joining them, in the present time, for what is going to be an act of worship, thus creating a situation where the time/space relationship is ambiguous and invites suspension of disbelief:

> Across the tremendous bridge
> of sixteen hundred years
> I come to stand in worship with you
> As I stood among my faithful congregation long ago.

The introduction, which from a narrative point of view is clearly separated from the episodes that follow, as they are all concerned with Nicolas' life, presents the cantata as an act of worship in which the contemplation of episodes from the life of the Saint are only one element. At the end of Nicolas' 'welcome' speech, the congregation responds with an invocation to God:

> Help us, Lord! to find the hidden road
> That leads from love to greater Love
> from faith to greater Faith
> Strengthen us, O Lord!
> Screw up our strength to serve Thee with simplicity.

Only after this invocation, that has associations with the Choruses' hymn in *The Rape of Lucretia* and the Abbott's addresses in the church parables, the narration begins, alternating lyrical and dramatic episodes. In the narration the time dimension fluctuates between present and past, although we can look at it as a 'dramatic' present, with no difference between the present of the congregation and the historical present of the episodes that are more 'enacted' than narrated.

A good example of the alternation of epic and dramatic within the same scene is the fourth episode, 'He journeys to Palestine', where the Tenors and Basses of the chorus start by narrating in unison the events that lead to a storm. During the storm the narration is taken over by the Sopranos and Altos of the semi-chorus, while the Tenors and Basses become characters in the action, now dramatized, impersonating the sailors on the boat, returning to their role of narrators only to introduce Nicolas' prayer. Nicolas himself, a *dramatis persona* during the prayer, becomes the narrator at the end of the episode when he remembers the events that followed the end of the storm. The reason for the whole episode seems to be the fact that Nicolas wants to lead the congregation in an act of prayer. It is important to note that the tenor maintains through the whole cantata his identity within the enactment of the story: whether he is expressing himself 'lyrically' or 'dramatically', he is always himself, Nicolas, a dramatic character, not a narrator talking about someone else. While the chorus alternate between being part of the congregation and being a character, the tenor is on a different dramatic level, as he is 'pretending' not only in front of the audience, but also in front of the chorus.

Even more interesting is episode VII, 'Nicolas and the Pickled boys', which is in effect a dramatic scene, with the chorus impersonating the main characters opposed to Nicolas, the pilgrims and the parents of the three boys that have disappeared. In what appears to be an 'epic' work, written for presentation within the normal conventions of the genre, Britten introduces a theatrical gesture, requiring that three small boys, representing the three boys that Nicolas has resuscitated, enter the auditorium singing 'Alleluia'. Such a simple gesture evokes in the audience a feeling of being involved in the dramatic action: the barriers between audience and performers are broken, and the event becomes a communal experience. In *Saint Nicolas* this is reinforced by the involvement of the audience, whose members are required to join in during the two hymns, at the central climax and at the end of the work. In the prefatory note to the printed study score Britten requires that 'the conductor must be cool headed and should turn to the congregation/audience to conduct them in the two hymns'.[447] John Culshaw testifies how these hymns have the power to 'shake normally impervious men to their foundation',[448] probably because, according to Christopher Palmer, they 'touch something deep down in our subconscious, something older than the present organization of our nature, something innocent of the fall from grace'.[449]

Imogen Holst defines the work as a 'meeting place, half-way between opera and oratorio', and describing the performance in Aldeburgh Parish Church during the 1948 Festival she also writes:

> Hearing Britten's Saint Nicolas sung by village choral societies in the overcrowded parish church at Aldeburgh last summer was an exhilarating experience. To begin with, there was the enormous satisfaction of being allowed to join in the singing of both the hymns in the cantata. Audiences are often given the courtesy-title of 'congregation' when they turn up to listen to a concert in a church, but they are very seldom given the chance of justifying their existence. This was only one of the barriers that Saint Nicolas removed during the afternoon. There was also the appropriate absence of any rigid boundaries between sacred and secular music.[450]

Donald Mitchell, in tracing a line that connects *Peter Grimes* with the church parables, identifies in *Saint Nicolas* the first work 'which significantly blurs the distinction between the kind of musical events we expect to find in a church on the one hand and in the theatre on the other'.[451]

> the thrilling revival of the Pickled Boys is re-enacted not only for our ears but also for our eyes. *Saint Nicolas* indeed, which freely introduces the dramatic gestures - 'opera', if you like - into an arena from which the

---

[447] Benjamin Britten *Saint Nicolas* op.42, miniature score (London: Boosey and Hawkes, 1949).
[448] PALMER 1984, p.81.
[449] PALMER 1984, p.82; on the subject see also MITCHELL 1950.
[450] HOLST 1948, p.24.
[451] In PALMER 1984, p.212.

dramatic convention has been excluded in recent (but not distant) centuries, already formulates a principle which is vastly enlarged and developed in the parables. One could call the incident of the Pickled Boys a *parable in miniature*.[452]

Mitchell also mentions, as one would expect, *Noye's Fludde* as a milestone on the way to the parables, but he stresses how 'the cantata particularly shows that Britten's creative mind has long been concerned with the kind of dramatic possibilities he comprehensively exploits in *The Burning Fiery Furnace* and *The Prodigal Son*.'[453] Mitchell does not mention that some of the elements that are at the root of the parables, and that they share with the cantata, were already present in *Lucretia*: there might be no recitatives in the later works, but the same principle of alternation between epic and dramatic, narration and enactment, oratorio and opera are there.

In the dramatic style that Britten will exploit at its maximum degree in the church parables there are recurrent elements: a parable-like subject, spareness, stylization, a somewhat ritualistic manner of delivery, sometimes enhanced by repetition at various levels (musical, textual, dramatic). One idea that seems to be always present is the involvement of the audience. Britten engages the audience not only by creating a strong dramatic impact in a work that is not expected to be 'dramatic', but also by asking for a suspension of disbelief through a distortion of the accepted time/space relationship (as in *Saint Nicolas* and in *The Rape of Lucretia*); he also involves us through the simple directness of active participation in the music-making.

Britten always seems to want to make the audience conscious of the fact that they are part of the performance, not simply passive spectators. Furthermore, works like *Saint Nicolas* and *Noye's Fludde* were written for a group of amateurs (a few professionals are required), and they provide the opportunity for a significant musical experience in which anybody can take part. The root for this seems to be Britten's interest in communication: his willingness to exploit the dramatic possibilities of mixing genres and to involve audiences directly both aim for the same

---

[452] PALMER 1984, pp.212–213 (italics in the original).
[453] PALMER 1984, p.213.

result, to make the communication more effective. By trying to increase the impact he hopes his work will have the composer wants to make sure that his message is going to be received, even if not necessarily liked.[454]

Britten asks audiences to be 'part of the business' also in *The Little Sweep* op.45 (1949), the children's opera that is part of *Let's Make an Opera*, composed in 1949. This 'entertainment for young people' could seem far away from the 'sacred' dimension to which *Saint Nicolas* and *Noye's Fludde* obviously belong, although it is another work written mainly with amateur performers in mind, and it too challenges the accepted perception of the relationship between 'those who do' and 'those who watch':

> By the time the curtain goes up there is no longer any dividing-line between audience and performer or between amateur and professional, so there need be no fear of any self-consciousness, either on or off the stage. And as soon as the story begins to unfold, one realizes that there is no dividing-line in Britten, whether he writes a tragic opera for grown-ups or a light-hearted entertainment for children.[455]

The Little Sweep does not present any moral ambiguities, nor is it a meditation about a great spiritual truth. It is a short simple work, that uses spoken dialogue instead of recitative, and whose composition is based on simple formulae. Nonetheless, its interest in the present context lies in the fact that

> it is, of course, another Britten parable about cruelty and compassion, good and evil, with its origin in the Blake poem he was to set some years later, but one needs not to become too portentous in this context. Britten relies on children's natural perception to draw the moral; he does not labour it, nor need we. The music makes the point infallibly.[456]

Although apparently only an entertainment for children, a work that appeals to them because it speaks to them directly and constitutes a very good introduction to the world of opera,[457] in essence *The Little Sweep* is

---

[454] See BRITTEN 1963, p.89.
[455] HOLST 1952, p.283.
[456] KENNEDY 1981, p.193.
[457] On this subject see 'A Children's Symposium on Britten's Children's opera', *Music Survey* II/4 (Spring 1950), pp.237–240.

not too far away from other 'more serious' works by Britten, including the church parables. Talking of the subject of the first children's opera, Arnold Whittall comments:

> It is perhaps a pity that its Suffolk-oriented subject-matter is not more contemporary — or timeless; it depends very much on cheerfully accepted nineteenth-century social distinctions, and the music, though surprisingly unsuperficial for a score written down in a fortnight, does nevertheless have the blandness of a conception in which entertaining and moralizing get in each other's way. Britten did not repeat the experiment for nine years, and in *Noye's Fludde* skilfully avoided the more patronizing aspects of the *Little Sweep*'s subject matter by taking a universal myth as theme.[458]

In many ways, it is not surprising that Britten had chosen a Suffolk tale to present to English children: its straightforward metaphor can be more easily accepted if children can recognize themselves in the characters. It is also another example of the composer's need to make the subject of his works his own, a need born out of the desire to construct something to which audiences can easily relate, and therefore make their own.

I believe this idea is at the root of the 'invention' of the church parable, where it manifests itself at its best in his need to take some distance from the Japanese source through the filter of English medieval drama. *Noye's Fludde* is certainly the link that helped the passage from Nô play to church parable: Britten had already used a text from the Chester Miracle Plays in *Canticle II*, and just as on that occasion he worked on the text himself, adapting the original medieval play by cutting it and reorganizing lines. In his preface to the score of *Noye's Fludde* he wrote:

> The mediaeval Chester Miracle Plays were performed by ordinary people: local craftsmen and tradesmen of the town and their families, with choristers from the local church or cathedral for the children's parts. Each Guild performed one play from the cycle on a cart (called a *pageant*). This cart moved around the town from place to place, and on it the performance had to be entirely contained. The scenic devices, though carefully worked out, had to be extremely simple. *Noye's Fludde*, set to

---

[458] WHITTALL 1982, p.124.

music, is intended for the same style of presentation – though not necessarily on a cart. Some big building should be used, preferably a church – but not a theatre – large enough to accommodate actors and orchestra, with the action raised on rostra but not on a stage removed from the congregation. No attempt should be made to hide the orchestra from the sight. The conductor should be to the side, but placed so that he can easily step forward to conduct the congregation, which has to play a large part in the proceedings.[459]

Noye's Fludde is very much in the same line of the works we have previously discussed, as it is another work written with children and amateurs in mind, and another work that requires the involvement of the audience in the two hymns (after the building of the ark and at the end). It also offered a 'traditional' solution to the composer's concern of integrating opera and oratorio, as in a way medieval theatre contains the roots for both. Britten had been very interested in the dramatic conventions proper to the early forms of liturgical drama, as it is testified by his extensive annotations in his personal copy of Karl Young's *The Drama of the Mediaeval Church*;[460] these deal mainly with dramatic style[461] and are a fascinating testimony of Britten's involvement with dramaturgical issues. At the same time *Noye's Fludde* is a work which integrates some ideas Britten had recently discovered in a trip to the Far East, as Mervyn Cooke points out:

> The gamelan and Nô-orchestra both take an active visual part in the proceedings, performing on the same levels as the action and in full view of the spectators. That Britten had this practice in mind when establishing the dramatic conventions for *Noye's Fludde* is suggested by his introductory note. The work is an obvious attempt to fuse theatre movement, gesture, music and religious devotion by means of a synthesis between elements of the mediaeval mystery play and oriental theatre.[462]

---

[459] Benjamin Britten, *Noye's Fludde* op.59, study score (London: Boosey and Hawkes, 1958).
[460] Karl Young *The Drama of the Mediaeval Church* , 2 vols. (Oxford, University Press, 1933). According to COOKE 1998, p.162, the copy (now in the Britten–Pears Library), came into Britten's possession in the mid-1950s.
[461] See COOKE 1998, pp.160–165.
[462] COOKE 1985, p.83.

CHURCH PARABLE

In November 1955 Britten and Pears went on an international tour that lasted four months They had some dates in Europe and the Middle East, but mainly they visited the Far East: India, Ceylon, Indonesia, Singapore, Thailand, Bali and Japan.[463] Britten was extremely fascinated by his encounter with musical cultures new to him, and the experience, in particular his encounters with Gamelan music and Nô Theatre,[464] influenced all his work from then on. Peter Pears recalled how 'The sight and sounds of those dancers and the gamelan orchestra had a profound influence on him. Above all, his journey reinforced the conviction that you could get a world of orchestral colour from really quite tiny resources'.[465] Britten himself gives a retrospective account of his encounter with the Japanese theatre in a note to the libretto of *Curlew River*:

> It was in Tokyo in January 1956 that I saw a Nō-drama for the first time; and I was lucky enough during my brief stay there to see two different performances of the same play — *Sumida-gawa*. The whole occasion made a tremendous impression upon me, the simple touching story, the economy of style, the intense slowness of the action, the marvellous skill and control of the performers, the beautiful costumes, the mixture of chanting, speech, singing, which with the three instruments made up the strange music – it all offered a totally new 'operatic' experience. There was no conductor – the instrumentalists sat on the stage, so did the chorus, and the chief characters made their entrance down a long ramp. The lighting was strictly non-theatrical. The cast was all male, the one female character wearing an exquisite mask which made no attempt to hide the male jowl beneath it. The memory of this play has seldom left my mind in the years since. Was there not something – many things – to be learnt from it? The solemn dedication and skill of the performers were a lesson to any singer or actor of any country and any language. Was it not possible to use just such a story – the simple one of a demented mother seeking her lost child – with an English background (for there was no question in any case of a pastiche from the ancient Japanese)? Surely the Medieval Religious Drama in England would

---

[463] For a detailed report on the trip see COOKE 1998.
[464] I adhere here to the spelling Nô, but where there are variant spellings, particularly in Britten's letters, I preserve the original orthography.
[465] Interview in *A time there was...*

have had a comparable setting – an all-male cast of ecclesiastics – a simple austere staging in a church – a very limited instrumental accompaniment – a moral story? And so we came from *Sumida-gawa* to *Curlew River* and a Church in the Fens, but with the same story and similar characters; and whereas in Tokyo the music was the ancient Japanese music jealously preserved by successive generations, here I have started the work with that wonderful plainsong hymn 'Te lucis ante terminum', and from it the whole piece may be said to have grown.[466]

It is interesting to note how Britten describes the Japanese theatre as 'a totally new *operatic* experience', revealing his perception of the Japanese performance not as something belonging to a different world, but simply as a variation of musical drama nearer to his experience. He underlines other elements which, as we have seen, have been characteristic of his own dramatic work: simplicity of plot, spareness of means, extreme stylization (characters are recognized by the props they carry, for example a bamboo frond to represent madness, a little gong for sadness, a staff for the ferryman).[467] There is also the element of strangeness in the music, a strangeness that is not only connected to the exoticism of the music, but can become a poetic and dramatic device insofar as it projects the listener into a world different from his own. One element Britten does not mention, but that must have contributed to the strength of the impact, is the particular relationship between performers and listeners in this specific form of Japanese theatre, because the Nô stage projects well into the auditorium, subtly strengthening the audience's participation in the drama.[468] It is therefore not surprising that Britten was so fascinated by the experience to the point of wanting to recreate it in his own work.

Peter Alexander[469] has clearly illustrated how the transition from *Sumidagawa* to *Curlew River* was anything but straightforward: in his study he discusses the process of writing the libretto and the complexity of

---

[466] Benjamin Britten, back cover of the libretto for *Curlew River* (London: Faber, 1964). It is interesting to note that Britten's report is similar to Artaud's desription of Balinese performance in *The Theatre and its Double* (ARTAUD 1958, pp.57–59); see also INNES 1981, p.14. Britten talked of the impact the Japanese theatre had on him on various occasions, see COOKE 1998, in particular Chapter 5.
[467] See COOKE 1998, p.119, also for an introductory overview of Nô theatre.
[468] COOKE 1998, p.132.
[469] ALEXANDER 1988. The process of composition of the libretto of *Curlew River* is discussed to a greater extent by COOKE 1998, Chapter 6.

adapting the Japanese play. The study also assesses Britten's leading role in the shaping of the text; the project was in the back of the composer's mind for several years, and during that period it was postponed several times. When talking about his habit of delaying important projects Britten says:

> I get terribly worked up about a thing, then cool off, & then, if the idea was originally a good one, come back with renewed vigour to it. The work has gone on boiling in the back of the old mind, & usually to good effect. Grimes was like this (I delayed over one year on starting the music after Slater had finished the first draft of the libretto) – so was the Spring Symphony, & The Turn of the Screw.[470]

'If the idea was originally a good one'. After *Gloriana* Britten had discussed with William Plomer, its librettist, at least three other projects, all children's operas: one based on Beatrix Potter's *The Tale of Mister Tod*, one on an original idea for a space-travel story, *Tyco the Vegan*, and another, to complement *The Little Sweep* in a double-bill on the subject of a Greek Myth. None of these projects were carried further than initial discussion, which may be because Britten was not terribly interested in them.[471] The fact that Britten held on to the *Sumidagawa* project for eight years testifies how dear it was to his heart.

Plomer was the obvious choice as librettist: not only he was well acquainted with Japanese culture,[472] but he had been the one to suggest, on hearing about the Eastern trip, that Britten should see a Nô play[473] (although Mervyn Cooke has recently shown how Britten's interest in Japanese theatre could be traced as far back as 1938).[474] Once back in England, Britten mentioned to Plomer the play *Sumidagawa*, expressing his interest in creating a work from it, and thus starting what was to be a very long and complex process.[475] The correspondence between Plomer and the composer is a fascinating testimony to the way in which Britten's

---

[470] Letter to Ronald Duncan, dated 3 February 1957, quoted in CARPENTER 1992, p.378.
[471] Copyright problems apparently were the main reason for the dismissal of the Potter project. See TOOGOOD 1994, p.29.
[472] Plomer had lived in Japan for almost three years. See ALEXANDER 1988, p.233.
[473] See Plomer's letter to Britten dated 6 October 1955, Britten-Pears Library.
[474] Britten had been involved with Ronald Duncan in an attempt to stage a Nô play in an English translation for Ezra Pound; see COOKE 1998, pp.24–25.
[475] Britten to Plomer, 13 May 1956.

creative mind worked, as well as constituting a precious example of his working process, and part of it is worth quoting.[476]

More than a year after Britten's return from Japan, Plomer mentioned the Japanese play in a letter,[477] and Britten's reply re-stated his interest in the project:

> The 'Sumidagawa' doesn't come into any <u>immediate</u> plans. I've rather put it to the back of my mind; but anytime you feel you'd like to talk about it, it can be brought forward again. It is something I'm deeply interested in, & determined to do sometime. Isn't it a curiously moving and disturbing story?[478]

One year later still, Britten had not started work on the *Sumidagawa* project, and in July 1958 he wrote to Plomer: 'I can't write about the No play idea now, except to say that it's boiling up inside me, but that I have so many things to talk to you… about the style & all that… before I start on it'.[479] By October 1958, Plomer had started working on the libretto, and as usual Britten influenced the process: 'I am very keen on as many nice evocative Japanese words as possible', he wrote to the librettist.[480] Plomer replied: 'I have made some progress with a first draft of Sumida — and find the language assuming great simplicity — as in a fairy tale or legend'.[481] At the end of October Britten wrote 'I long to see what you have been doing over Sumidagawa, & to talk endlessly with you about it. I am more and more excited about it, & I have to keep my ideas in chains in case they don't run parallel to yours'.[482] In November Plomer completed a preliminary draft of the libretto, and Britten responded: 'What a wonderful play it is, & I cannot thank you enough for working with me on it. The more I think of it, the more I feel we should stick as far as possible to the original style & look of it — but oh, to find some equivalent to those extraordinary noises the Japanese musicians made!'.[483]

---

[476] The correspondence between Plomer and Britten is in the Britten–Pears Library holdings. Part of the correspondence relating to *Curlew River* is quoted in ALEXANDER 1988 and COOKE 1998.
[477] Plomer to Britten, 5 July 1957.
[478] Britten to Plomer, 10 July 1957.
[479] Britten to Plomer, 12 July 1958.
[480] Britten to Plomer, 8 October 1958.
[481] Plomer to Britten, 21 October 1958.
[482] Britten to Plomer, 29 October 1958.
[483] Britten to Plomer, 16 November 1958.

According to this statement, Britten initially wanted to be as near to the original style as possible, and Mervyn Cooke as pointed out how the first draft is substantially different from the final text of *Curlew River*, this being an indication that the authors were 'contemplating a faithful treatment of the play reflecting its Japanese characteristics':[484]

> His first draft libretto [...] takes the form of a straightforward paraphrase of the Japanese Classics Translation Committee's authorized translation and is entitled *Sumida River*. It is handwritten throughout and differs very little from the original text. Both the Japanese names and the numbered sections of the translation are retained, the latter undoubtedly helping Britten in his perception of the play's structure. There is some versification of the original prose, but much of the phraseology is identical and many verbal expressions from the translation were retained in the final version of the libretto completed some five years later. [...] The initial draft differs from the final text of *Curlew River* in several important respects. Most striking are the absence of the quasi-liturgical framework subsequently imposed on the presentation of the story and the retention of all the Buddhist references, which were also to be modified at a later stage of the work's development.[485]

Britten did not start working on the libretto immediately because of his many other commitments. In March he was still working on other projects, in particular the cantata commissioned for the anniversary of the University of Basle,[486] but his heart was already with the Nô play: 'In a month or so it should be done & I'll get to work on what really interests me. I think the Noh libretto is wonderful'.[487] Things did not go quite as planned, and one year later Britten had still not written any music to the libretto; instead, by April 1959, notwithstanding the above quoted statement, major changes in his conception of the work had taken place, with a shift towards the idea of early medieval drama and of Christian ideas. This change is illustrated by a fascinating letter from the composer to the librettist, that I believe is worth quoting almost in full:

---

[484] COOKE 1998, p.139.
[485] COOKE 1998, p.139.
[486] *Cantata Academica* op.62, first performed in Basel by the Basel Chamber Choir and Orchestra under Paul Sacher on 1 July 1960.
[487] Britten to Plomer, 8 March 1959.

I rather hope that you are feeling strong & courageous when you open this letter, my dear, because I fear it's going to be long-winded, and maybe a trifle disturbing. Anyhow it doesn't need an immediate answer – only something to think about & which we can discuss when we meet. It is about the Noh play. A new idea has come into our (Peter's & my) heads about it – put in, because for many reasons it would be best if done in one of the churches here – I won't go into the practical reasons here, which are pretty important, but the artistic ones include placing of orchestra, long entrances, beauty of sound (if in Orford church) & contact with audience. This lead [*sic*] us to the idea of making it a Christian work (Here you can stop reading and have another sip of coffee to give you courage to proceed...). I think one of the best ways of writing what I feel about this is to weigh the matter — pros. & cons.

Pros.The little bits of Zen-Bhuddism [*sic*], which don't mean much to me could be replaced by something which <u>does</u>. The story is one which stands strongly wherever it is placed. I have been <u>very</u> worried lest the work should seem a <u>pastiche</u> of a Noh play, which however well done, would seem false & thin. I <u>can't</u> write Japanesy music, but might be led into trying if the rest of the production (setting, clothes, moves) were Japanese. <u>Masks</u> – for which no solution has yet presented itself, & remains a colossal problem for the singer. The chorus could move freely, if we wanted it.

<u>Cons.</u> We should lose the magic of Japanese names, & atmosphere – obviously very dear to you, & dear to me too. No very good reason for Peter to do a female part, unless in an accepted style.

Actually, to answer the <u>cons</u>, if we made it Mediaeval, or possibly earlier, it would be accurate that no women should be used; also if the style were kept very artificial, very influenced by the Noh, then it wouldn't seem so odd for a woman to be played by a man, especially if the dresses were very carefully & strongly designed. There is nothing, I realise, to replace the magic of 'Shimosa', or 'Miyako', or even 'Namu Amida' — altho' 'Kyrie Eleison' is pretty good. But we might get a very strong atmosphere (which I personally love) if we set it in pre-conquest East Anglia (where there were shrines galore).[488]

It is possible that Britten's initial shyness in tackling the libretto might have been influenced by the fact that he could not commit to the

---

[488] Britten to Plomer, 15 April 1959.

philosophical content of the play, and maybe he was unconsciously looking for a solution. This certainly appears to be the strongest motivation in his change of direction, indicated also in the concern regarding the 'contact with the audience'.

By May 1959 the provisional title for the work had become 'The River'. In the summer of the same year Britten found himself in the situation of having to postpone the work again. He wrote to the librettist:

> I fear I must postpone this piece, still near to my heart, for a year. For many reasons. Partly time, because of my change of location, moving it from Japan to Mediaeval England, we are well behind our schedule. [...] The other reason is that we are going this coming winter to rebuild the Jubilee Hall, make it a proper little Opera House, with dressing rooms, bigger stage, bigger orchestral pit, changing & increasing the seating, etc, etc, and we must have a new big opera to open it with next June. The 'River', being for a church, wouldn't do, also, it is scarcely Festive.[489]

For one year all work on 'The River' was suspended, and by August 1960 Britten seemed impatient to resume work on what had by now become *Curlew River*:

> I am much looking forward to starting on Curlew River. I'd love to talk about one or two bits fairly soon, but it's thrilling that it is so beautifully & convincingly shaped now. By-the-way I saw the Play of Daniel the other day... which was an object lesson in how not to do a mediaeval play... glorious, accurate scholarship, I know, every detail being perfectly copied visually & aurally, without any style or taste or genuine understanding – one of the most hideous hours I've ever spent. We must think very carefully about the look of our thing.[490]

Britten is probably referring to Noah Greenberg's production of the play; Greenberg had produced the *Ludus Danielis* with the New York Pro Musica in 1958, and he subsequently toured Europe.[491] This letter is

---

[489] Britten to Plomer, 17 August 1959.
[490] Britten to Plomer, 4 August 1960.
[491] I am indebted to David Fallows for this information. See also *The Play of Daniel*, ed. by W.L. Smoldon, revised edition (Sutton, The Plainsong and Mediaeval Music Society, 1976), in particular the introduction. Notwithstanding Britten's negative comment, a comparison

further testimony of how closely Britten was involved in all the stages of the production, from the first moment, down to the last, attending to all the details, as is the following one, written to Plomer four years later, when finally the work was planned to be performed at the 1964 Aldeburgh Festival:

> I have had some excellent talks with Colin Graham... He is getting on well with his ideas, & I think they are good. One scheme we have developed is this: the Chorus, seated at one side, is going eventually to give the appearance of being in the boat. There-fore, on arrival on the other side they all will get out & cross to a new position around the Shrine; this will happen on p.15 (typed script) after 'For this boy he never knew'.[492]

Britten had been able to start the composition process on *Curlew River* only in the winter of 1964, eight years after the first work on the project. In the context of Britten's working methods and routine this is definitely an exception. The score of *Curlew River* was composed mainly in Venice (the completion date reads Venice-Aldeburgh Maundy Thursday 1964). Some of the composition process is described by Britten himself in a long letter to Plomer written from Palazzo Mocenigo in Venice:

> When we arrived I was tireder than I thought (nothing like birthdays, Christmases and operas[493] to make one feel one's age), & honestly I still couldn't quite see the style of it all clearly enough. I was still very drawn towards the Nô, too close for comfort. However, a few days here, although Arctic in temperature, the Gothic beauty & warmth, and above all the occasional Masses one attended, began to make their effect. It was a slow start, but after that it rushed ahead, & after little more than a month I am well towards the end. Apart from the usual bits that need clarifying, I am very pleased with it. Honestly I would have loved to have you at my side all the time; there have been so many problems. But you have other things to do, & so I have made my own changes, & we must just work at them together at the earliest moment, and see that we are both happy. There is nothing major at all. It has only been the infinite little details,

---

between the beginning of the *Play of Daniel* and of *Curlew River* is quite revealing, see WATSON 1985, p.7.
[492] Britten to Plomer, 4 January 1964.
[493] Britten had just finished working on a new production of *Billy Budd*.

which, until the music begins to take over, one can never anticipate – lengths of line & verses, for instance… A few points. The Ceremonial robing now takes place <u>after</u> the Abbot's prologue (reasons are mostly practical). I've referred to the <u>Land</u> of East (or West) rather than <u>Kingdom</u> (rhythmic problem). To emphasise the river, & Curlew, idea, I like to refer to the <u>River</u> people, as opposed to <u>Village</u> p. (less contemporary too, I feel). I liked the idea of keeping the mystery a little longer, & so on page 2 & 3 (typed script), I have kept the burial anonymous (no boy mentioned yet). In the great narration on the boat – I've inserted a reference to the boy as being a <u>Christian</u> – & therefore the Northman as a <u>pagan</u>. Do you mind?

As you obviously didn't have time to do me a new piece for the Chorus getting out of the boat I used the river chorus from page 12 again, & it works well. I am sorry to have bothered you about this, because I ought to have spotted it before, as the best solution.

I have omitted referring to the boy's name (Siward) anywhere – it didn't seem necessary – so on page 16 one cuts from 'Pray tell me, tell me what his name was' – to 'Oh how should I know?'

I have had to concoct a big <u>ensemble</u> after her revelation on page 17 – which I have done with Colin's help, mostly from phrases used elsewhere. Similarly I have concocted a big <u>really</u> Crazy scene for Madwoman on top of 18 – but used nothing, I think, which hasn't appeared before, except one idea pinched from the Nô. I have made her confuse the Curlew river with the bird, & suggested the boy has flown away with the young Curlew birds – 'like the four young birds that left their nest.' (Nô) But of course it can be changed if you object.

I have a big new idea, which I think is good – I am just approaching the big moment round the Tomb. I would like to use one of those great Gregorian plain-chant tunes. It will somehow tie the whole thing together, & match the entrance and exit chant (for which I am using '<u>Te lucis ante terminum</u>') The one I have my eye on is: '<u>Custodes hominum</u>' from the Feast of the Holy Guardian Angels, a magnificent tune & suitable too. If you agree with our feeling that it should be sung in English could you possibly do a translation – it is quite short, needs to be metrically exact, but not rhyming – ?

> There are many small points, but these are the few major ones. The more I work on the libretto, the more I admire and love it, and find it always stimulating and exciting. I do thank you for doing it.[494]

The impact of the 'occasional Masses one attended' was certainly strong; in February 1964 the changes in the common liturgy indicated by the Second Vatican Council, which had taken place the previous years, had not yet been widely adopted, and is therefore likely that Britten attended liturgical celebrations in Latin, in which plainchant was still relevant. The insertion of the Gregorian tune is not a new concept for Britten, as he had used plainsong (real, modified or fake) from *The Company of Heaven* (1937) onwards, in particular in his *Sinfonia da Requiem*, where he had quoted from the *Dies Irae* of the Requiem Mass in order to increase the familiarity of the listeners with the sound-world of the new work;[495] the device can also be associated with the use of well-known hymns for audience participation in *Saint Nicolas* and *Noye's Fludde*. Plomer seemed very happy with the idea of the liturgical connection suggested by the use of the Gregorian chant, 'The Gregorian plain-chant idea is one of those revelations that you get',[496] and in general with the overall result:

> Curlew River seems to me a work of extraordinary originality, unity, force and vitality, and how I long to hear the full effect of it and to trace the course of each instrument and study the texture of the singing. I am so happy [...] that the change of gear from the buddhist idiom to a Christian one has been complete. Only you could have seen the possibility of transposing a Nô play into the European Medieval tradition, and only you could have brought it off with such tense and haunting effect.[497]

Towards the end of the compositional process Britten expressed his concern that the work could be seen as a weird operatic experiment: 'I have been looking for a subtitle which will make clear it is not an opera, in the accepted sense, and must be done in church. Do you like Curlew River – a parable for Church performance? We all like the parable-idea'[498] (and we have seen how in the context of Britten's aesthetic it was

---

[494] Britten to Plomer, 15 February 1964.
[495] See above, Chapter 1.
[496] Plomer to Britten, 20 February 1964.
[497] Plomer to Britten, 2 March 1964.
[498] Britten to Plomer, 2 April 1964.

not completely a new idea). Plomer replied 'When young I was taught that a parable was "an earthly story with a heavenly meaning". The *Concise Oxford Dictionary* says: "Fictitious narrative used to typify moral or spiritual relations." Exactly!',[499] and only few days later he wrote:

> Yesterday I spent some time with Colin Graham, who showed me the model, which is most exciting and well planned and made, and is going to make the greatest possible effect in the formalization of the whole piece without the least suggestion of false japonaiserie. In fact I almost feel that you are evolving, with Curlew River, something of great originality, a new style really of operatic-church parable.[500]

Apparently Plomer had been the one to suggest the processional entrance of the monks, and the ceremonial robing, although according to Colin Graham, who had spent a considerable amount of time in Venice working with the composer, the idea of the ceremonial robing derived from their experience of the preparation for the Mass in the chapel of San Giorgio Maggiore.[501] The procession and the ceremonial robing constitute an excuse for a prologue, a device that Britten had used quite regularly in previous works, as for example in *Lucretia, Billy Budd, The Turn of the Screw* (where the Prologue was added at the very last moment), and even *Saint Nicolas*. The use of Latin text might seem strange in a work that had changed radically in order to accommodate an English audience, but at the same time can be explained by the desire to use a language that while historically and culturally justified could still evoke a sense of strangeness in the audience (similar to the ancient Japanese use in the Nô), therefore constituting an effective vehicle to introduce the sacral dimension of the performance. Humphrey Carpenter comments that 'the effect is that of a distancing device, which provides a preparation and a warning before we enter the enclosed world of these operas'.[502] This comment echoes Britten's own statement in the Aspen speech about the attitude one should have when taking part in a concert.[503] It is certainly

---

[499] Plomer to Britten, 3 April 1964.
[500] Plomer to Britten, 9 April 1964.
[501] GRAHAM 1979, p.48.
[502] CARPENTER 1992, p.339.
[503] 'Music [...] demands some preparation, some effort, a journey to a special place, saving up for a ticket, some homework on the programme perhaps, some clarification of the ears and sharpening of the instincts' (BRITTEN 1964, p.20).

appropriate in the case of the church parables. Britten was very concerned that the work should not have a 'traditional' performance: the dramatic convention he uses, the style of performance are part of the conception of the work, and should therefore be respected, to the point that the published score of *Curlew River* contains more than twenty pages of performance instructions for the production:

> The movement and production details should be as spare and economical as possible: the miming, which plays an integral part, is symbolic and should be pared down to its quintessence. Once the spectator becomes geared to the convention his emotions are imperceptibly but passionately involved in a drama doubly distilled by the very economy of its theatrical means. Such involvement can be shattered by a single uncontrolled, weak, or unnecessary gesture. Every movement of the hand or tilt of the head should assume immense meaning and, although formalized, must be designed and executed with the outmost intensity. [...] The lighting should be as simple as possible, and no attempt should be made to achieve theatrical effects. [...] The action of the story itself should be as formalized as a ritual: unlike naturalistic acting, emotion should never be expressed with the face or the eyes but always be a rehearsed ritualistic movement of the hands, head or body.[504]

Some of these production notes are similar to the ones that were published in 1958 to accompany the full score of *Noye's Fludde*. In those again the stress was on avoiding theatrical lighting, and any kind of naturalistic acting. Even regarding the costumes for the animals, the notes stress how they do not need 'proper costumes': 'the children have to be brought in to help *represent* the animals, they should have animals' heads or masks over some basic form of modern dress (without jackets). They could even, as in the early street days, carry some symbol or picture of the animal they represent'.[505] This style of symbolized representation is very similar to that of the Japanese performance that had such a profound effect on Britten, but in *Noye's Fludde* it is not perceived as having been borrowed from a non-Western aesthetic; one can see how the two works, born from different cultural contexts, presented similar characteristics.

---

[504] Benjamin Britten, *Curlew River: A Parable for Church Performance* op.71 (London: Faber, 1964), pp.143–145 (the production notes are by Colin Graham).

[505] Benjamin Britten and Colin Graham, *Noye's Fludde: Notes on the Production* (London: Boosey and Hawkes, 1958).

Colin Graham has recognized Britten's leading influence in his approach to the staging: 'When [Britten] asked me to do the opera, he also particularly asked that I should read as much as I could about Noh plays but under no circumstances go to see one as he wanted our stylised movement to have its own style and not be a pastiche – thus echoing his musical approach'.[506] Graham also recalls that 'final details of the music were worked out simultaneously with the dramatic ideas'.[507] So Britten had been in control of the whole process of writing the libretto, and now the production reflected his own idea of what the work was supposed to be: no *Japonaiserie*, but a special theatrical and musical experience with only a hint of the operatic. I think this reinforces the perception that Britten not only did not want to 're-create' a Nô play, he ultimately wanted to develop a form of theatre which shared with the Nô some characteristics, but whose stylistic essence could be said to be born out of a Western experience of those characteristics, in the light of what can be defined an 'universal' form of theatre. This might have been an unconscious reason of his attraction to the Nô theatre to begin with, an hypothesis that might be supported by an early statement made by the composer in his 1958 broadcast to Japan:

> I shall never forget the impact made on me by the Japanese theatre – the tremendous Kabuki, but above all the profound Nô plays. I count the last amongst the greatest theatrical experiences of my life. [...] The deep solemnity and *self*lessness of the acting, the perfect shaping of the drama (like a great Greek tragedy) coupled with the strength and universality of the stories are something which every Western artist can learn from.[508]

Beyond the intrinsically Japanese aesthetic and stylistic elements of the performance, what Britten seems to single out is the universality of a theatrical experience that narrates a story of great spiritual profundity with great dramatic impact through stylized gesture, poetry and music, and I would also add, to a didactic end. Mervyn Cooke has pointed out how musically the work was more influenced by the Gagaku, a form of Japanese ceremonial music, rather than the Nô, a indication that Britten was 'more attracted to the dramatic quality of Nô rather than its musical

---

[506] Quoted in COOKE 1998, p.154.
[507] COOKE 1998, p.154.
[508] BRITTEN 1991, p.19; also quoted in COOKE 1998, p.120.

idiom',[509] a dramatic quality that Daniel Allbright defines as 'hieratically intense'.[510] The reference to Greek tragedy also is not too hazardous, because, as Mae Smethurst has demonstrated,[511] the two forms share many similarities, amongst which is the philosophical, religious background they both inhabit: the theatre as a sacred space where a didactic exercise takes place. This is also a similarity shared with the medieval theatre, and Mervyn Cooke has pointed out how the Nô and mediaeval European drama, forms that developed approximately at the same time, have many common features.[512] Although the development of the church parable as a form was triggered by the Japanese experience, that Britten had something quite different at the back of his mind is evident in how *Curlew River* developed. It did maintain several of the original stylistic features, although re-visited, but the result is radically different in content and expression. The most striking difference, which is a direct consequence of the Christianization of the story, is the ending: in the Japanese original the spirit of the child disappears for ever, leaving the mother grieving on the grave, but in *Curlew River* the appearance of the child becomes as a miracle by which the madwoman is healed.

> Britten's decision to Christianize the plot of *Sumidagawa* marks a significant and philosophically radical departure from the aesthetic effect of the Japanese original. To the uninitiated Westerner, many Nô play seem highly static in their dramatic effect because stage action and plot developments are less important than the philosophical contemplation expected from cognoscenti of the genre. The aesthetic principles of Nô theatre are both complex and subtle, and are based on three categories of artistic 'beauty' […] which are expressed through a sophisticated process of dramatic symbolism. Britten evidently had little interest in this fundamental dimension of Nô, and his attempt to replace it with a dramatic momentum more typical of Western theatre might well disappoint a connoisseur of Nô aesthetic. […] Plomer's Christianized text has a dramatic shape of its own […]. In *Curlew River* the Mother makes no reference to God or Heaven until she is freed from her madness by the apparition of the spirit and sings 'Amen'. Britten's drama might therefore be seen as a spiritual progression towards this climactic and cathartic moment.[513]

---

[509] COOKE 1998, p.154, p.166.
[510] ALLBRIGHT 2000, p.89.
[511] See SMETHURST 1989.
[512] See COOKE 1998, p.160.
[513] COOKE 1998, pp.153–4.

This climactic dramatic structure, seen as a spiritual progression towards a cathartic ending, is maintained in the two later parables, that progressively distance themselves from the Japanese experience: in particular, in their use of the chorus, but also the relationship between the characters[514] and the development of the story, that somehow does not have the directionality and dramatic cogency *of Curlew River*, but appears more episodic. At the same time, the Christianization of what was a pagan story brings us back to *The Rape of Lucretia*,[515] as do other elements, amongst which is the stylization of the acting.

A very strong similarity is constituted by the presence of the Abbot's addresses at the beginning and the end of the church parables, which brings us back to the Choruses in *Lucretia*, particularly to the final commentary. There again we had a story used as a metaphor for a didactic exercise of religious nature, although there is an obvious difference: in the chamber opera the final address was attempting to give Christian hope to the audience after evil, in the form of Tarquinius, had triumphed. In the church parables on the other hand what we see is the dramatization of stories where good does triumph, and where the presence of God is tangible. The abbot in *Curlew River* and *The Burning Fiery Furnace* talks of 'performing a mystery' (in *The Prodigal Son* the abbot enters on stage already dressed as The Tempter, so the introduction is different from the almost formulaic beginning of the previous church parables), and we could say that in all the three works we are presented a miracle: the healing of the madwoman, the young Jew's immunity (and Nebuchadnezzar's conversion to 'the most high God'), and the father's love. It would therefore seem that in the church parables Britten has become much more assertive in his didactic intent.

There are of course other elements that link the parables not only to *Lucretia*, but to the some of the works that precede them, in particular *Saint Nicholas*, *Noye's Fludde* and the Canticles. The didactic intent is the most obvious, but also relevant is the connection with the early Medieval theatre: as we have suggested the morality play, as the antecedent of oratorio, is in the background of the conception of

---

[514] See COOKE 1998, Chapter 7.
[515] COOKE 1987, 'The prophecy of Lucretia', has already discussed the relationship of the first chamber opera with the church parables.

Lucretia,[516] and *Saint Nicolas*, can be related to the same form, although not directly, in his integration of epic and dramatic, as well as in his subject matter and in the involvement of the congregation in the hymns. The relationship with the audience is of course another key element, as Mervyn Cooke points out:

> The Nô stage projects well into the auditorium, subtly strengthening the audience participation in the drama. This concept of an experience shared between actors and onlookers is once again an important part of Britten's ideal in all the three Church Parables, and might be traced back to the direct audience participation in *Saint Nicolas* (1948), *Let's make an opera* (1949) and *Noye's Fludde* - the latter a seminal work in the development of the Parable style, dating as it does from the year following Britten's visit to Japan.[517]

The concept of audience participation can also be traced back to *Lucretia*, as we have previously discussed: by moving between the different levels of the action the Choruses, although wearing historical costumes, become contemporary of the audience, that is thus involved in the representation.

There is no doubt that Britten was extremely satisfied with the format of the church parables, and it is difficult to assess how, should his state of health have been different, he would have continued to develop and use the parable format. We know that later in life Britten had also contemplated setting a text derived from the Chester nativity plays, and although the project was never brought to completion a typed libretto, dated 5 October 1974, survives.[518] Mervyn Cooke points out how the work seems to combine some of the elements presents in *Noye's Fludde*, for example the participation of the congregation in various hymns, but at the same time integrates one of the elements of the parables, the singing of a plainsong at the beginning, and the use of the dance in a way similar to that developed in *Death in Venice* (the dancers were intended to portray various characters, as well as the animals around the crib and the sheep in the fields).[519] An element that throws an interesting light on what could have been the dramaturgy of Britten's next parable is illustrated in

---

[516] See also HADDON SQUIRE 1946, p.1.
[517] COOKE 1998, p.132.
[518] COOKE 1998, p.161.
[519] COOKE 1998, p.162.

a passage that the composer highlighted in his personal copy of Karl Young's *The Drama of the Mediaeval Church*, relative to a play concerning the adoration: 'The conclusion of this scene is unique in that after adoring the Child themselves, the shepherds invite the congregation to do likewise'.[520] The congregational adoration of the Holy infant (or the Cross) is a practice still common in the Christian liturgy, at least in Italy, where during Advent and Holy week the congregation is invited to join in a procession and prostrate themselves in front of a statue. Had Britten integrated this last element he would have created an even more involving theatrical experience that not only had the elements of sacrality he had been developing with the church parables, but that would have really become not only ritualistic, but an almost liturgical experience.

Thanks to a series of fortunate circumstances during the 1950s Britten was able to experience different types of theatre which shared some features with the ideal that he had already attempted to put into practice with *The Rape of Lucretia*. Both the Medieval play and the Nô theatre share a common *plateau* of archetypal theatrical elements, which are also common to Greek tragedy:[521] a theatrical form constituting in essence a ritualised act of religious devotion, which uses a chorus and male actors wearing masks, on a austere the stage, whose design is spare and symbolic, and whose style of performance is highly stylized to the point of being ritualistic. On top of all this, they use symbolism with a didactic intent. I believe that from these elements Britten was able to identify a kind of theatre that, beyond the cultural and historical connotations, had a quality of universality, in terms of both space and time, and also responded to his desire for sacrality in the performance. It is interesting to note though that the existing trilogy constitutes a sort of cycle and that when the three works are performed together they offer a comparison with the traditional mode of performance of Nô theatre (a cycle of plays performed in a single day)[522] and also with Greek tragedy, traditionally performed in cycles of three plays in a day during the festivities dedicated to Dionysus.

---

[520] YOUNG 1933, vol.II, p.89, quoted in COOKE 1998, p.164.
[521] See HOOVER 1988, p.146; on the subject see also AYLEN 1985, GOULD 1990 and SMETHURST 1989.
[522] See COOKE 1998, p.132.

This is the kind of theatre at which Britten was aiming in what might superficially seem a mixture of genres, but can also be read as a process of filtering in order to achieve a form of 'purified' theatre, which suited his vision of the function of dramatic performance which we outlined in the second chapter; a form of theatre that from the church parables will go even further back to its roots, Greek tragedy, with what becomes then a theatre parable, *Death in Venice*, where the integration of opera and oratorio is complicated, as we shall see, by the introduction of dance. In some ways Britten had already introduced the concept of dance in the church parables, as they are 'as closely choreographed as a ballet',[523] but in the last work dance assumes a new expressive strength which is totally integrated in the conception of the work and becomes a further dramatic level.

HOLY THEATRE

In an illuminating analysis of the work, Gary Watson[524] has identified in *Curlew River* an example of what Peter Brook, starting from Antonin Artaud's theories of the theatre, refers to as 'holy theatre'. For Artaud, theatre must break with actuality: 'Its object is not to resolve social or psychological conflicts, to serve as a battlefield for moral passions, but to express objectively certain secret truths'.[525] Theatre is in essence a 'social organ committed to the public revelation of mystical truths',[526] aiming for spiritual revelations. As a corollary to this statement, Peter Brook explains that 'all religions assert that the invisible is visible all the time. But here's the crunch. Religious teaching – including Zen – asserts that this visible-invisible cannot be seen automatically – it can only be seen given certain conditions'.[527] Holy theatre, which is a form of holy art, is an aid to this, as it tries to offer conditions that make such perception possible. These conditions include the use of ritual, the explorations of dream states or the instinctive and subconscious levels of the psyche, the use of symbolism and the deliberate subordination of physical to spiritual reality.

---

[523] ALLBRIGHT 2000, p.99.
[524] WATSON 1985.
[525] ARTAUD 1958, p.70.
[526] ARTAUD 1958, p.46.
[527] BROOK 1972, p.63.

It is quite easy to see how these traits emerge in Britten's works after the early experience of *Johnson over Jordan*, progressively assuming greater importance. Furthermore, all forms of avant-garde holy theatre express the same desire 'to return to man's "roots" – whether the psyche or pre-history – which is reflected on a stylistic level by the return of "original" forms of drama, Dionysian ritual and the mysteries at Eleusis, tribal drama from New Guinea and archaic survivals like the Balinese dance';[528] this can extend to include Nô theatre and medieval liturgical drama. Watson presents an interesting clarification of the use of ritual in a theatrical context:

> The word ritual refers to the prescribed and ordered practices associated with religious rite or ceremony, whose function is to provide a formal vehicle for the metaphysical transportation from a state of mundane awareness to one of mystical awareness, transcending limitations of space and time. A distinction needs to be made between holy and secular ritual: most theatre involves ritual in the 'modern' sense in some form. In the more complex process, the audience 'suspends its disbelief', a notion originally conceived by Coleridge (*Biographia Litteraria*, Chapter XIV) to describe the nature of poetic faith, but eminently suited to describe the state of mind required of a theatrical audience. But such dramatic rituals do not necessarily express a 'holy purpose'. It is the purpose then, of the particular ritual through which a play unfolds, that determines whether the ritual-as-play does or does not constitute 'holy theatre'. If the (dramatic) ritual aims to provide access for actors and audience to a perception of themselves and their world which transcends their physical-psychological actuality, then this ritual and the play or drama it embraces may be considered as 'holy'.[529]

This seems to have been Britten's aim: to use a form of theatre that corresponds to the definition of 'holy' in order to communicate in a suitable context spiritual truths which provide access to a higher perception of the world and of humanity.

---

[528] INNES 1981, p.50.
[529] WATSON 1985, p.3–4.

THEATRE-PARABLE

In terms of interpretation, *Curlew River* and the other church parables are straightforward works, once we become acquainted with their particular dramaturgy. The didactic intent is obvious from the start, and the message very clear: *spes*, *fides* and *caritas* are the respective subjects of what becomes a moral meditation in dramatic terms (an archetypal means of religious teaching). Their intent is not only to provoke questions, they communicate a given truth. I believe they are the product of a deep change in Britten's relationship with the theatre which took place after the experience of *The Turn of the Screw*. In 1955 the composer had written to Edith Sitwell, whose poem 'Still falls the rain' he had just set in his *Canticle III*, saying: 'I feel with this work and the Turn of the Screw... that I am on the threshold of a new musical world... your great poem has dragged something from me that was latent there, & showed me what lies before me'.[530] It is not only Britten's sound world that changes, and I believe that the change also involved a different approach to the content of the works (it might be argued that it was rather the sound world that had to change as a consequence, but this is an issue that goes beyond the limits set in the present work). In Britten's dramatic works after *The Turn of the Screw*[531] we are no longer faced with psychologically distressing (on the part of the listener) moral ambiguities, but rather with the assertion of timeless truths in the pseudo-religious environment of the theatre, whether sacred or not.

It would seem that from the beginning of the 1960s Britten had changed his attitude towards the 'message' he was trying to convey, maybe because of factors we are not yet able to identify. Even the first work that follows the parables, the television opera *Owen Wingrave*, notwithstanding the more traditional dramatic format, is in essence a modern parable about peace: there is no ambiguity about the character, although his death is mysterious. In Owen's monologue[532] we have a rhetorical rhythm that echoes that of a sermon (and could even be

---

[530] Quoted by Philip Reed in a programme note for *Canticle III: Still falls the Rain* op.55, in *Aldeburgh October Britten Festival 1994*, p.60.

[531] I would consider *A Midsummer Night's Dream* an exception from this point of view, as the circumstances of its creation reinforce the perception that the work was born as a festive theatrical *divertissement*, where the element of parody has great relevance.

[532] See Donald Mitchell's discussion of the *Wingrave* monologue in COOKE 1999, pp.190–195.

reminiscent of some pages of the Bible, for example St Paul's Second Letter to the Corinthians):

> In peace I have found my image,
> I have found myself.
> In peace I rejoice amongst men
> and yet walk alone,
> in peace I will guard this balance
> so that it is not broken.
> For peace is not lazy, but vigilant,
> peace is not acquiescent, but searching,
> peace is not weak, but strong like a bird's wing
> bearing its weight in the dazzling air.
> Peace is not silent, it is the voice of love.
> Oh you with your bugbears, your arrogance, your greed,
> your intolerance, your selfish morals
> and petty victories,
> peace is not won by your wars.
> Peace is not confused, not sentimental, not afraid.
> Peace is positive, is passionate, committing –
> more than war itself.
> Only in peace can I be free.

It is important to remember that *Wingrave* was commissioned and composed during the years of the Vietnam war, at a time when pacifism was again, as in the 1930s, an extremely relevant issue,[533] and it is not surprising that Britten would have wanted to use the chance of a medium as popular as television to give his contribution to the debate. The 'holy' or 'parable' aspect of the artistic work seems to have taken over, not only in theory but also in its practical implications, of form and content. And after the moral meditations about the fundamentals of Christian faith and about pacifism, Britten's longstanding belief, one is left to wonder what is the truth that the composer wanted to communicate in his last parable, *Death in Venice*.

---

[533] See EVANS, JOHN 1984, 'Owen Wingrave…', p.229.

CHAPTER 6
THE TASTE OF KNOWLEDGE

> Death in Venice *embodies unequivocally the powerful sexual drive that was Britten's towards the young (and sometimes very young) male.*
> *(Donald Mitchell)* [534]

Anyone familiar with the scholarship lavished upon Der Tod in Venedig will know how perfect a trap the story is for generalization — even those not made in haste — and how unavailable its full value is to those with a specialist's focus. It is all too easy to write about such a work in impertinent clinical or scholarly jargon. Merely uncovering beyond a certain point its bare outlines is in a way shameful. Literary anatomists can nevertheless be shameless, and so over the years the story has been burdened with just such jargon ('manic replacive object', 'disintegration of artistic sublimation'), farfetched psychoanalysis ('Tadzio as an ecstasy-provoking embodiment of the maternal breast'), silly moralizing ('Why does Aschenbach never envisage fruitful love between himself and Tadzio, or any healing or beneficial outcome of his love? He could have introduced himself to the family with propriety, and sought appropriate expression of love'), mercilessly reductive simplification ('a story ... of latent and unrecognised homosexuality leading to self-destruction') or mere revulsion (D.H. Lawrence calling the story 'absolutely, almost intentionally unwholesome'). It is easy for critics to say too much and, it would seem, nearly impossible to say too little about Der Tod in Venedig, where silence rather than assertiveness would often be more telling. As

---
[534] MITCHELL 1987, p.21.

yet another commentator upon the action of the story Britten, we shall see, exercised more discretion than many of his scholarly counterparts — though he too was for 'operatic' as well as interpretative reasons unable to avoid simplifying the original. Still, Death in Venice ennobles Mann's story. [...] Its focus remains on the universal level and does not merely communicate a moral tale for pederasts.[535]

Britten's last opera is considered at the same time a testament and a public confession made by the composer who had in some ways lived all his life 'in the closet': we know that the composer wished to make public the truth about his relationship with Pears, and Donald Mitchell reports how Britten himself had stated that *'Death in Venice* is everything that Peter and I have stood for'.[536]

Mitchell, agreeing that the opera is 'autobiographical in character',[537] argues that probably 'he [Britten] was not just referring to the opera's frank avowal of his own Tadzio-oriented homosexuality but also to the obligatory consequential constraints, the absence of which was ultimately Aschenbach's undoing';[538] he also locates the focus of the drama as being less in the sexually oriented approach of a repressed paedophile's journey towards self-destruction and more in the artistic struggle towards keeping the balance 'between order and chaos'.[539] Still, in Mitchell's reading, Aschenbach is driven to self-destruction, an impression shared by Mervyn Cooke, who describes the opera as the story of an attraction culminating in corruption and death.[540] Indeed, Mann's novella involves a 'deeply negative and (in Mann's words) pathological approach to homosexuality as such'.[541] Britten's decision to set such a text is seen as a consequence of his 'internalisation', a psychological process which implies 'the acceptance of society's values and judgements by the

---

[535] SCHMIDGALL 1977 p.324, p.338. The four quotations are taken respectively from (1) Raymond Taybox, *'Death in Venice*: The Aesthetic Object as Dream Guide', *American Imago* 26 (1969), p.135; (2) A.E.Dyson 'The Stranger God: *Death in Venice*', *The Critical Quarterly* XIII (1971), p.19; (3) Albert J. Guerard *André Gide* (1951), p.113; (4) D.H. Lawrence *Selected Literary Criticism*, ed. A. Beal (1966), p.264.
[536] MITCHELL 1987, p. 207, note 15.
[537] MITCHELL 1987, p.21.
[538] MITCHELL 1987, p.207, note 15.
[539] MITCHELL 1987, p.22. Mitchell refers here to a letter written by W.H. Auden to the young Britten probably in 1942, where he talks about 'the dangers' that beset an artist (quoted in MITCHELL 1981, p.161).
[540] COOKE 1998, p.245.
[541] HINDLEY 1990, p.511.

victim',[542] an argument Philip Brett has discussed on several occasions. We are therefore left with the impression that this last confession has the composer drowned in his own sense of guilt, with no hope, no resolution. Clifford Hindley, holding the theory that Britten in his operas was trying to show the positive aspects of same–sex love,[543] sees in the last opera 'an affirmative vision of Platonism[544] as a genuine option for the artist, developed and amplified by an emphasis on the significance of a real relationship with the beloved for the artist himself';[545] it is only the refusal of that ideal, again a consequence of the internalisation of society's pressure, with its consequent self-doubt and frustration, that 'leads to introverted sterility and degradation'.[546] Indeed Arnold Whittall recognises a 'great tragic irony' in the fact that his profession of faith in the 'Hymn to Apollo' leads the protagonist 'not to the fulfilment of love, but to a lonely death, with no hint of Christian consolation'.[547] Notwithstanding the positive potential, then, here again Aschenbach is destroyed.

In his review after the first performance of the opera Edward Greenfield wrote that '*Death in Venice* becomes the longest and greatest of the church parables, that is, a story of a pilgrim and his tempter';[548] but unlike the previous parables, it would seem that here the tempter prevails. While I have no doubt that the work transfers the philosophical and aesthetic results offered by the church parables in the theatre, I believe there must be a more positive reading of this 'theatre-parable' than the one envisaged by the commentators: there must be redemption for Aschenbach. At some level of this complex many-layered work I think lies a reading that does not exclude those previously outlined, but that by including them sees the work, in a broader perspective, as a synthesis of Britten's understanding of life. The philosophical position he presents is the one he reached through his own life-experience: the choice of a character so near to him, portrayed by Peter Pears, not only his lover but his theatrical 'alter-ego', is no coincidence. Through a complex musico-dramatic structure which is

---

[542] BRETT 1987, p.357. See also BRETT 1983, in particular p.192.
[543] In particular see HINDLEY 1990, 1995 and 1999.
[544] Here 'Platonism' means the Platonic philosophy of love for a beautiful youth as expressed primarily in *Phaedrus* and *Symposium*. See HINDLEY 1992, in particular p.407.
[545] HINDLEY 1990, p.523.
[546] HINDLEY 1990, p.523.
[547] WHITTALL 1995, p.297.
[548] *Guardian*, 18 June 1973.

not only a solution for the problems presented by the novella, but also represents a synthesis of his work in the theatre, Britten communicates his answer to some of the questions which have been a common theme in his works, what David Matthews has defined 'his quest for transcendence'.[549]

As Clifford Hindley has pointed out, 'the development of a new interpretation of the story provided by his literary original is a marked feature of Britten's practice',[550] and *Death in Venice* is no exception: in their reading of the novella Britten and Piper add new levels of meaning, and the work of creating the libretto is not simply a process of adaptation for the stage, it is a real re-thinking of the story, a total re-interpretation. A comparison between the libretto and the novella, together with an analysis of the working process and of the musico-dramatic structure, can demonstrate how, even before a word of it was set to music, *Der Tod in Venedig* and *Death in Venice* were two different tales, signifying different experiences and communicating different perspectives on reality. I believe Britten chose as his metaphor a tale about homoeroticism not because this was his subject, but because this was his own experience; his subject is life, and the problem of balance between 'order and chaos' in life rather than in art, not least because for him, as we have suggested, life and art were not two different worlds.

THE LITERARY SOURCE : *DER TOD IN VENEDIG*[551]

When Thomas Mann published *Der Tod in Venedig* in 1912, he was already one of the most respected European writers. The novel that had brought him to fame in 1901, *Buddenbrooks*, a grand family epic about the rise and fall of a merchant family in Lübeck in which Mann had portrayed his difficult personal relationship as *fin de siècle* intellectual against the *bourgeoisie* and its values, had soon become a paradigm of European history. The theme of the ambiguous relationship between the artist and those values becomes central in Mann's literary experience, and he explores it in a series of characters that all reflect the same personality,

---

[549] MATTHEWS 1987, p.157.
[550] HINDLEY 1990, p.511.
[551] For a general overview on Mann and the novel I referred to a selection of literary criticism, and especially: LUKACS 1956, pp.162–164, 190–192; HELLER 1984; REED T.J. 1971, pp.9–51, and 1984, pp.147–178; Roberto Fertonani, 'L'aria nativa di Thomas Mann', in MANN 1977, pp.ix–xix, and 'Introduzione', in: *Thomas Mann. La morte a Venezia* (Milano: Mondadori, 1970), pp.29–50; Giacomo Manzoni, 'Prefazione', in: *Thomas Mann. Doctor Faustus* (Milano: Mondadori, 1980), pp.viii–xxvi; SCHOFFMAN 1990; ZINKIN 1970.

characterised by diversity, aloofness, a searching spirituality, always on the edge of illness (illness that is often a requisite of the artistic experience, and is identified with it, as Mann explains in his 1938 essay 'Freud und die Zukunft'),[552] and exemplified in a few short novels: *Tristan* (1902), *Tonio Kröger* (1903) and finally *Der Tod in Venedig*. Mann had a special passion for this *petit roman*, the most perfect work of his first creative period, up to the First World War. It interprets in a tragic way the dialectic relationship between life and art: the special sensibility of the main character makes him a favourite victim of the most irrational of cosmic forces, love, often linked in the nineteenth century with death. *Der Tod in Venedig* is a paradigmatic work for Mann, for it concludes his early period of self-quest but at the same time is at the root of the final masterwork, *Doktor Faustus*, a work that tackles the same subject, art seen as sin.

The subject of the novella is, in Mann's words, 'passion as confusion and as a stripping of dignity',[553] and the original idea had been an episode of Goethe's life: in his late years, the poet had fallen violently in love with a seventeen–year old girl in Marienbad, Ulrike von Levetzov, finally experiencing in his own flesh that same destructive force of Eros, that had been the subject of one of his most celebrated books, *Die Wahlverwandtschaften*, which Mann held as the stylistic model for *Der Tod in Venedig*. When in 1911 Mann spent some time with his wife in Venice, the basic idea had developed into its final shape through the contours of a personal experience lived by the author; in a later autobiographical essay of 1930 Mann confesses how nothing in the novella was purely invented.[554] While writing, Mann was able to follow in the Austrian press the last hours of Gustav Mahler's life, an inspiration for the character of Gustav von Aschenbach;[555] in Venice he was also haunted by the memory of Richard Wagner, who had died there in 1883, and whose autobiography had appeared that very year.[556] Part of the character of Aschenbach was also inspired by the personality of August

---

[552] See MANN, 1980, p.137.
[553] Letter to Carl Maria von Weber, see MANN 1970, p.103.
[554] See MANN, 1983, p.711.
[555] Mann states this in *Rede und Antwort* (1922), and the statement is at the basis of Luchino Visconti's choice of making the main character a musician instead of a writer in his cinematographic transposition of the novella.
[556] Richard Wagner, *Mein Leben* (Munich, 1911).

von Platen, a German poet who died in Siracusa in 1835, famous both for his cult of the classical world and for his homoerotic tendencies.

Notwithstanding the explicit references to well-known personalities such as Mahler or Platen, the character of Aschenbach is nonetheless full of the existential and cultural problems of its author, and constitutes a projection of Mann himself, although he cannot be completely identified with him. Fundamental to Mann's literary quest was a need for self-understanding, of which the autobiographical character of the novella is a consequence: the conflicts created by the tension between inner needs and the conventions of a bourgeois society are the author's own inner conflicts. An important trait was his moral unease derived from an awareness of the importance of erotic tension in the artistic process, an unease intensified by the fact that for him such a tension was basically homoerotic: at the beginning of the century Mann had conducted an ambiguous relationship with the painter Paul Ehrenberg, although in 1905 the thirty-year-old writer re-established his social and sexual 'normality' by marrying Katja Pringsheim, the young and well-educated daughter of a wealthy Jew, who bore him six children. Mann was extremely worried about his early years and his erotic ambivalence, to the point that, once exiled, he took great care to make sure his diaries were destroyed.[557]

Mann's personal attitude towards homosexuality, the same one that is at the root of *Der Tod in Venedig*, is well explained by the artist himself in a famous letter to the critic Carl Maria von Weber dated 4 July 1920, a document extremely relevant in the present context, because it is one of the main sources used by Britten and Piper in their re-working of the novella. In this letter Mann not only gives an interpretation of the work, he also clarifies some of its themes, explaining how the main object of his enquiries was essentially aesthetic in nature: erotic passion, regardless of its sexual orientation, and its consequences. It also presents the theme of art likened to illness, as far as illness is a consequence of passion, the source of the creative stimulus:

> My dear Herr Weber
> [...]I should not want you and others to have the impression that a mode of feeling which I respect because it is almost necessarily infused with *mind* (far

---

[557] On the subject see HELLER 1984.

more necessarily so, at any rate, than the 'normal' mode) should be something that I would want to deny or, insofar as it is accessible to me (and I may say, with few reservations, that it is), wish to disavow. You cleverly and clearly recognised the *artistic* reason why this might seem to be the case. It is inherent in the difference between the Dionysian spirit of lyricism, whose outpouring is irresponsible and individualistic, and the Apollonian, objectively controlled, morally and socially responsible epic. What I was after was an equilibrium of sensuality and morality such as I found perfected in the *Elective Affinities*, which I read five times, if I remember rightly, while working on *Death in Venice*. But that the novella is at its core of a hymnic type, indeed of hymnic origin, cannot have escaped you. The painful process of objectivation, imposed on me by the inner necessities of my nature, is described in the introduction in the otherwise miscarried *Gesang vom Kindchen*.

> Do you recall? High frenzy, extraordinary emotion
> Once may have come over you too, casting you down
> So that you lay, brow in hands, your soul rising
> In hymnic praise. Amid tears the struggling spirit+
> Pressed forward to speak in song. But alas there was no change.
> For a sobering effort began then, a chilling command to control.
> Behold, *the intoxicated song turned into a moral fable.*

But the artistic reason for the misunderstanding is just one among others; the purely intellectual reasons are actually more important. For example, there is the naturalistic bent of my generation (so foreign to you young people), which compelled me to see the 'case' *also* in a pathological light, and to alternate this motif (the climacterium) with the symbolic motif (Tadzio as Hermes Psychopompos). Something still more a matter of intellect, because more personal, was added: the altogether non-'Greek' but rather Protestant, puritan ('bourgeois') basic state of mind not only of the story's protagonists but also of myself; in other words, our fundamentally mistrustful, fundamentally pessimistic relationship to passion in general. Hans Blüher, whose writings fascinate me (certainly the idea of his 'Role of the Erotic', etc., is greatly and profoundly Germanic) once defined eros as the 'affirmation of a human being, irrespective of his worth'. This definition comprehends all the irony of eros. But a moralist - whose point of view, to be sure, can be only taken *ironice* - would have to comment: 'That's a fine kind of affirmation, "irrespective of worth". No thanks!'. But more seriously: passion as confusion and as a stripping of dignity was really the subject of my tale - what I originally wanted to deal with was not anything homoerotic at all. It was the story - seen grotesquely - of the aged Goethe and that little girl in Marienbad whom he was absolutely determined to marry, with the acquiescence of her social-climbing procuress of a mother and despite the outraged horror of his own family, with the girl not wanting it at all - this story with all its terribly comic, shameful, awesomely ridiculous situations, this embarrassing, touching, and grandiose story which I may someday write after all. What was added to the amalgam at the time was a personal, lyrical travel experience that determined me to carry things to an extreme by introducing the motif of 'forbidden love'.... [...] I did not want to close without having said something further about my relationship to that emotional tendency. You will not demand of me that I place it absolutely above the more common variety. There could be only one reason to place it absolutely below: that of its 'unnaturalness', a term which Goethe long ago rejected on good grounds. Obviously the law of polarity does not hold unconditionally; the male need not necessarily be attracted by the female. Experience refutes the idea that an attraction to the same sex is necessarily allied to 'effeminacy'. Experience also teaches, to be sure, that degeneracy, hermaphroditism, intermediate creatures, in short, repulsively pathological elements may be and are frequently involved. That is the medical side of it, which is important but has nothing to do with the intellectual and cultural side of it. On the other hand, it can scarcely be suggested that say, Michelangelo, Frederick the Great, Winckelmann, Platen, Stefan George were or are unmanly or feminine men. In such cases we see the polarity simply failing, and we observe a masculinity so pronounced that even in erotic matters only the masculine has importance and interest. It does not surprise me for a moment that a natural law (that of polarity) ceases to operate in a realm that in spite of its sensuality has very little to do with nature, far more to do with mind. [...] As for myself, my interest is somewhat divided between Blüher's two basic forms of social organisation, the family and associations of men. I am a family founder and a father by instinct and conviction. I love my children, deepest of all a little girl who very much resembles my wife – to a point that a Frenchman would call idolatry. There you have the 'bourgeois'. But if we were to speak of eroticism, of unbourgeois intellectually sensual adventures, things would have to be viewed a little differently. The problem of eroticism, indeed the problem of beauty, seems to me comprehended in the tension of life and mind. I have intimated as much in an unexpected context. 'The relationship of life and mind', I say in the *Betrachtungen*, 'is an extremely delicate, difficult, agitating, painful relation charged with *irony and eroticism'*. And I go on to speak of a 'covert' yearning which perhaps constitutes the truly philosophical and poetical relationship of mind to life. 'For yearning passes back and forth between mind and life. Life, too, longs for mind. Two worlds whose relation is erotic without clarification of the sexual polarity, without one representing the male and the other the female principle: such are life and mind. *Therefore there is no union between them, but only the brief, inebriating illusion of union and understanding, an eternal tension without resolution...It is the problem of beauty* that the mind feels life and life feels mind as "beautiful".... The mind that loves is not fanatical; it is ingenious, political; it woos, and its wooing is erotic irony...' [...] Tell me whether one can 'betray' oneself any better than that. My idea of eroticism, my *experience* of it, is completely expressed in those lines. But finally, what else have we here if not the translation of one of the world's most beautiful love poems into the language of criticism and prose, the poem whose final stanza begins: 'Wer das tiefste *gedacht*, liebt das *Lebendigste*'.[558] This wonderful poem contains the whole justification of the emotional tendency in question, and the whole explanation of it, which is mine also..[559]

Mann's elucidation of his own personal thoughts about homosexuality is very interesting, because regardless of the poetic aura that surrounds his reasoning, and the philosophical and aesthetic context that frames it, there is a shadow of apology: the bourgeois spirit had won the battle. This might explain why Aschenbach is destroyed by his homoerotic passion: with Aschenbach dies the young Thomas and his 'sexual inversion'.[560] The novel, with its catastrophic ending, is in a way a cathartic experience for its author.

---

[558] 'He whose thought has plumbed deepest, loves life at its height', Friedrich Hölderlin, *Sokrates und Alkibiades*, which is also one of the poems set by Britten in his *Sechs Hölderlin-Fragmente*, op.61.
[559] MANN 1970, pp.102–106.
[560] HELLER 1984, p.157.

The homoerotic subject has of course been one of the main reasons for considering the opera autobiographical as well. There is, though, an interesting difference, as Mann writes the novella in his mid-thirties, in order to exorcise his same-sex oriented sexual attraction through the creative act: he projects himself into a character that is 25 years his senior, and builds up a scenario in which he analyses the possible consequences of him giving in to that instinctive side of himself that so much worried his moral sense. Basically he has to kill that part of himself that Aschenbach represents: there is no hope for Aschenbach in the novella, and his degradation is total. When Britten writes his opera, he is approaching the end of his life, a life that has been creative and, we can assume, emotionally fulfilling. The difference in the treatment of the subject is, paradoxically, exactly in the autobiographical detail, because Mann, distancing his character from himself, created a perfect alter-ego for a sixty-year-old Britten. While the young writer faces problems concerning artistic creation and the contradictions that ensue, the famous and mature composer transfers the novella to a different level, making the content his own, and adding to it his personal experience.

Beyond the homoerotic context, the central theme of the novella is translated in the conflict between 'mind' and 'life' and their relationship, which is expressed in the search for 'beauty'. The tension around the absolute idea of 'beauty' is seen as the driving force of the artistic experience, and 'mind' and 'life' can easily be identified in the two opposite poles of human nature, the Apollonian and Dionysian principles (which can also be seen as the bourgeois and bohemian souls): the Apollonian Aschenbach is overwhelmed by a Dionysian orgy. Mann's novella is a meditation in the form of a moral tale about the contradictions inherent in a search that, in its struggle for 'beauty', and therefore, according to classical thought, 'goodness', faces the degeneration caused by the irrationality of instinct and primordial forces. It is the everlasting conflict between Apollo and Dionysus, whose presence is implicit in the novella, a testimony of the ideological influence of Nietzsche and Schopenhauer on Mann.[561] Their influence is tangible not only in the references to classical literature, but also in the direct filiation from *Die*

---

[561] Mann dedicated two essays to the German philosophers, 'Schopenhauer' (New York, 1939) and 'Nietzsches Philosophie im Lichte unserer Erfahrung' (Stockholm: Bermann-Fischer, 1948). See MANN 1980.

Geburt der Tragödie of the dichotomies between discipline and dissolute living, order and chaos, Apollo and Dionysus.

The philosophical mood of the novella is expressed in very elaborate language, that often trespasses over the borders between prose and poetry, in the romantic tradition of German literature. In the moments of Aschenbach's extreme excitement, when he is lost in his erotic fantasies, Mann shows his stylistic mastery by introducing in the prose rhythm dactyls or even full hexameters, for example in the orgiastic dream the night before Aschenbach's death. There is also continuous and frequent use of traditional rhetorical figures that give to the prose a richness down to the smallest detail. This elaborate prose is further complicated by the literary application of the leitmotif technique, another homage to Wagner: in different situations similar images, if not textual repetitions, recall each other, creating an intricate structure somehow reminiscent of the Wagnerian *Musikdrama*.[562]

Aschenbach does not talk with anyone; he never speaks to Tadzio, and the only interaction is a smile, a look from the boy, who remains for the reader just a distant image. Aschenbach's own stream of thoughts is inserted into the 'objective' narration of the novella, structured in brief inner monologues, as a commentator on the processes that are happening in the undefined area between subconscious and consciousness. The tale is built on two intersecting levels: on one the author objectively, sometimes with cold irony and without any emotional participation, narrates the descent into hell of a character at the same time far away from its creator and yet so similar; on the other Aschenbach is the protagonist and spectator of the tragedy he is living. The action is created by Aschenbach's process of progressive self-awareness, by his objectivation of his own experience, his obsessive retelling of the events he has captured with morbid interest: the meetings with Tadzio, all the physical details, the boy's reaction to his silent adoration, the influence of the weather and of the landscape on his frame of mind. The world is presented through the looking glass of Aschenbach's egocentric narcissism, and outer action is replaced by inner monologue. The novella, far from relying on action or presenting vivacious dialogues, is in essence

---

[562] Mann had already used Wagnerian material in *Tristan*, and would more famously in *Doktor Faustus*: see SCHOFFMANN 1990.

a long inner monologue for two voices: the narrator and the protagonist, who are the same person. In the monologues the protagonist analyses his own behaviour articulately, using a sophisticated prose; a refined exercise in style, full of literary and philosophical references, and filled with an extreme symbolism, difficult to interpret. It is easy to see how there would be major obstacles in the 'dramatisation' of a tale that is primarily the ordered stream of consciousness of a single mind, and it is therefore not surprising that Myfawny Piper's first reaction to the prospect of writing a libretto from Mann's novella should have been quite negative.

THE LIBRETTO

> In September 1970, just after he had completed the final score of *Owen Wingrave*, Benjamin Britten asked me if I would work with him on another opera, on a subject that he had been brooding over for many years. When I heard that it was *Death in Venice* my first reaction was – impossible! My second, that if Britten said so, it could be done.[563]

Britten was no stranger to adapting apparently unsuitable work for the stage: the success of *The Turn of the Screw* constituted an imposing precedent. Even so, the dramatic content of James' novella was evident from the start, and the characters interacted at different levels. With *Der Tod in Venedig* the situation was slightly different: as we have seen the novella is basically a long monologue. Aschenbach does not interact with anybody: his sporadic contacts with the 'outer world' are the triggers for further inner questioning, and he does not communicate with people around him. There are no other 'full' characters in the novella, because Aschenbach is the only person we know anything about: we see everybody else filtered through Aschenbach's own perception, a perception that is often the fruit of his own fertile imagination, as is evident in the case of Tadzio.

In a later letter to Britten Piper writes: 'I'm overjoyed at the idea of working with you again. It is a wonderful idea - a very difficult one, but I look forward immensely to tackling it. I think it a perfect subject for you at the moment and I think, by its nature, it will be quite unlike any other

---

[563] PIPER 1992, p.20.

operatic work'.[564] Such comment is an indication of the way the adaptation was approached: not following the typical conventions of opera, but responding to the inner structure of the novella. The librettist did not try to construct an opera made of recitatives and arias, inventing words for Tadzio or for other characters as she had done for *The Turn of the Screw*. Instead Britten and Piper looked for dramatic solutions that would preserve the particular qualities of the novella and of its protagonist, solutions which pre-dated the actual writing of the words. The process of transposition from novella to libretto has been amply discussed and analysed [565] and there is therefore no need to discuss it in detail here; I will nonetheless overview some elements which I consider of relevance in the present context.

In a preliminary meeting of the English Opera Group in March 1971 the production of the new opera was scheduled for September 1972. Because of copyright problems[566] the work was delayed, and a new date for the first performance was set for June 1973. Britten and Piper started work on the libretto in January 1971, during a holiday in France. Once back in England, the collaboration continued mainly by post or via the phone, and is well documented.[567] The text they used is the 1928 English translation by H.T. Lowe-Porter; Britten's copy is richly annotated, another testimony to his involvement from the earliest stages of the work. By July 1971 a draft of the first act was completed, and in October Britten, Pears and the Pipers travelled to Venice to immerse themselves in the atmosphere and to do some research.[568] The musical composition started in October 1971, but Britten had to stop several times due to his deteriorating health, which led to major heart surgery in May 1973.

It was only in February 1973 that the libretto assumed its definitive shape: until then there had still been indecision about the number of acts. The definitive version was different from the first printed edition, as

---

[564] Letter to Britten, dated 11November 1970. All the correspondence between Piper and Britten and the working material for the libretto, including the sketches and the autographs, is part of the collection at the Britten–Pears Library in Aldeburgh.
[565] Mainly in MITCHELL 1987, but also in EVANS, JOHN 1983 and DIANA 1997. Of particular interest are also CORSE 1987 and 1989 and PALMER 1984.
[566] Warner Bros had previously acquired the rights of the novella for Visconti's cinematographic transposition.
[567] All the material related to the collaboration is part of the collection at the Britten–Pears Library in Aldeburgh.
[568] In particular, they collected songs in the Venetian dialect.

corrections were still being made during the rehearsal period. In an interview Myfawny Piper states:

> The intention had been to produce the work in eighteen months and so we had to make our first analysis without very much preliminary research. This, I now think, was an advantage, since we were forced to use the text to solve its own problems; to make ourselves so familiar with the symbolism and the reality, the realism and fantasy, with all their cross-references and echoes that even if we had not Mann's rich *prolegomena*, his *kind* of dramatic thinking became natural to us in the course of composition.[569]

It is possible that given a less punishing schedule Britten and Piper would have altered the perspective through which the work is narrated; of course they could have written the libretto from an external point of view, looking at the story through the eyes of a spectator, and the result might have been scenically richer, reproducing life in a Grand Hotel in the charming atmosphere of *fin de siècle* Venice. But Britten created *Death in Venice* from inside out, and I do not believe he would have done it any other way, because his interest was focused on the literary, philosophical and psychological levels of the narration, certainly the most anti-dramatic and therefore difficult in this context, but nonetheless the ones which seem to have been dearest to him: 'why' Aschenbach thinks, sees and lives what he sees, thinks and lives, rather than 'how' or 'when'.

The sequence of events in the opera is substantially the same as narrated by Mann, with few omissions or alterations.[570] In the novella Aschenbach travels initially for a holiday to the Adriatic coast, only going to Venice later. For Mann this was an autobiographical touch; it was eliminated in the opera, as it does not add anything essential to the action, but would indeed delay it. In the initial scheme of the opera the action was divided into numerous short scenes, alternating ensemble with monologues; the definitive version presents longer scenes, without a clear-cut separation between Aschenbach's meditations and the events that trigger them. It is interesting to note that the first four chapters of the novella become act I of the opera, while the fifth chapter alone is the basis for act II; this is

---

[569] MITCHELL 1987, p.46 (italics in original).
[570] For a detailed synopsis of the opera see MITCHELL 1987, p.76-85.

partly because the first chapters include long descriptions, that have been drastically condensed.

Although the tale is a long narration without many dialogues, the text of the libretto derives almost exclusively from Mann's own text, with few alterations or insertions. Nevertheless, even if there seem to be few differences between the two texts, Britten's Aschenbach, who necessarily has to speak in the first person, is very different from Mann's character, whose thoughts we know only through the mediation of the writer. In a way, the opera protagonist has a stronger personality: by speaking his thoughts out loud he takes full responsibility for his actions. The change in the narration from the third to the first person implies a completely different perspective, which is reflected also in the content, although this would not seem a necessary condition. The words that the librettist chose are sometimes more explicit than in the novella, and throw a different light on Aschenbach's thought.[571]

Britten's and Piper's strict respect for Mann's text is rooted in an attempt not to alter the delicate structural balance of the novella, whose subject is such an easy trap for generalisation. As the librettist points out, the problems created by the libretto could only be solved by the novella itself and its literary and philosophical background; for these reasons she researched in detail the origin of the novella, its sources and its literary, stylistic and ideological context. Her notebooks are a fascinating testimony to her unceasing effort to find an appropriate language for such a complex subject. The main difficulty was the need to find a balance between the simplicity of language requested by the composer and the extreme wordiness of the text; as she comments, 'all those words of Mann at first seemed necessary for our full understanding'.[572] This is because the narration is focused on the thoughts, visions and dreams of a single man, and the audience needs to understand what kind of person Aschenbach is, because what happened to him could only have happened to that kind of person: a solitary man, not used to talking about what he sees and feels, and whose experiences are at the same time more intense and less articulate than those of ordinary people, who can analyse his feelings but not express them. He is a writer who has dedicated his life to

---

[571] This appears evident when we compare in details the two texts.
[572] PIPER 1979, p.15.

literature, and it is quite normal that he would read his experiences in the context of his own altered perception of reality: being the 'perfect Nietzschean artist', he is completely alienated from reality. These are elements which can hardly be characterised by the music, and need to be told in words; but an excess of explanation could have made the work particularly static, making the opera just a long monologue, with virtually no action.

The Musico-Dramatic Structure[573]

Britten managed to avoid such danger, and *Death in Venice* is the ultimate example of his ability to create new forms or modify existing ones in order to present his chosen subject in the way he considered the most effective. He creates an unusual formal structure, that allows him greater respect for the original, by dividing the 'action', which is often no more than intellectual 're-action', between three levels, associated with three 'modalities' which imply different styles of language and music:

1. **Narration**, where Aschenbach is his own observer. In these sections he is the detached and rational writer, analysing his own condition in the light of his past, present and future experience, thus presenting to the audience all the elements necessary to their comprehension of the story; this device also allows him to articulate what in the novella are mainly inner monologues. He is presented alone on stage, often in his room, therefore in a situation away from the public sphere. These scenes are written in elaborate prose, and are set as recitatives with a bare instrumental accompaniment.

2. **Action**, where Aschenbach interacts with his surroundings: the boat, the hotel, the streets of Venice. The dialogue is always constituted by brief exchanges between Aschenbach and the people he meets, and the musical accompaniment is orchestral.

---

[573] As in the previous chapters, I will concentrate solely on some dramaturgical aspects which I consider relevant to the present discussion, without attempting an exhaustive analysis of the work. For detailed analysis of the musical structure and language of the opera see related sections in CORSE 1987, pp.131-148; EVANS, JOHN 1983, Chapters 8-14; EVANS, PETER 1989, pp.523-547; KENNEDY 1981, pp.253-259; WHITTALL 1982, pp.258-263; MITCHELL 1987; ROSEBERRY 1987; EVANS, JOHN 1987; PALMER 1987; COOKE 1998, Chapter 8. Amongst the articles devoted to the work see in particular TRAVIS 1987, and CORSE 1989.

3. **Oneiric dimension**, where Aschenbach relates to Tadzio in a dreamlike context. The sense of abstraction, of distance from reality is conveyed not only through the use of verse, but also of dance, the means of expression of the Polish family, and by the presence of a percussion orchestra inspired by the gamelan.[574]

In this way Britten creates a 'music-drama in which speech, music and dance all have an integral place',[575] but which at the same time maintains the character of a monodrama, as it is centred around Aschenbach: the audience is presented with the facts only by the protagonist himself, through his meditations and comments, or through his reaction to explanations or news given to him. For this reason, Aschenbach is the only character to have a defined psychological reality.

The opera begins with one of Aschenbach's monologues. The overture does not occur until before scene iii. The two first scenes are therefore a sort of prologue, although not in the traditional sense: they are more a sort of prelude to the action, in which the reasons for the action that follows are introduced. The first scene is one of the most problematic, because the librettist needed to present Aschenbach in detail, with all the information given in the first chapter of the novella. It would not have been appropriate to have an external narrator, as in the prologue in *The Turn of the Screw,* because it is essential that Aschenbach himself should speak the narrative, presenting himself and his ideas, to reinforce the sense of monodrama; on the other hand, a long monologue would have delayed the beginning of the dramatic action for too long. In her solution, the librettist does not reveal everything in the first scene, but distributes references to Aschenbach's own aesthetic and to his past in various monologues throughout the scenes that follow. In this way, the audience gets to know Aschenbach progressively, deepening its knowledge as the action develops. At the same time, the contrast between Aschenbach's vision of himself at the beginning and his perception of himself as the plot develops is increased by continuous self-reference in the monologues. This does not happen in the novella, where it is the function of the writer/narrator to analyse Aschenbach's development. This is one of the most dramatically poignant changes in the adaptation, because this

---

[574] See COOKE 1998, in particular Chapter 9, pp.220–44.
[575] PIPER 1979, p.15.

'reduction by distribution' allows the librettist to present all the information without creating a long narration that would be anti-dramatic and torn away from the action; the distribution allows a balanced unfolding of 'action' and 'narration', which determines the rhythm of the action itself, a rhythm that changes towards the end, when the moments of self-analysis become rarer.

The presence of a prologue, although not indicated as such, indicates also a similarity with the church parables. The first two scenes, in the final version integrated into act I, were intended as separate during the working process, and the fact that they precede the Overture reinforces the feeling that they have a function comparable to the processional prelude at the beginning of the parables:[576] they are a way of leading the audience into a different dimension, where the theatrical ritual is taking place. In *Death in Venice* the idea of moving into a different dimension is reinforced by the fact that before the overture Aschenbach falls asleep (on the boat, scene ii), therefore we do not know whether he ever wakes up, or whether what we see is only his dream.

Another feature of the operatic version is the creation of a second major role, sung by a baritone, that represents Aschenbach's fate embodied in the figure of Dionysus, hidden behind different masks: the Traveller, the Elderly Fop, the Old Gondolier, the Leader of the Players, the Hotel Barber and the Hotel Manager. The idea was conceived after considering the critical literature about the novella, in particular T.J. Reed's introductory essay to his translation.[577] Reed points out how these characters have a double function, the realistic and the symbolic:[578] they are figures that, notwithstanding their ordinary appearance, guide Aschenbach in his journey towards his own destiny. The baritone role was called *Death's Messenger* in the early version of the libretto. It was only later on that Britten and Piper decided to represent visibly the inner conflict between Apollonian and Dionysian forces, introducing the role of Apollo, sung by a countertenor (the most un-earthly voice, but also a voice that because of its *tessitura* we could somehow associate with that aspect of Tadzio that is a representation of absolute beauty and therefore order), and adding Dionysus to the list of roles sung by the baritone. In

---
[576] And of other Britten's opera: see CARPENTER 1992, p.339.
[577] REED, T.J. 1971, pp.9-51.
[578] REED, T.J. 1971, p.14.

this way the figure of Dionysus becomes predominant, representing the overriding power of that part of Aschenbach's personality – the passionate side - that he has contained and repressed all his life, as it finally takes over. The fact that all these characters are unified in a single figure, a projection of Aschenbach's psyche, reinforces the idea that in the opera he is the only player, who in facing his destiny finally comes to terms with himself.

Only Tadzio could have contested Aschenbach's supremacy, and this is the character that presented most problems to the librettist, as in the novella he never speaks. Aschenbach does not have any kind of spoken communication with the boy or his family, and although the reader in the novella knows every thought of Aschenbach concerning Tadzio, we have no hint of what the boy might think. Of course Myfanwy Piper was not new to silent characters, as she had already invented words for Peter Quint in *Turn of the Screw*. But in this instance they decided otherwise: as Piper points out, 'the implication is that, unlike the Ghosts in *The Turn of the Screw*, what he thought or said would have been of no interest to us'.[579] What the boy thinks, speaks or even feels is not important: his function is simply 'to be', and to be 'ideal', a representation of the Platonic idea of beauty. If he spoke he would appear human, and his main attribute is being 'superhuman', at least in Aschenbach's vision, which is the only one we are concerned with. The audience must know Tadzio only through Aschenbach's perception, not as he is. By giving the role of Tadzio and his family to dancers Britten and Piper manage to amplify these characteristics.

According to the librettist it was not a straightforward aesthetic decision, as 'it arose out of the nature of the theatrical performance. Only dancers find it natural to be on stage for any length of time in silence, and only dancers can express the triviality and pleasures of human behaviour without speech'.[580] It was a very fortunate solution, because it bears other consequences: Tadzio's function as a symbol is enhanced by the stylisation of movement proper to dance, and his insurmountable remoteness from Aschenbach is accentuated by the fact that his mode of

---

[579] MITCHELL 1987, p.47.
[580] MITCHELL 1987, p.47.

expression is completely different from Aschenbach's own rigidity in literary prose dress, making communication between the two impossible.

Britten had a clear idea of the aesthetic status of dance within the opera, and as in the case of the church parables and *Noye's Fludde* he provides the printed score with specific production notes:

> Clearly each production of *Death in Venice* must find its own approach to the movement and gestures which should characterize Tadzio and his family. It should be understood, however, that from the outset the composer envisaged a style of movement that requires for its materialization the collaboration of a choreographer. This style, self-evidently, must be less than fully-fledged ballet. On the other hand, it is essential to avoid a completely naturalistic style of movement for the boy and his family. This could in no way realize the composer's basic intention, which was, through the use of appropriately stylized movement, to suggest the 'other' and different world of action inhabited by Tadzio, his family and friends, especially as seen through Aschenbach's eyes. For the same reason, it is emphasized that the beach games, etc., of the children and of Tadzio and his friends throughout the opera are of crucial dramatic significance.[581]

This statement leaves no doubt about the dramatic importance of the dance sequences, which are not simply a diversion or a filler, but a central idea in the conception of the opera; as Donald Mitchell points out, 'ballet is raised in *Death in Venice* to a new formal, dramatic and expressive status'.[582] The root of this development can be traced back to Britten's encounter with the Nô theatre: the 'non-naturalistic' style of movement advocated for the dancers recalls the ritualistic and abstract gestures of the Japanese theatre, which Britten had already tried to reproduce in the church parables.[583] Of course the musical accompaniment of the dance sequences, with their gamelan inspired percussion orchestra, is connected with the Balinese theatre, in which dance has a ritualistic meaning.

The presence of stylization and ritualistic gestures and movement is a feature that the last opera shares with the church parables, together with the spareness and stylization of the staging. Colin Graham, who directed the

---

[581] BRITTEN 1975, p.xiii.
[582] MITCHELL 1984, p.240.
[583] See also ROSEBERRY 1987, p.97.

original production, testifies how Britten 'was particularly keen on finding an unconventional way to stage *Death in Venice* [...] no scene had to be presented in a literal way; there had to be some form of stylization':[584] the staging has to allude, rather than describe, another obvious influence of the Japanese theatre. In the early stages of the planning of the opera Britten had also envisaged the possibility of having, for the dance sequences, a percussion orchestra visible on stage.[585] This solution was later discarded for practical reasons, but it is a detail that reinforces the connection with the Eastern aesthetic (both the gamelan and Nô orchestra have an active visual rôle, being on stage), and with the church parables.

But *Death in Venice* is not simply a succesor to the church parables, it is rather an enrichment of the basic idea they represent, as it incorporates other dramaturgical solutions that Britten had previously put into practice. The idea of the interaction of three levels of action, already present in *The Rape of Lucretia*, is here re-visited in a different context, but with similar consequences. These three levels, which Britten had defined from the very early stages of the work,[586] and that we have identified as 'narration', 'action' and 'oneiric dimension', can be likened to the three narrative modalities, previously outlined in chapter 4, of epic, dramatic and lyrical. We are thus presented again with the interaction of epic and dramatic, in which we had identified the fusion of the opera and oratorio. What is interesting is that here the epic narrative is not given to the Chorus. *Death in Venice* is not a chamber opera, and requires the presence of a 'proper' chorus, an ensemble of background characters without individual traits that fulfils what is its traditional operatic rôle (as the Hotel guests and waiters, gondoliers, street-vendors, citizens of Venice, tourists, youths and girls on the boat, and even the choir in St Mark's). In this work its function is also to provide an aid to the staging, as it describes the action (as in the Games of Apollo) or visual elements that are not physically presented on stage (for example the inscription on the graveyard chapel).[587] It does nonetheless differ from the chorus in the church parables, where, as we have seen, Britten had already achieved a

---

[584] MITCHELL 1987, p.56.
[585] MITCHELL 1987, p.4.
[586] MITCHELL 1987, p.4.
[587] In this sense its function is comparable to some aspects of the rôles of the Female and Male Chorus in *The rape of Lucretia*.

fusion between Nô and classic tragedy. In the Japanese theatre the chorus does not comment upon the action, nor is it a character:

> the chorus fills in dialogue for the actors during dance sequences; it makes no commentary on the action as does the chorus in the Greek tragedy, nor does it have any special identity as part of the cast. Its members merely take up the voice of the actors from time to time like a dispassionate, heavenly choir.[588]

In the classical tragedy the chorus is nearer to being a collective character, and it takes on practical duties, as it introduces the audience to the story (in the Japanese theatre the characters often introduce themselves), describes the events between the acts and comments upon the action. It can also be noted that in the tragedy the function of the Chorus, and in particular of the Corypheus, is similar to that of the 'historian' in the oratorio, and of the Evangelist in the Passions.[589] The Chorus in *Curlew River* is still very dependent on the Japanese model, but reveals the Western influence in the way it describes and comments on the action. These functions in the last opera are taken on not by the traditional chorus, but by the protagonist in his 'narrative', i.e. epic, modality.

It is through Aschenbach's monologues that we are introduced to the story and he comments upon the action, which is basically articulated through the development of his own reflections and behaviour. As we have already mentioned, these long monologues presented a major problem within the structure of the work, both from a dramatic and musical point of view, and also from a practical one: the effort requested from the tenor was quite overwhelming. At first Britten's idea was to have these sections simply spoken, as Myfawny Piper explains:

> From several points of view [Britten] would have liked to have these passages spoken. It would have underlined the dryness and the isolation of this incorrigible writer; it would have provided a rest from singing for Aschenbach, and it would have done what we had intended to do at the

---

[588] HOOVER 1981, p.151.
[589] D'AMICO 1982, p.25

outset, create a music-drama in which speech, music and dance all had an integral place.[590]

Nonetheless, the contrast between these sections and the musical ones would have been too strong. Britten was looking for something 'even further from the stylization of song than conventional recitative',[591] which could render not so much the sense of discourse, but of thought-flow. As Peter Evans points out, Schoenberg's *Sprechgesang* 'would not ideally answer his purpose since its aim is to suggest in a somewhat musicalized form (and often enough in a form intentionally distorted to Expressionistic ends) the contours and rhythms of natural speech'.[592] Britten's solution is in Hans Keller's opinion exactly the opposite of *Sprechgesang*: 'Where Schoenberg rhythmicizes and de-pitches, Britten pitches and de-rhythmicizes'.[593] Aschenbach's recitatives are melodic lines without any rhythmic indication: 'Britten restricted his notation to exact indications of pitch, and left his singer (Peter Pears in the original production) to find convincing "thought"- rather than "speech"- rhythms'.[594]

This idea of 'free style' recitatives was derived from Pears's interpretation of the recitatives in the oratorios of Schütz. While Britten was working on *Death in Venice*, between December 1971 and December 1972, his partner had been involved in several projects connected with the 300th anniversary of Schütz's death, and had sung the rôle of the Evangelist in the *Auferstehungs Historia*, in the *Historia der Geburt Gottes* and in the *Matthäus-Passion*. Britten had been very impressed by Pears's delivery of these recitatives, determined only in the melody, and decided to use a similar device. Furthermore, the melodic shape of Aschenbach's recitatives derives from Pears's natural verbal inflections in reading Piper's text, which Britten noted. Philip Langridge, an outstanding interpreter of Aschenbach, has emphasized how these recitatives are something quite unusual for a singer:

---

[590] Quoted in EVANS, JOHN 1985, p.133.
[591] EVANS, PETER 1989, p.524.
[592] EVANS, PETER 1989, p.524.
[593] KELLER 1979, p.xxxi.
[594] EVANS, PETER 1989, p.524.

> It's magical for an actor because you're not constrained by the barlines that most composers put in. You can absolutely take your own speed – obviously having discussed it with the producer, and so on – with the pianist weaving auras around you, so to speak. You can just suddenly let the penny drop, at a given moment, or you can take a little longer for it to drop, or you can rush through the whole thing. You can do it exactly as you want. Aschenbach's mind is very wayward, and therefore so is the music that Britten writes for him. Even when there's no rhythm, there's pitch, and then you have to try to forget that pitch and sound as if you're speaking. It's a cross between singing, speaking, *Sprechgesang*, all those things – but it's actually something quite individual. It's really very like a soliloquy that a Shakespearean actor has to deliver.[595]

In the performance notes on the published score Britten had specified:

> These Recitatives, which are conceived as interior monologues (or soliloquies) for Aschenbach, should be sung freely, with varying speeds, according to their meaning and dramatic text. They should always be declamatory in style, rather than lyrical. On the other hand, they should never be sung exclusively in the manner of *recitativo secco*, but always with some expression. It is further emphasized that these Recitatives form an integral part of the composer's conception of the opera, and their length and location have been precisely calculated in relation to the pace and development of the drama.[596]

The stress on a 'declamatory' delivery of the text emphasizes how these recitatives are 'epic' in their character; the fortuitous connection with Schütz's sacred stories fits perfectly in the aesthetic context of Britten's concerns in the theatre, as it refers to the Christian Choruses in *The Rape of Lucretia*. There is also another link to the church parables, where Britten had already developed a form of unmeasured notation.[597]

DIDACTIC THEATRE

There is a further element that Britten incorporates into the musico-dramatic structure of *Death in Venice*, an element that can be linked to Brecht's theory of epic theatre, which in my opinion reinforces the status

---

[595] In an interview for the *Royal Opera House News Magazine* (January/February 1992), p.7.
[596] BRITTEN 1975, p.xiii.
[597] See KENNEDY 1981, p.254.

of the last opera as a didactic piece, and that is the attention to naturalistic details. Britten and Piper spent some time in Venice researching gondoliers' cries, as well as song in the original dialect for the Strolling Players in scene x. Other realistic touches are the adoption of the original languages for the Hotel guests in scene iv, and for the Venetian citizens (for example, the strawberry-seller or the beggar-woman). This attention to found materials is extended to the music, as Britten quotes a Gregorian hymn in the scene inside St. Mark's (scene ix), and the first Delphic hymn in the music for Apollo.

In a work that could easily lead the audience away from reality and capture them within Aschenbach's fantasy, these features, exactly because they are remote from the abstractness and symbolism of the protagonist's world, could be read as a way of producing what Brecht defines as the 'estrangement effect', a sort of detachment from the story on the side of the audience, who are induced to cease the suspension of disbelief. If we accept this possibility we can then extend this reading also to Aschenbach's monologues, that become 'estrangement' devices. Within Brecht's conception of didactic theatre, the estrangement effect is a way of avoiding the danger that the audience may 'fling itself into the story as it were a river and let itself be carried vaguely hither and thither. [...] The episodes must not succeed one another indistinguishably but must give us a chance to interpose our judgement'.[598]

A drama can be 'estranged' in its entirety through a prologue or through the projection of titles; the individual characters can 'estrange' themselves by introducing themselves to the audience, or by talking about themselves in third person (and this certainly applies to Aschenbach). Furthermore, the staging is 'estranged' when it does not reproduce any longer a 'real' place (and we have seen how Britten wanted for the opera a stylized staging, which is also implied in the score). All these devices are aimed at achieving for the audience an 'epideictic detachment' that serves the theatre in its scientific-pedagogical modality, whose objective is 'to interpret a story and to communicate it to the audience through appropriate estrangement effects'.[599]

---

[598] Bertold Brecht quoted in SZONDI 1987, pp.72–3.
[599] SZONDI 1987, pp.72–3.

> The events unfolding on stage no longer completely fill out the performance the way dramatic events had previously. This earlier dramatic practice led to the elimination of the fact of the performance (noted historically in the disappearance of the Prologue during the Renaissance). The flow of events is now the object of a stage narrative - the stage is to these events what the narrator is to the object of his narration. It is only the confrontation of the two that produces the totality of the work. Likewise, the spectator is not excluded from the play; neither is he pulled into the play by his suggestive power (caught in its illusion) in such a way that he ceases to be a spectator. Instead, as spectator, he is confronted by the events, which are proposed as an object for his consideration. [...] The dramatic concern with ends is replaced by an epic freedom to pause and reflect. Since the active individual has now become the object of the theatrical performance, the performance itself can go beyond this individual and ask questions about the casual grounds for his actions.[600]

These ideas easily fit Britten's last opera; the comparison with Brecht's theory of epic theatre is useful in highlighting how in this work the composer applies dramaturgical solutions which are found in a mode of theatre which purposefully uses every device to a didactic end. Britten might not have consciously adopted Brecht's theory, which as we have seen he had already encountered in his collaboration with Auden, but he certainly came to very similar solutions; and it is interesting to remember here that Brecht himself had been greatly influenced by his encounter with Japanese theatre.[601]

Thus, in *Death in Venice* we have a *summa* of Britten's formal research on the theatre, with a work that on the basis of its aesthetic status can rightfully be defined as a 'theatre parable'. At the same time, it is interesting to note how in its formal apparatus the work shares many similarities with what we can consider the archetypal form of Western

---

[600] SZONDI 1987, p.71.
[601] On the subject see WIRTH 1972. The Nô theatre had a great influence also on William Butler Yeats, another theorist of theatre at the beginning of the century, but his theatre, highly ritualistic, does not have the same didactic and social intent as Brecht's. On the subject one can refer to O' DRISCOLL 1975, in particular to the articles by Richard Taylor, 'Assimilation and Accomplishment: Nô drama and an unpublished source for *At the Hawk's Well*', pp. 137–158, and James W. Flannery, 'W.B.Yeats, Gordon Craig and the Visual Arts of the Theatre', pp.82–108.

theatre, Greek tragedy;[602] Eric Roseberry, for example, recognizes in the sonata-like scheme of the opera 'a metaphor for the unfolding of a Greek tragedy, its three stages standing for protasis, epitasis and catastrophe'.[603] According to John Drummond, in the Attic tragedy we find a coincidence of the three basic forms of *music-drama*:[604] the 'narrative', represented by the narration, the 'ceremonial', represented by the action, and the 'enthusiastic', represented by the dance.[605] We can easily see how these three forms can relate to the three narrative modalities of epic, dramatic and lyrical, and to the three levels of action in *Death in Venice*. I believe the parallel between the 'enthusiastic' form of *music-drama* and the oneiric dimension in *Death in Venice* is particularly appropriate: 'enthusiasm', the possession by the god, is 'a loss of identity, a submergence of self in divine rapture',[606] and Aschenbach, possessed by the irrational force of love, loses himself in Tadzio's world.

By adding the lyrical dimension of the dance Britten expands the formal results achieved with the opera-oratorio and the church parables, still maintaining their principal characteristic. As such, the formal structure of the last opera suggests that we as still dealing with a form of 'holy' theatre, a work that aims to provide access for the audience to a higher perception of reality and to a spiritual truth, although the last opera seems to be foreign to the Christian background that justified the ritualistic form and the symbolism of its predecessors. And it is here that the parallel with the classical tragedy moves from a formal level to a level of content.

APOLLO AND DIONYSUS

In his letter to Carl Maria von Weber Mann identified in the tension between 'life' and 'mind' the central theme of the novella; this theme acquires even greater emphasis in the opera, where it is translated into the opposition between Apollo and Dionysus, representing rational and irrational forces. Donald Mitchell has identified in a letter written by W.H. Auden to Britten before his return to England in 1942 the seeds of what he defines 'the very topic that was Britten's concern throughout his

---

[602] Greek tragedy and Nô theatre at the same time share many similarities and a common ground, as demonstrated in SMETHURST 1989.
[603] ROSEBERRY 1987, p.91.
[604] A form of dramatic ritual in which music plays a fundamental rôle.
[605] DRUMMOND 1980, p.68.
[606] DRUMMOND 1980, p.70.

later creative life, and formed the substance – the heart – of his last opera'.[607] Writes Auden:

> I think I know something about the dangers that beset you as a man and as an artist, because they are my own. Goodness and [Beauty] are the results of a perfect balance between Order and Chaos, Bohemianism and Bourgeois Convention. Bohemian chaos alone ends in a mad jumble of beautiful scraps; Bourgeois convention alone ends in large unfeeling corpses. Every artist except the supreme masters has a bias one way or the other. The best pair of opposite I can think of in music are Wagner and Strauss. (Technical skills always comes from the bourgeois side of one's nature). For middle-class Englishmen like you and me, the danger is of course the second. Your attraction to thin-as-a-board juveniles, i.e. to the sexless and innocent, is a symptom of this. And I am certain too that it is your denial and evasion of the demands of disorder that is responsible for your attacks of ill-health, ie sickness is your substitute for the Bohemian.[608]

The same year Britten had written to his brother in law: 'in art, as you know, the bias is... to anarchy and romantic "freedom". A carefully chosen discipline is the only possible course'.[609] We are thus in no doubt that Britten was deeply concerned by this dichotomy, that at the end of his creative life he represented on stage in *Death in Venice*.

According to Piper, the idea of representing the conflict between Apollo and Dionysus, only implied in the novella, was derived from Euripides' *Bacchae*;[610] this work, whose subject is Dionysus' revenge against his enemies, exemplifies the opposition which is at the core of Greek tragedy: that between Apollo, representing rationality and ordered life, and Dionysus, representing the irrational and mysterious. It was a solution initially intended only for scene xiii, 'The Dream', where Aschenbach's two sides fight for predominance, and was born as a consequence of the decision to introduce an off-stage voice. To begin with the voice should have been a boy treble's representing Tadzio, whom Piper identified with Apollo, as she explains in a letter:

---

[607] MITCHELL 1981, p.163.
[608] MITCHELL 1981, p.161.
[609] Quoted in EVANS, PETER 1992, p.478.
[610] MITCHELL 1987, p.51.

> I have gone back to *Phaedrus*, in my struggle over the verses for the end of act I, and I have made an interesting discovery which I think would wholly justify your using a voice that could be Tadzio's for Apollo in the dream. All that rather arch stuff of Mann's (my page 48) about 'Sly arch-lover as he was, he said the subtlest thing of all etc.'. I think he refers to the passage in *Phaedrus* where Socrates says that the lover tries to see and to induce in his beloved the attribute of the God of whom in his heavenly state – and therefore even more in his mental state – was a devotee, i.e. if the lover was a devotee of Mars he would see his love as a war-like character.[611] There is no doubt in my mind that Aschenbach was a devotee of Apollo, that Apollo is the god he put up against Dionysus and that Tadzio therefore can and does represent Apollo in his mind, so that in his 'distraught' state a voice that could be Tadzio's would be dramatically right.[612]

Only at a later stage it was decided to have the part sung by a countertenor representing Apollo, and to extend the conflict to the dream and to the whole opera: talking about the dream Piper says 'It seemed, to me, that however the producer and the choreographer decided to stage the dream, the dialogue must be between the two sides of Aschenbach's nature: the Apollonian and the Dionysian'.[613]

The voice off-stage becomes thus the voice of Aschenbach's Apollonian conscience. In this way Tadzio loses completely the 'active' rôle he had in the novella as a personification of Hermes or Fate, becoming only an image, a reflection of beauty. He also loses his identification with Eros, which in a Freudian context represents the vital force opposed to Thanatos, recognizable in the novella in the figure of the *Death's messenger*.[614] This is an aspect which differentiates the libretto from the novella, because Eros and Thanatos, although associated with conscious and unconscious, represent the basic instincts of self-preservation and self-destruction, two forces very different from those represented by Apollo and Dionysus.[615]

---

[611] *Phaedrus*, xxxiii.
[612] Piper letter to Britten, dated 28 February 1972, at the Britten–Pears Library in Aldeburgh.
[613] MITCHELL 1987, p.51.
[614] As identified by REED 1971, p.15.
[615] We can therefore see how it is important to look at the opera not on the basis of the critical interpretation of the novella, but approaching it from the different perspective presented by the libretto.

The materialization on stage of the two gods to represent Aschenbach's inner conflict is a brilliant solution, but at the same time can be read as a further similarity with a form of theatre which is a ritualistic dramatic enquiry about the philosophical questions that face man: because if the conflict between Apollo and Dionysus is the subject of tragedy, its object is the understanding of life and death. *Death in Venice* is a parable about the meaning of life, about the philosophical understanding reached by Britten through his own personal experience. On the basis of what we have discussed in the previous chapters I find it very difficult to believe that at the end of the opera Aschenbach dies a broken and defeated man, believing that his pursuit of ideal beauty in the real world has lead him to the abyss: this might have been true in Mann's novella, but it would not respond to Britten's basic intent to communicate a constructive spiritual truth through his work. Instead, I believe in *Death in Venice* Britten reveals the solution to a problem that is central to his artistic life, the loss of innocence, a problem that he now puts into a wider spiritual and metaphysical context.

'DOES BEAUTY LEAD TO WISDOM?'

> For Ben, the opera was, in some sort of way, a summing-up of what he felt. [...] At the end, Aschenbach asks what it is he has spent his life searching for. Knowledge? A lost innocence? And must the pursuit of beauty, of love, lead only to chaos? All questions Ben constantly asked himself.[616]

The core of the opera is recognized in the monologue Aschenbach addresses to himself towards the end, when he realizes to what extremes his passion has led him: not only has he made a fool of himself by trying to appear younger (his visit to the barber transforming him into the Old Fop by whom he had been disgusted at the beginning), but, disowning the philosophy of self-possession that had shaped his life, he has even wished for him and Tadzio to be the only survivors to the plague: 'What is reason, moral sense, what is art itself, compared to the rewards of chaos. The city's secret, desperate, disastrous, destroying, is my hope. I will not speak. What if all were dead, and only we two left alive?'.[617] According

---

[616] Peter Pears interviewed in *A Time there was...*
[617] *Death in Venice*, scene xii.

to most commentators, from this moment on, with what is defined 'Aschenbach's last connected statement', we assist to his 'ultimate descent into the abyss', his corruption and death: 'After this memorable farewell we are to hear no more than a few pitiful ejaculations from the "flabby, rouged lips" of a degraded hero cast in the soliloquizing mould of Hamlet, whose musing incapacity for direct speech and resolute action is the cause of his degradation'.[618] Indeed, in the novella Aschenbach is described at this point as delirious: 'His eyelids were closed, there was only a swift, sidelong glint of the eyeballs now and again, something between a question and a leer; while the rouged and flabby mouth uttered single words of the sentences shaped in his disordered brain by the fantastic logic that governs our dreams'.[619]

I think this does not quite correspond to the impression we get from the opera, where the libretto presents one of the few but fundamental alterations of the original. In the opera, Aschenbach seems to re-conquer a moment of lucidity just before plunging in the Socratic meditation:

> Chaos, chaos and sickness.
> What if all were dead
> and only we two left alive?

By restating the absurd hope that he had already expressed in scene xii, Aschenbach finally becomes aware of the abyss he has plunged into. We are aware that he has regained lucidity when he repeats sentences from his initial monologue, but this time not using the first person:

> O Aschenbach...
> Famous as a master...
> Self-discipline...your strength...
> All folly, all pretence –

It is not the proud 'I, Aschenbach' of the first scene, but a compassionate cry: he does not recognise himself any longer in the image he had presented before, which he now considers, as he tells us, 'All folly, all pretence'. The fact that Aschenbach addresses himself is the main

---

[618] ROSEBERRY 1987, p.90.
[619] MANN 1971, p.76.

difference between the libretto and the novella, where the character seems completely lost in his dream world. In Britten's reading, instead, it looks as if Aschenbach has just woken up: he has looked into the abyss, but finally, although tired and ill, he has got a glimpse of understanding.

> O perilous sweetness
> the wisdom poets crave.
> Socrates knew, Socrates told us.

It is at this point that Piper faced what she defines as 'the most embarrasing task' in her work as a librettist, 'to précis bits from Plato in the Phaedrus song'.[620] The text of the monologue masterfully reduces in a few lines what in the original is a quite long passage, and manages to convey in a strong and concise way the essence of Socrates' speech:

> Does Beauty lead to Wisdom, Phaedrus?
> Yes, but through the senses.
> Can poets take this way then
> For senses lead to passion, Phaedrus.
> Passion leads to knowledge
> Knowledge to forgiveness
> To compassion with the abyss.
> Should we then reject it, Phaedrus,
> The wisdom poets crave,
> Seeking only form and pure detachment
> Simplicity and discipline?
> But this is beauty, Phaedrus
> Discovered through the senses
> And senses lead to passion, Phaedrus
> And passion to the abyss.
> And now, Phaedrus, I will go
> But you stay here
> And when your eyes no longer see me
> Then you go too.

---

[620] MITCHELL 1987, p.51.

It is not in the content of the monologue that Britten and Mann differ, but in its perception of the character: Britten's Aschenbach is no longer a passive victim of events, but he is able to look at himself in a detached way, and the text of the monologue then becomes charged with 'irony'. In her discussion of the opera Sandra Corse sees in this scene the ultimate tragic irony of the opera:

> Finally, then, Aschenbach comes to a full realization of what his present situation and his whole life have meant. That he has returned to his thinking self, though greatly altered; that he has awakened not only from the dream on the beach but from the dream that has constituted his whole stay in Venice, is suggested by the music: the harp and piano arpeggios sound together for the first time since the opening pages of the score. As Aschenbach contemplates the 'wisdom poets crave' (act 2, scene 16), the melodic line moves in parallel whole steps recalling the opening lines of the opera. Aschenbach goes on to muse aloud on the doctrine of Socrates, which he newly understands. This passage reflects the fundamental dilemma of Aschenbach's life, Plato's theory of poetry, and the opera. [...] There is for the artist no escape from a dependence on physical, sensual knowledge. Thus, the artistic isolation and mastery Aschenbach has so highly prized also lead to passion and 'the abyss'. Aschenbach has failed to realize until too late that the sensual cannot be denied; he has failed to appreciate the ultimate irony of his life. Now, he has fallen, and although he has gained wisdom, there is nothing left for him but a humiliating end.[621]

This is the conclusion presented by Thomas Mann, which does not contemplate, as he explained in his letter to Carl Maria von Weber, a solution to the dichotomy between beauty and eros. The irony is in the incompatibility of the two tensions, the Apollonian, representing 'mind', and the Dionysian, representing 'life', because it is not possible to reach beauty following only the former, and the latter, being an 'illness', would lead to self-destruction, as in Aschenbach's case.

In his introductory essay to the novella T. J. Reed underlines how for Mann the work had to move from his original hymnic impulse, which would have suggested 'a celebration of the subject', and become a moral

---

[621] CORSE 1987, P.147.

criticism, as Mann explains in the letter we have quoted.[622] Reed sees in this development of the story the influence on the writer of an essay by György Lukács, entitled 'Sehnsucht nach Form', in which the theme of Platonic love is received with pessimism, for 'what men, and poets, yearn for on earth is often all too earthly, and their efforts at sublimation are almost bound to fail'.[623] According to Reed, this was another chance encounter that enriched the already complex background of the story, as Lukács 'pointed to the Platonic framework which so sympathetically accommodated Mann's perennial themes and impulses, and he sounded a warning note which echoed Mann's own scepticism as to whether a writer can ever achieve true dignity, and anticipated his story's final conclusions'.[624] Nonetheless, Reed is wary of accepting the idea that all of Mann's reception of Socratic texts had been coloured by Lukács's critical spirit, and contemplates an 'original' or alternative reading of the novella on the basis of what he defines as 'the striking ambivalence' of the story's closing scene.

> Aschenbach dies on the beach, looking seawards, and Tadzio stands before him, seeming to point out to lead the way 'ins Verheißungsvoll-Ungeheuer'. This configuration is clearly modelled on a passage in the *Symposium* which describes the progressive initiation of the lover of beauty into ever higher things. When he has left behind him all particular forms, the beauty of the forms, the beauty of the soul, the beauty of institutions, he approaches and contemplates the 'vast sea of beauty', he grows strong 'on that shore' and comes to see the vision of a single ultimate beauty which embraces all he has experienced'.[625]

Thus for Reed the death-scene is ambivalent, because it could be an apotheosis of Aschenbach just as well as the conclusion of a moral criticism: Aschenbach's passion for Tadzio becomes the proper culmination of his increased devotion to formal beauty, and Tadzio's beauty would have been 'the impetus to pass beyond particular forms to the contemplation of beauty itself'.[626]

---

[622] See REED. T.J. 1971, pp.40–41.
[623] REED. T.J. 1971, p.42. We have already commented on Mann's personal need to 'destroy' his alter-ego.
[624] REED. T.J. 1971, p.43.
[625] REED. T.J. 1971, p.44.
[626] REED. T.J. 1971, p.44.

With the nature of Mann's original conception in mind, as hinted by the words 'hymnisch' and 'Gesang' and by what he said of the first impulse to write, we can see how the other details of his story might have fallen into place with a very different function. The sordid old dandy, instead of being a pointer forward to Aschenbach's cosmetic rejuvenation, could have been a figure to contrast with Aschenbach's nobler feeling. The dionysian element in the work could have been, not a degrading, but a revitalising agent: the purpose of the Thracian orgies, as Mann had read, was to release the disciplined individual into the collective and bring him into contact with the god – a kind of inspiration. Aschenbach's rather forced deliberate attempt to be reborn would have been a preparation only, confirmed by this more dynamic, emotionally liberating rebirth. To have evoked such a process would indeed have qualified a work for the Nietzschean title of 'trunkenes Lied' which Mann aspired to, it would have been the work of a 'Dichter'. It is the failure to achieve this that Mann laments in the *Gesang vom Kindchen*.[627]

It is important to remember that Piper and Britten referred to Reed for their interpretation of the story. I believe that what they did was to re-visit in the theatre, in the best classical tragic tradition, a story, which can be looked at as a mythological tale, presenting their own philosophical understanding of the subject and coming to a new interpretation, thus giving also a voice to what Reed's defines as 'Mann's original alternative'.

Clifford Hindley has already suggested how Britten might have been well aware of Platonism, and discussed the possible influence that those ideas might have had on the opera.[628] Still for Hindley Aschenbach's end is a consequence of his failure to contemplate as a possible option a sublimated relationship with the boy:

> Reduced to its simplest terms, [Aschenbach's story] provides an affirmative vision of Platonism as a genuine option for the artist, developed and amplified by an emphasis on the significance of a real relationship with the beloved for the artist himself. Refusal of that ideal through a combination of self-doubt and the pressure of society (a

---

[627] REED. T.J. 1971, p.45. Reed refers here to Mann's quoted letter to Carl Maria von Weber, and to the last section but one of Nietzsche's *Also sprach Zarathustra*.
[628] See HINDLEY 1990, 1992 and 1999.

continuing theme of Britten's operas) leads to introverted sterility and degradation.[629]

I believe it is exactly the concept of degradation, of a 'humiliating end' that the opera challenges by presenting the Phaedrus monologue as a moment of clarity rather than of delirium. By addressing himself in third person Aschenbach objectivizes the situation, taking distance from his behaviour, and finally understands: not the unavoidability of the abyss, but exactly its opposite.

I would like to suggest that in Britten's reading of the story the last monologue is indeed charged with irony, but of a different kind: not the tragic irony of Mann, but a sort of Socratic irony, where the statement of a negative concept serves as a partial assertion of a truth that is often its opposite.[630] The concepts expressed in the monologue are mainly derived from the *Symposium*, which, like *Phaedrus*, is not a dialectic or maieutic dialogue, but an assertive one, in which instead of trying to undermine others' convictions Socrates positively states his theory of Eros.[631] It is important to remember how in this theory what is fundamental is the erotic feeling, which alone is able to inspire and lead to knowledge, without the need for a physical realization of the love: Socrates is praised in the dialogue for his ability to inspire the deepest feelings, but also for his chastity. Desire unfulfilled deepens the feeling, and leads to the *sophia*.[632]

This theory is complicated in *Death in Venice* by the insertion of the Apollo-Dionysus dichotomy: the experience that Tadzio has triggered in Aschenbach has been intoxicating, and liberating at the same time, as it has put Aschenbach in touch with a side of himself he had previously avoided. Tadzio's rare beauty was the only thing that could have led the Apollonian and restrained Aschenbach to lose control and abandon himself to the

---

[629] HINDLEY 1990, p.523.
[630] The Greek work 'eironeia' was used for an understatement in the nature of dissimulation, and it is especially exemplified in the assumed ignorance which Socrates adopted as a method of dialectic, the Socratic irony. In tragedy what is called tragic irony is the device of making a character use words which mean one thing to him and another to those acquainted with the real issue.
[631] On the subject see HINDLEY 1992, in particular pp.407–408.
[632] I refer here to the overview of Platonic philosophy presented in CHÂTELET 1976, especially p.61.

feeling and the sensation, therefore to the knowledge of the Dionysian part. When Aschenbach wakes up after the dream (scene xiii) and accepts his defeat, before giving himself completely up to the irrational forces, he comments: 'O the taste of knowledge'. This statement had previously appeared during the pursuit in scene ix, when Aschenbach has commented upon the new contrasting emotions that possess him while he is following the Polish family through the city's labyrinth:

> O voluptuous days,
> O the joy I suffer:
> feverish chase,
> exquisite fear,
> the taste of knowledge.

This is a detail not present in Mann, and I believe it aims to reinforce the idea of the importance of Aschenbach's finally experiencing those wanton feelings he had denied himself all his life, because 'not proper', and likely to lead into an abyss of debauchery. Although Aschenbach does humiliates himself, he does not fall into the abyss - he merely glances into it: and it is exactly that glance that brings him enlightenment.

I think we can look at the music to support such reading: the Phaedrus monologue is set as an arietta in a simple ternary form, a moment of delicate formal balance whose lyricism surprises us after the dark musical atmosphere that had accompanied the frantic chase through the city infested by the plague. Even more surprising is the appearance of the C major tonality, a real oasis of calm and serenity, that is difficult to associate with a moment of ironic disillusion. In a comparison with the mad scene in *Peter Grimes*, an emotional climax where Grimes 'disjointedly dredged up snatches of hope, despair, accusation from the past', Eric Roseberry finds 'strange' the spiritual serenity that Britten attains in this arietta, which he defines as 'a still, held moment, a climax of quietness'.[633] It probably would not be so strange if we looked at it as the attainment of wisdom, rather than a moment of derangement. Such a reading would also justify the 'extraordinarily atmospheric ending', the 'final apotheosis'[634] that has its roots in the alternative reading of the

---
[633] ROSEBERRY 1987, p.96.
[634] WHITTALL 1982, p.262; ROSEBERRY 1987 p.96

story proposed by Reed. It is the music indeed which suggests an interpretation in which Aschenbach's death is not a tragedy, but a triumph. Here Britten breaks off from Mann, whose character is destroyed from a passion he lives as perversion: in the opera the character through the fire of passion is purified, and finally reaches the wisdom he has been looking for, albeit on the wrong path. At the end of the opera Apollo and Dyonisus have found in him a balance.

In this way the opera deals also with the problem of the search for identity, that often compromises self-understanding in a struggle for self-identification: the image that the artist has carefully built for himself and the world through his whole lifetime is destroyed in an instant, when the repressed forces of the true self claim their reward. In Britten's rendering such discovery does not lead to annihilation: it is a moment of enlightenment, a catharsis. With the Phaedrus monologue Maia's veil is broken, and the artist can look upon himself and his own struggle with irony, but also finally with compassion. Aschenbach's death is not a moment of destruction, but his final liberation.

With *Death in Venice* Britten's continues his 'didactic' work in the theatre with a parable about self-knowledge and the self-awareness that produces an apprehension of life and of the world. Without underestimating the relevance of the autobiographical connection, I believe the composer chooses a story about a homoerotic passion not because homoeroticism is his subject, but because it represented his personal experience: it is not so much the need for self-understanding proper to Mann that drives the composer, but rather Britten's need for communication.

Looking for its significance in the wider context of Britten's thought, I believe the end of the opera represent a final step in his concern with the issue of innocence: Britten seems to finally come to terms with the fact that loss of innocence is a necessary evil. In the quest for wisdom experience, however painful, is a necessary step to reach knowledge: all his life Aschenbach has believed that restraint was the way to achieve balance, but restraint has only limited his understanding. Wisdom is achieved by maintaining strength within passion, and by stopping short of the abyss, not by avoiding knowledge: it is the archetypal concept of the initiation, and extremes of passion are our initiation to life. Knowledge brings understanding, and through understanding we can reach wisdom, which is still pure, but not naive, as is innocence.

Of course this reading of the last opera implies a perspective in which death is not seen as a negative event, but in his late works Britten has often touched on the theme of the ambiguity of death, for the example in the fourth canticle, *The Journey of the Magi*, where death and birth are somehow equated.[635] An echo of this same concept is expressed in one of Britten's most devastating settings, *Before life and after*, from *Winter Words*, where the contrast between innocence and experience is also present:

> A time there was – as one may guess
> and as, indeed, earth's testimonies tell –
> Before the birth of consciousness
> When all went well [...]
>
> But the disease of feeling germed,
> and primal rightness took the tinct of wrong;
> Ere nescience shall be reaffirmed
> How long, how long?

The last opera is thus a resolution of a problem that had been central in Britten's artistic work: life is finally seen as an experiential journey, leading to the rediscovery of the bliss that Hardy associates with nescience.

The composer restated the message of *Death in Venice* in his third string quartet, one of his last compositions,[636] and a work that is seen to continue on a purely musical level 'Aschenbach's quest for transcendence'. As David Matthews comments 'what lies beyond death is beyond the scope of most artists, but Britten, close to his own death, came as near as anyone to providing a clue'. [637]

---

[635] See WHITTALL 1982, pp.255–256.
[636] Composed in October–November 1975, first performed on 19 December 1976, two weeks after the composer's death.
[637] MATTHEWS 1987, p.161.

CONCLUSIONS

Commenting on Britten's consistency in terms of themes, concerns and preoccupations, Donald Mitchell says:

> If I am right about Britten's consistency, it should be possible to draw a meaningful line of development between his first full-blooded and full-scale opera, *Peter Grimes* (1945), and the ritual and restraint that comprise the chief distinguishing features of the church parables. Is this position tenable? Or does the division between opera house and church constitute an unbridgeable gulf?[638]

I hope with the present work I have succeeded in demonstrating not only that such position is tenable, but that the line of consistency extends well before *Grimes* - as it includes *Paul Bunyan* and Britten's politically committed work in the 1930s - and beyond the church parables. I also hope to have shown how constant is Britten's effort to create a bridge over what Mitchell defines the 'unbridgeable gulf' between opera house and church, an effort whose final product is a work that not only integrates opera and oratorio, but looks further back to the origin of Western theatre by taking Greek tragedy as its model.

The connection with classic theatre well responds to Britten's desire of using the theatre to communicate his beliefs, ethical and political. In early Greek society the poet is a 'master of truth', and the dramatist is a poet: tragedy is a journey of investigation on the meaning of life, a journey that

---

[638] MITCHELL 1984, 'The church parables...', p.212.

takes place in the theatre.[639] As we have seen, Britten's preoccupation with the function of the artist within society was connected with his belief in the artist's special sensibility, and therefore his capacity 'of being right about many things, long before their time':[640] for Britten too the artist is a 'master of truth'.

The tension with contemporary society seems to be born in Britten out of the frustration caused by the fact that, unlike ancient Greece, in his world the artist is not recognised as such, rather he is seen as a unnecessary commodity. Thus his constant effort to assert himself as a constructive part of society, and his desire to be accepted as the voice of society's consciousness, a desire that produced its early fruits in the years of his collaboration with Auden, but that continued to exercise its influence throughout his career, although often in a subtle way. I believe here lies the root of his dramaturgical search for the most effective form of theatre, a form that not only allowed him to express his beliefs, but to do so in the most communicative way: for Britten what is important is that his message is understood. The content of his message ultimately is an investigation of the meaning of life. Britten's constant preoccupation with the problem of the loss of innocence is just one of the aspects of the perennial question that philosophers and poets have asked themselves for centuries: what is the meaning of life after the fall, what is the meaning of history.

The composer seems to have spent his life posing himself these same questions, and trying, through his work, to provide answers. The solution he finally presents in *Death in Venice* not only has an echo of one of the core concept of Greek thought, that 'know thyself' that was inscribed on the entrance of the temple of Apollo in Delphis, but is also the same offered by transpersonal psychology: life as an experiential journey that after the fall of grace brings us back to Eden with the newly acquired gift of self-awareness, a quality of which innocence, in its naivety, is devoid.[641] Thus Britten's thought comes to the same conclusions reached in the twentieth-century in other fields, in the context of what Erich Fromm has defined 'radical humanism',[642] a philosophical view of the world and of man's destiny on earth that, reacting against the mechanistic

---

[639] See SEGAL 1986, p.79.
[640] BRITTEN 1951, p.5.
[641] On the subject see WILBER 1983.
[642] FROMM 1970, p.13.

constructions of positivism, brings man and his inner life back at the centre of the universe.

This interest in 'man' and his psychological processes seems to be an explanation for the international success of this composer that, by asserting his particularity as a gay Englishman, has risen to levels of universality. The progressive distancing from the cultural situation that produced his works has demonstrated how they survive the challenge of time better than other contemporary works, and that they were not just a fashionable product of post-war England. And while performances of his works become more and more common outside the English speaking world, it is particularly his operatic output that is reaching new audiences every day.

The universality of these works, paired with their dramatic craftsmanship and intelligence, allows them to speak in a direct way to audiences everywhere, despite the fact that they were consciously written for a specific audience and a specific place. Their strength is also a fruit of the strength of the convictions that produced them, and of Britten's constant effort to say what he meant, a characteristic that according to the composer's himself was Frank Bridges's greatest lesson.[643] I believe that his dramaturgical search was an attempt to be true to such lesson, and also to the idea that art is a socially responsible activity, and it is not about self-expression but, as suggested by Artaud,[644] is about the expression of truth, whatever this truth is perceived to be.

---

[643] See KENNEDY 1981, p.6.
[644] See ARTAUD 1985, p.70, and also BROOK 1972, p.63.

SELECTED BIBLIOGRAPHY

ABBATE Carolyn
Unsung Voices: opera and musical narrative in the nineteenth century (Princeton: Princeton University Press, 1991).

AITKEN Ian
Film and Reform: John Grierson and the documentary film movement (London: Routledge, 1992).

ALEXANDER Peter
'A study of the origins of Britten's "Curlew River"', *Music and Letters*, LXIX (1988), pp.229–243.
William Plomer: a Biography (Oxford: Oxford University Press, 1989).

ALLARD Joe
'Lucretia as literature I', in *Aldeburgh October Festival Programme Book* 1996, p.12.

ALLBRIGHT Daniel
Untwisting the serpent: modernism in music, literature and other arts, ed. by Daniel Allbright (Chicago: University of Chicago Press, 2000).

ALLEGRI Luigi
Teatro e spettacolo nel Medioevo (Bari: Laterza, 1988).

ARTAUD Antonin
The Theatre and Its Double, trans. by Mary Caroline Richards (New York: Grove Press, 1958).

ASSAGIOLI Roberto
Psychosynthesis (Rome: Institute of Psychosynthesis, 1927).
The Act of Will (London: Wilwood House, 1977).

AUDEN Wystan Hugh

'Reflexions sur la musique et l'opéra', *La Revue Musicale* CCXV (1952), pp.3-11.

'The world of opera', in *Secondary worlds* (London: Faber, 1968), pp.76-102.

'Some reflections on music and opera', in *The essence of the opera*, ed. by Ulrich Weisstein (New York: Norton, 1969), pp.353-360.

"Paul Bunyan": the libretto of the operetta by Benjamin Britten (London: Faber, 1988).

The Language of Learning and the Language of Love. Uncollected writings, new interpretations, ed. by K. Bucknell and N. Jenkins (Oxford: Clarendon, 1994).

AXTON Maurice

English drama: forms and development (London: Cambridge University Press, 1977).

AYLEN Leo

The Greek theatre (London: Associated University Press, 1985).

AYLESWORTH Thomas G.

Broadway to Hollywood: musicals from stage to screen (London: Hamlyn, 1985).

BACHARACH Arthur

British music of our time (Harmondsworth: Pelican, 1946).

BANFIELD Stephen

'British opera in retrospect', *Musical Times* CXXVII (1986), pp.205-207.

Sensibility and English song: critical studies of the early 20th century (Cambridge: Cambridge University Press, 1985).

BANKS Paul

Britten's "Gloriana": Essays and Sources, ed. by Paul Banks (Aldeburgh: Britten–Pears Library; Woodbridge: Boydell Press, 1993) (Aldeburgh Studies in Music, 1).

The Making of "Peter Grimes", ed. by Paul Banks (Aldeburgh: The Britten Estate; Woodbridge: The Boydell Press, 1996).

Benjamin Britten: a Catalogue of the Published Works, ed. by Paul Banks (Aldeburgh: The Britten–Pears Library, 1999).

BARTHES Roland

Image. Music. Text (London: Fontana, 1977).

BASSI Adriano
Benjamin Britten (Milano: Targa, 1989).

BEDFORD Steuart
'The struggle with the word', in *Peter Pears: a tribute on his 75th birthday*, ed. by Marion Thorpe (London: Faber, 1985), pp.5–7.

BENNETT G.M.
A Performer's Analysis and Discussion of the Five Canticles of Benjamin Britten (DMA, Southwestern Baptist Theological Seminary, 1988).

BENTLEY Eric
The Playwright as Thinker. A study of drama in modern times (New York: Meridian, 1955).

BERTHIER Philippe
Littérature et opéra. Colloque de Cerisy 1985, ed. by Philippe Berthier (Grenoble: Presse Universitaire, 1987).

BETZ Albrecht
Hanns Eisler, Political Musician (Cambridge: Cambridge University Press, 1982).

BIANCONI Lorenzo
La drammaturgia musicale, ed. by Lorenzo Bianconi (Bologna: Il Mulino, 1986).

BLOUNT Gilbert L.
'Britten's "Curlew River": a cultural composite', in *Literature East and West (Japanese issue)* XV–XVI/1-2 (Dec. 1971- June 1972), pp.632–646.

BLYTH Alan
Remembering Britten (London: Hutchinson, 1981).

BLYTHE Ronald
Aldeburgh anthology (London: Faber, 1972).

BOCCIA Bruno
'"The Turn of the Screw" di Benjamin Britten', *Rassegna Musicale* XXII (1962), pp.270–276.

BONAVIA Ferruccio
'New Britten opera heard in England', *New York Times*, 13 July 1946.

BORMAN Gerald Martin
American Musical Comedy: from "Adonis" to "Dreamgirls" (New York: Oxford University Press, 1982).
American Musical Revue: from "The passing show" to "Superbabies" (New York: Oxford University Press, 1985).

BORWICK Susan
'Weill's and Brecht's theories on music in drama', *Journal of Musicological Research* 4 (1982), pp.39–67.

BOWLES Edmund
'The role of musical instruments in medieval sacred drama', *Musical Quarterly* XLV (1959), pp.67–84.

BOYS Henry
'"The Rape of Lucretia": musico-dramatic analysis', in: *"The Rape of Lucretia": a symposium*, ed. by Benjamin Britten and Eric Crozier (London: The Bodley Head, 1948), pp.75–101.

BRECHT Bertold
'The rise and fall of the city of Mahagonny', translated by Wystan Hugh Auden and Chester Kalmann, in: *Bertold Brecht: Collected Plays*, ed. by Ralph Manneim (London: Eyre Methuen, 1979).

BRETT Philip
'Britten and Grimes', *Musical Times* CXVIII (1977), pp.995–1000.
Benjamin Britten: "Peter Grimes", ed. by Philip Brett (Cambridge: Cambridge University Press, 1983).
'Grimes and Lucretia', in: *Music and theatre: essays in honour of Winton Dean*, edited by Nigel Fortune (Cambridge: Cambridge University Press, 1987), pp.353–365.

'Britten's Dream', in *Musicology and difference: Gender and Sexuality in Music Scholarship* (Berkeley: University of California Press, 1993), pp.259–280.

Queering the Pitch: The New Gay and Lesbian Musicology, ed. by P. Brett, E. Wood and G. Thomas (London: Routledge, 1994).

'The Growth of the Libretto', in *The Making of "Peter Grimes"*, ed. by Paul Banks, (Aldeburgh: The Britten Estate; Woodbridge: The Boydell Press, 1996), pp.53–78.

'Toeing the Line', *Musical Times* CXXXVII (September 1996), pp.7–13.

'"Grimes at his exercise": sex, politics and violence in the librettos of "Peter Grimes"', in *Siren songs: representations of gender and sexuality in opera*, ed. by Mary Ann Smart (Princeton: Princeton University Press, 2000), pp.237–249.

'Benjamin Britten', in *The New Grove Dictionary of Music*, 2nd edition, ed. by Stanley Sadie and John Tyrrell (London: Macmillan, 2001).

BREWSTER Robert G.

The relationship between poetry and music in the original solo-vocal works of Benjamin Britten through 1965 (PhD, Washington University, 1967).

BRITTEN Benjamin

'Composer would knock out fascists by mighty songs', *Toronto Daily Star*, 21 June 1939.

'An English composer sees America', *Tempo* I/2 (American edition, April 1940), p.1–3.

'England and the folk-art problem', *Modern Music* 8/2 (1941), pp.71–75.

'How to become a composer', *The Listener,* 7 November 1942, p.624.

'Conversation with Benjamin Britten', *Tempo* 6 (old series, February. 1944), pp.4–5.

'"*Peter Grimes*": introduction', in: *Benjamin Britten: "Peter Grimes"*, ed. by Eric Crozier (London: The Bodley Head, 1945), pp.7–8.

"The Rape of Lucretia": a Symposium, ed. by Benjamin Britten and Eric Crozier (London: The Bodley Head, 1948).

'Address on being made an Honorary Freeman of Lowestoft', *Tempo* XXI (1951), pp.3–5.

"Noye's Fludde": Notes on the Production, with Colin Graham (London: Boosey and Hawkes, 1958).

'The composer's "dream"', *Observer*, 5 June 1960 [reprint in: *The Britten Companion*, ed. by Christopher Palmer (London: Faber, 1984), pp.177–180].

'On writing English operas', *Opera* XII (1961), pp.7–8.

'Thoughts on writing an opera: an interview with Benjamin Britten' *Boston Symphony Concert Bulletin* 15 (n.d), p.820.

'Benjamin Britten on receiving an honorary degree from Hull University', *The London Magazine* III/7 (October 1963), pp.89–91.

On Receiving the First Aspen Award (London: Faber, 1964).

'Profile: Benjamin Britten', *The Observer,* 27 October 1964.

"Curlew River". A parable for church performance op.71 (London: Faber, 1965).

'Benjamin Britten talks to Edmund Tracey', *Sadler's Wells Magazine* (Autumn 1966), pp.35–41.

'Early influences: a tribute to Frank Bridge (1879-1941)' *Composer* 19 (Spring 1966), pp.2–3.

'Communicator, an interview with England's best known composer' *Opera News* XXXI/16 (February 1967), p.16.

'No Ivory Tower: Benjamin Britten talks to Opera News', *Opera News* XXXIII/23 (April 1969), pp.8–11.

'How I became a composer', *The Radio Listener's Weekend Book*, ed. by John Pringle (London: Odhams, n.d.), pp.108–112.

Benjamin Britten: a complete catalogue of his published works (London: Boosey and Hawkes, Faber, 1973).

Benjamin Britten. Morte a Venezia, programme book (Venezia: Teatro La Fenice, 1973).

Death in Venice op.88 (London: Faber, 1975).

'Britten on "Oedipus Rex" and "Lady Macbeth"', *Tempo*, 120 (1977), pp.10–12.

'New Year's message to the people of Japan, 3 December 1957', in *Aldeburgh Festival Programme Book* XLIV (1991), pp.18–19.

BROOK Peter
The Empty Space (Middlesex: Pelican Books, 1972).

BROWN David
'Stimulus and form in Britten's work', *Music and Letters* XXXIX (1958), pp.218–226.

BRUNEL Pierre
L'opéra (Paris: Bordas, 1980).

BURROWS Jill
'Lucretia as literature II', in *Aldeburgh October Festival Programme Book* 1996, p.13.
'The death of Lucretia: myth, motivation and meaning' in *The Rape of Lucretia*, programme book (London: English National Opera, 2001).

CAMPBELL Clare
'Music and poetry; with some note on Benjamin Britten's setting of words', *Critical Quartely* (autumn 1964), pp.253−263.

CAMPLING Christopher R.
The Food of Love. Reflections on Music and Faith (London: SCM Press, 1997).

CARENA Carlo
Platone: Dialoghi, ed. by C. Carena, translated by Francesco Acri (Milano: Einaudi, 1970).

CARLSON Marvin
Theories of the Theatre (Ithaca: Cornell University Press, 1984).

CARPENTER Humphrey
Wystan Hugh Auden: a biography (London: Allen, 1981).
Benjamin Britten: a biography (London: Faber, 1992).

CESCOTTI Diego
'Britten e la favola del "Bel marinaio"', *Rivista Italiana di Musicologia* XXI (1986), pp.170−193.

CHÂTELET François
La Filosofia Pagana, ed. by F. Châtelet (Milano: Rizzoli, 1976) (Storia della Filosofia: Idee e Dottrine, Vol.I).

CHIARI, Joseph
The contemporary French theatre: the flight from naturalism (London: Rockliff, 1958).

CHIARINI Paolo
Brecht, Lukacs e il realismo (Bari: Laterza, 1983).

CONE Edward T.
The Composer's Voice (Berkeley: University of California Press, 1974).
Music: A View from the Delft (Chicago: University Press, 1989).

CONRAD Peter
Romantic opera and literary form (Berkeley: University of California Press, 1977).
A song of love and death (London: Chatto, 1986).

COOKE Mervyn
Britten and Bali: a study in stylistic synthesis (MPhil., University of Cambridge, 1985).
'Britten and the gamelan: Balinese influences in "Death in Venice"', in: *Benjamin Britten: "Death in Venice"*, ed. by Donald Mitchell (Cambridge: Cambridge University Press, 1987), pp.115−128.
'The prophecy of Lucretia', *Aldeburgh Festival Programme Book* XL (1987), pp.54−55.
'Britten and Bali', *Journal of Musicological Research* 7/4 (1988), pp.307−339.
'Britten and the shô', *Musical Times* 129 (1988), pp.231−233.
Oriental influences in the music of Benjamin Britten (PhD, University of Cambridge,1989).
Benjamin Britten: "Billy Budd", ed. by Philip Reed and Mervyn Cooke (Cambridge: Cambridge University Press, 1993).
'From Nô to Nebuchadnezzar', in *On Mahler and Britten. Essays in honour of Donald Mitchell on his seventieth birthday*, ed. by Philip Reed (Aldeburgh: Britten–Pears Library; Woodbridge The Boydell Press, 1994), pp.135−145.
Britten: War Requiem (Cambridge: Cambridge University Press, 1996).
Britten and the Far East (Aldeburgh: Britten–Pears Library; Woodbridge: Boydell Press, 1998) (Aldeburgh Studies in Music 4).
The Cambridge Companion to Benjamin Britten, ed. by Mervyn Cooke (Cambridge: Cambridge University Press, 1999).

CORSE Sandra
Opera and the use of language: Mozart, Verdi and Britten (London, Toronto: Associated University Press, 1978).
'From narrative to music: Benjamin Britten's "The Turn of the Screw"', *University of Toronto Quarterly* LI (1981), pp.161−174.

'Britten's "Death in Venice": literary and musical structure', *Musical Quarterly* LVVIII (1989), pp.344-365.

CROFT Andy
A Weapon in the Struggle. The Cultural History of the Communist Party in Britain, ed. by Andy Croft (London: Pluto Press, 1998).

CROZIER Eric
Opera in English, ed. by Eric Crozier (London: The Bodley Head, 1945) (Sadler's Wells Opera Books 1).
Benjamin Britten: 'Peter Grimes' (London: The Bodley Head, 1946) (Sadler's Wells Opera Books 3).
'Benjamin Britten's second opera: "The Rape of Lucretia"', *Tempo* 14 (1946), pp.11-12.
'Lucretia: 1946', in *'The Rape of Lucretia': a symposium*, ed. by Benjamin Britten ed Eric Crozier (London: The Bodley Head, 1948), pp.55-60.
'Writing an opera', in *Aldeburgh Anthology*, ed. by Ronald Blythe (London: Faber, 1972), pp.199-202.
'The writing of "Billy Budd"', *Opera Quarterly* IV (1986), pp.11-27.
'Within each other's heart: our first Lucretia' (Nancy Evans and Eric Crozier), in *The Rape of Lucretia* CD Booklet, EMI CMS 7647272, 1993, pp.20-26.

DAHLHAUS Carl
Grundlagen der Musikgeschichte (Köln: Arno Volk, 1977); *Fondamenti di storiografia musicale*, Italian translation by Gian Antonio de Toni (Fiesole: Discanto, 1980).
Esthetics of Music, translated by W.A. Austin (Cambridge: Cambridge University Press, 1982).
Analysis and value judgement (New York: Pendragon, 1983).
'Euripide, il teatro dell'assurdo e l'opera in musica' in *La drammaturgia musicale*, ed. by Lorenzo Bianconi (Bologna: Il Mulino, 1986), pp.291-308.
'Drammaturgia dell'opera italiana', in *Storia dell'opera italiana* (Torino: EDT, 1989) vol.VI, pp.77-162.
'What is a musical drama?', *Cambridge Opera Journal* I (1989), pp.95-111.

D'AMICO Silvio
Storia del teatro drammatico (Milano: Bulzoni, 1982).

DEAN Winton
'English Music Today', *The Score* 8 (1953), pp.5–16.
'Death in Venice', *Musical Times* CXIV/1566 (1973), pp.819–820.
'Britten's "inner insecurity"', *Opera* XLIII (1992), pp.536–541.

DEAVEL Gary
A study of two operas by Benjamin Britten: "Peter Grimes" and "The Turn of the Screw" (PhD, University of Rochester, 1970).

DELMORE J.P.
Benjamin Britten's canticles and their literary, thematic and musical unity with his opera (DMA, Arizona University, 1991).

DE MARINIS Marco
Il nuovo teatro 1947–1970 (Milano: Bompiani, 1987).

DENT Edward J.
'The Future of British Opera', in *Opera in English*, ed. by Eric Crozier (London: The Bodley Head, 1945), pp.27–41.

DICKINSON Andrew
'Current chronicle: Britten's new opera', *Musical Quarterly* LX (1974), pp.470–478.

DOCHERTY Barbara
'Syllogism and symbol: Britten, Tippett and English text', *Contemporary Music Review* V (1989), pp.37–93.
'"When feeling becomes thought": Britten, text and biography', *Tempo* CLXXXIV (1993), pp.24–29.
'We know for whom we mourn', *Tempo* CXCII (1995), pp.22–27.

DONINGTON Robert
Opera and its symbols: the unity of words, music and staging (New Haven: Yale University Press, 1990).

DOWNES Oliver
'Second thoughts', *New York Times,* 9 January 1948.

DREW, David
'Brecht versus Opera: some comments', *The Score* 23 (1958), pp.7−10.
Kurt Weill: a handbook (London: Faber, 1987).

DRUMMOND John
Opera in perspective (Minneapolis: University of Minnesota Press, 1980).

DUNCAN Ronald
'"The Rape of Lucretia"; the libretto: the method of work', in *"The Rape of Lucretia": a symposium*, ed. by Benjamin Britten and Eric Crozier (London: The Bodley Head, 1948), pp.61−66.
'Benjamin Britten: a pen portrait', *Radio Times*, 3 March 1950, p.8.
'The problems of a librettist: is opera emotionally immature?' *Composer* 23 (1967), pp.6−9.
Working with Britten: a personal memoir (Welcombe: The Rebel Press, 1981).

ELIOT Thomas Stearns
The Three Voices of Poetry (New York: Cambridge University Press, 1954).
Opere, ed. by Roberto Sanesi (Milano: Bompiani, 1986).

ELLIOTT Graham
Benjamin Britten: the things spiritual (PhD, University of Wales, 1985).
'The operas of Benjamin Britten: a spiritual view', *Opera Quarterly* IV (1986), pp.28−44.

ELLIS Jim
'Strange meeting: Wilfred Owen, Benjamin Britten, Derek Jarman and the "War Requiem"', in *The work of opera: genre, nationhood and sexual difference*, ed. by Richard Dellamora and Daniel Fischlin (New York: Columbia University Press, 1997), pp.277−296.

EMSLIE Barry
'Billy Budd and the fear of words', *Cambridge Opera Journal* IV (1992), pp.43−59.

EVANS John

"Death in Venice": perspectives on an opera (PhD, Cardiff University College, 1983).

'Britten's Venice workshop: 1.The Sketch Book; 2.The composition sketch and revisions', *Soundings* XII (1984), pp.7-24; XIII (1985), pp.51–77.

'"Owen Wingrave": a case for pacifism', in *The Britten Companion*, ed. by Christopher Palmer (London: Faber, 1984), pp.227–237.

'On the recitatives of "Death in Venice"', in *Peter Pears: a tribute on his 75th birthday*, ed. by Marion Thorpe (London: Faber, 1985), pp.31–33.

'"Death in Venice": the Apollonian/Dionysian conflict', *Opera Quarterly* IV (1986), pp.102–116.

A Britten sourcebook, compiled by John Evans, Philip Reed and Paul Wilson (Aldeburgh: Britten–Pears Library, 1987).

'Twelve-note structures and tonal polarity', in *Benjamin Britten: "Death in Venice"*, ed. by Donald Mitchell (Cambridge: Cambridge University Press, 1987), pp.99–114.

EVANS Peter

'Britten's "Death in Venice"', *Opera* XXIV (1973), pp.490–496.

'Britten's television opera', *Musical Times* CXII (1971), pp.425–428.

'Britten's fourth creative decade', *Tempo* CVI (1973), pp.8–17.

'Benjamin Britten', in *The new Grove's dictionary of music and musicians*, 6th edition, ed. by Stanley Sadie (London: Macmillan, 1980).

The music of Benjamin Britten (London: Dent, 1979, 2/1989).

'Letters from a life: selected letters and diaries of Benjamin Britten' (review), *Tempo* (1992), pp.478–482.

EWEN David

The story of America's Musical Theater (Philadelphia: Chilton Book Company, 1961).

FIRMÉ Jacques

Opéra sans musique (Lausanne: L'age d'homme, 1982).

FLYNN William

'Britten the progressive', *Music Review* LXIV (1983), pp.44–52.

FORD, Boris
Benjamin Britten's Poets: an anthology of the poets he set to music, ed. by Boris Ford (Manchester: Carcanet, 1994).

FOREMAN Lewis
'Benjamin Britten and "The Rescue"', *Tempo* 166 (Sept. 1988), pp.28−33.

FROMM Erich
Voi sarete come dei (Roma: Ubaldini, 1970).

FULLER Michael
'Living on the edge', *Musical Times* CXLI (2000), pp.45−49.

GARBUTT John
'Music and motive in "Peter Grimes"', *Music and Letters* XL (1963), pp.335−342.

GARDA Michela
L'esperienza musicale. Teoria e storia della ricezione, a cura di Michela Garda e Gianmario Borio (Torino: EDT, 1989).

GARNHAM Maureen
As I saw it: Basil Douglas, Benjamin Britten and The English Opera Group 1955-57 (London: St. George's Publications, 1998).

GAULLE Xavier de
Benjamin Britten ou l'impossible quiétude (Paris: Actes Sud, 1996).

GISHFORD Anthony
A tribute to Benjamin Britten on his 50th birthday (London: Faber, 1963).

GOULD Thomas
The ancient quarrel between poetry and philosophy (Princeton: Princeton University Press, 1990).

GRAHAM Colin
'The Convention of "Curlew River"', Decca Set 310 (1965).
'Working with Britten', *Opera* XXVIII (1977), pp.130−137.

'Staging first productions 3', in *The operas of Benjamin Britten,* ed. by David Herbert (London: Hamilton, 1979), pp. 44–53.

GREENBERG, Noah
The Play of Herod: A Twelfth Century Musical Drama, ed. by Noah Greenberg and William L. Smoldon (New York: Oxford University Press, 1965).

GREENE Richard
Selected letters of Edith Sitwell, ed. by Richard Greene (London: Virago, 1997).

GREER Germaine
'Let's forget the rape shall we?', *The Guardian,* 1 June 2001.

GRUBBE G.M.A.
Aristotle on poetry and style, translated with an introduction by G.M.A. Grubbe (New York: Macmillan, 1958).

GUTHRIE Tyrone
'Production of opera', *The Score* 4 (1951), pp.52–56.

HADDON SQUIRE William
'The aesthetic hypothesis and "The Rape of Lucretia"', *Tempo* NS I (1946), pp.1–9.

HANDEL Darrel
'Britten's use of the passacaglia', *Tempo* XCIV (1970), pp.2–6.

HANLON Richard
'Notes from the Left: Communism and British Classical Music', in *A Weapon in the Struggle. The Cultural History of the Communist Party in Britain,* ed. by Andy Croft (London: Pluto Press, 1998), pp.68–86.

HARDY Forsyth
Grierson on Documentary, ed. by F. Hardy (London: Faber, 1979).

HAREWOOD Lord
'Britten's operas', *Opera* XXVIII (1977), pp.124–127.

HEADINGTON Christopher
Britten (London: Eyre Methuen, 1981).
Peter Pears: A Biography (London: Faber, 1992).

HELLER Erich
In the age of prose. Literary and philosophical essays (Cambridge: Cambridge University Press, 1984).

HERBERT David
The operas of Benjamin Britten: the complete librettos illustrated with designs of the first productions (London: Hamilton, 1979).

HEWISON Robert
Under Siege. Literary life in London 1939–1945 (London: Quartet Books, 1979).

HIGGINS Patrick
Heterosexual Dictatorship: Male Homosexuality in Post-war Britain (London: Fourth Estate, 1996).

HINDLEY Clifford
'Love and salvation in Britten's "Billy Budd"', *Music and Letters* LXX (1989), pp.363–370.
'Contemplation and reality: a study in Britten's "Death in Venice"', *Music and Letters* LXXI (1990), pp.511–523.
'Why does Miles die? A study of Britten's "The Turn of the Screw"', *Musical Quarterly* LXXIV (1990), pp.1–17.
'Homosexual self-affirmation and self-oppression in two Britten's operas', *Musical Quarterly* LXXVI (1992), pp.143–168.
'Platonic elements in Britten's "Death in Venice"', *Music and Letters* LXXIII (1992), pp.407–429.
'Britten, Auden and Johnny Inkslinger', *Perversions: the international journal of gay and lesbian studies* 2 (1994), pp.42–56.
'Britten's Parable Art: A Gay Reading', *History Workshop Journal* 40 (1995) pp.63–90.
'Eros in life and death: "Billy Budd" and "Death in Venice"', in *The Cambridge Companion to Benjamin Britten*, ed. by Mervyn Cooke (Cambridge: Cambridge University Press, 1999), pp.147–166.

HINTON Stephen
'Kurt Weill: "The Threepenny Opera"', ed. by Stephen Hinton (Cambridge: Cambridge University Press, 1990)

HODGSON Peter J.
Benjamin Britten: A Guide to Research (New York: Garland, 1996).

HOLLOWAY Robin
'The church parables (II): limits and renewals', in *The Britten Companion*, ed. by Christopher Palmer (London: Faber, 1984), pp.215–226.
'Benjamin Britten: Tributes and Memories', *Tempo* 120 (1977), pp.5–6.
'Strange Victory', *The Times Literary Supplement,* 13 September 1992, pp.5–6.

HOLST Imogen
'Britten's "Saint Nicolas"', *Tempo* 10 (Winter 1948-49), p.24.
'Britten and the young', in *Benjamin Britten: a commentary on his work by a group of specialists*, ed. by Hans Keller and Donald Mitchell (London: Rockliff, 1952), pp.283–290.
Britten (London: Faber, 1970).

HOOVER Thomas
Zen culture (London: Routledge, 1988).

HOPE-WALLACE Philip
'Opera productions in London', *The Score* 5 (1951), pp.61–64.

HOWARD Patricia
The operas of Benjamin Britten (Westport: Greenwood Press, 1969).
Benjamin Britten: "The Turn of the Screw" (Cambridge: Cambridge University Press, 1985).

INNES Christopher
Holy Theatre: Ritual and Avant guarde (Cambridge: Cambridge University Press, 1981).

JENNINGS John Wells
The Influence of W.H.Auden on Benjamin Britten (PhD, University of Illinois, 1979).

KAHNT Helmut
'"Mahagonny": Weill e Brecht si cimentano col teatro d'opera', in *La drammaturgia musicale*, a cura di Lorenzo Bianconi (Bologna: Il Mulino, 1986), pp.93−117.

KASSLER Jamie Croy
'Apollo and Dionysos: music theory and the western tradition of epistemology', in *Music and civilization. Essays in honour of Paul Henry Lang*, ed. by Edmond Strainchamps (New York: Norton, 1984).

KELLER Hans
Benjamin Britten: "The Rape of Lucretia"; "Albert Herring" (London: Boosey and Hawkes, 1947) (Covent Garden Operas).
'Britten and Mozart: a challenge in the form of variation on an unfamiliar theme', *Music and Letters* XXIX (1948), pp.17−30.
'Film Music', *Music Survey* II/4 (1950), pp.250−251.
Benjamin Britten: a commentary on his work by a group of specialists, ed. by Hans Keller and Donald Mitchell (London: Rockliff, 1952).
'Key characteristics', in *A tribute to Benjamin Britten on his 50th birthday*, ed. by Anthony Gishford, (London: Faber, 1963), pp.111−123.
'The world around Britten', *Tempo* LXVI-LXVII (1963), pp.32−36.
'Two interpretation of "Gloriana" as a music drama: 1. A reaffirmation, *Tempo* LXXIX (1966-67), pp.2−5.
'Introduction: operatic music and Britten', in *The operas of Benjamin Britten*, ed. by David Herbert, (London: Hamilton, 1979), pp.xiii−xxxi.
Criticism (London: Faber,1987).
Essays on Music, ed. by Christopher Wintle (Cambridge: University Press, 1994).
Three Psychoanalytic Notes on "Peter Grimes", ed. by Christopher Wintle (London: Institute of Advanced Musical Studies, King's College, 1995).

KEMP Ian
Michael Tippett: a symposium on his 60th birthday, ed. by Ian Kemp (London: Faber, 1965).

KENDALL Alan
Benjamin Britten (London: Macmillan, 1973).

KENNEDY Michael
Britten (London: Dent, 1981).
Portrait of Walton (London: Oxford University Press, 1990).
'The crowning masterpiece', *Opera* XLIII (1992), pp.510-514.

KERMAN Joseph
Opera as drama (London: Oxford University Press, 1957).
'A profile for American Musicology', *Journal of the American Musicological Society* 18 (1965), pp. 61-69.

KILDEA Paul
Selling Britten: a social and economic history (PhD, Oxford University, 1996).
'Britten, Auden and "otherness"', in *The Cambridge Companion to Benjamin Britten*, ed. by Mervyn Cooke (Cambridge: Cambridge University Press, 1999), pp.36-53.

KIMBALL Robert
The complete lyrics of Ira Gershwin, ed. by Robert Kimball (London: Pavillion, 1994).

KING W.G.
'Constant Composer', *New York Sun*, 27 April 1940.

KISHINAMI Yukiko
Britten's 'Sinfonia da Requiem': context, sources and genesis (PhD, University of London, 1998).

KIVY, Peter
'Opera talk: a Philosophical "Phantasie"', *Cambridge Opera Journal* 3/1 (1991), pp.63-77.

KNOWLES Dorothy
French drama of the inter-war years 1918-1939 (London: Harrap, 1967).

KORSYN Kevin
'Towards a new poetics of musical influence', *Music Analysis* 10 (1991), pp.3-72.

KOWALKE Kim

Mahagonny. A sourcebook, edited by Kim Kowalke, Joanna Lee and Edward Harsh (New York: Kurt Weill Foundation for Music, 1985).

LABIE Jean-François

'La musique de la langue anglaise', *L'Avant-scene Opera* CXLVI (1992), pp.4–9.

LANGER Suzanne

Feeling and form. A theory of art (New York: Scribners, 1953).

'The principle of assimilation', *The Score* 24 (1958), pp.42–53.

LAW Jack

'Linking the past with the present: a conversation with Nancy Evans and Eric Crozier', *Opera Quarterly* III/1 (1985), pp.72–79.

'Daring to eat a peach: Literary allusion in 'Albert Herring', *Opera Quarterly* V/1 (1987), pp.1–10.

'"I must get a better composer....but how?": The Early Letters and Diaries of Benjamin Britten' (review), *Opera Quarterly* IX/2 (1992), pp.31-51.

LEVIN, David J.

Opera through other eyes (Stanford: Stanford University Press, 1993).

LINDENBERGER Herbert

'Towards a theory of musical drama', *Yearbook of Comparative and General Literature* XXIX (1980), pp.5–9.

LUKACS György

Breve storia della letteratura tedesca dal Settecento ai giorni nostri (Torino: Einaudi, 1956).

McDIARMID Lucy

Saving civilization. Yeats, Eliot and Auden between the wars (Cambridge: Cambridge University Press, 1984).

McGIFFERT Genevieve

The musico-dramatic techniques of Benjamin Britten: a detailed study of "Peter Grimes" (PhD, University of Denver, 1970).

McKELLAR Shannon
'Re-Visioning the 'Missing' Scene: Critical and Tonal Trajectories in Britten's "Billy Budd"', *Journal of the Royal Musical Association* 122 (1997), pp.258–280.
Institutional voices: 5 Britten Operas (PhD, Oxford University, 1998).
'Music, Image and Ideology in Britten's "Owen Wingrave"', *Music and Letters* LXXX (1999), pp.390–410.

MACKERNESS Edward
A social history of English music (Westport: Greenwod, 1976).

MANN Thomas
Death in Venice, translated by H.T.Lowe-Porter (Harmondsworth: Penguin, 1955).
Letters of Thomas Mann 1889–1955, selected and translated from the German by Richard and Clara Winston (London: Secker and Warburg, 1970).
Romanzi brevi, ed. by Roberto Fertonani (Milano: Mondadori, 1977).
Saggi: Schopenhauer, Nietzsche, Freud, Italian translation by Italo Alighiero Chiusano (Milano: Mondadori, 1980).

MANN William
'The Incidental Music', in *Benjamin Britten: a commentary on his work by a group of specialists*, ed. by Hans Keller and Donald Mitchell (London: Rockliff, 1952), pp.295–310.

MARK Christopher
'Simplicity in early Britten', *Tempo* CXLVII (1983), pp.8–14.
'Contextually transformed tonality in Britten', *Musical Analysis* IV (1985), pp.265–287.

MARTIN George
'Benjamin Britten: twenty-five years of opera', *Yale Review* LX (1970), pp.24–44.

MARTORELLA Rosanne
The Sociology of Opera (New York: Prager, 1982).

MARX Robert
'Drama and the opera libretto', *Yale Theatre* IV (1973), pp.123–133.

MATTHEWS David
'The string quartets', in *The Britten Companion*, ed. by Christopher Palmer (London: Faber, 1984), pp.383−92.
'"Death in Venice" and the third quartet', in *Benjamin Britten: "Death in Venice"*, ed. by Donald Mitchell (Cambridge: Cambridge University Press, 1987), pp.154−162.

MAUS Fred
'Music as drama', *Music Theatre Spectrum* 10 (1988), pp.65−72.

MAUST Wilbur R.
Benjamin Britten: Music of Conscience and Compassion (Waterloo, Ontario: Conrad Grebel College, 1987).

MAYER Mark
A Structural and Stylistic Analysis of the Benjamin Britten "Curlew River" (EdD., Columbia University, 1983).

MERTZ Margaret
History, criticism and the sources of Benjamin Britten's "The Rape of Lucretia" (PhD, Harvard University, 1990).

MEYER Leonard B.
Style and Music (Philadelphia: Pennsylvania University Press, 1989).

MESSINIS Mario
'Da James a Britten', in: *Benjamin Britten:"The Turn of the Screw"*, programme book (Venezia: Teatro La Fenice, 1992), pp.47−55.

MILLIMAN Jo Ann
Britten's symbolic treatment of sleep, dream and death in his opera "Death in Venice", (PhD, University of South California, 1977).

MITCHELL Donald
'A note on "St. Nicolas": some points on Britten's style' *Music Survey* II/4 (1950), pp.220−226.
'Britten's revisionary practice: practical and creative', *Tempo* LXVI (1963), pp.15−22.

'Britten's "dramatic" legacy', *Opera* XXVIII (1977), pp.127−130.
Benjamin Britten 1913−1976: pictures from a life. A pictorial biography (London: Faber, 1978).
Britten and Auden in the thirties: the year 1936 (London: Faber, 1981).
'Catching on to the technique of "Pagoda-land"', *Tempo* CXLVI (1983), pp.13−24.
'Montagu Slater (1902−1956): who was he?', in *Benjamin Britten:"Peter Grimes"*, ed. by Philip Brett (Cambridge: Cambridge University Press, 1983), pp.22−43.
'Three lectures in China', unpublished, March 1983.
'Outline Model for a Biography of Benjamin Britten (1913−1976)', in *Festschrift Albi Rosenthal* (Tutzing: Hans Schneider, 1984), pp.239−251.
'"Death in Venice": the dark side of perfection', in *The Britten Companion*, ed. by Christopher Palmer (London: Faber, 1984), pp.238−249.
'Mapreading: Benjamin Britten in conversation with Donald Mitchell', in *The Britten Companion*, ed. by Christopher Palmer (London: Faber, 1984), pp 87−96.
'The church parables (I): ritual and restraint', in *The Britten Companion*, ed. by Christopher Palmer (London: Faber, 1984), pp.211−214.
Benjamin Britten: "Death in Venice", (Cambridge: Cambridge University Press, 1987) (Cambridge Opera Handbooks).
Letters from a life: the selected letters of Benjamin Britten 1913−1976, edited by Donald Mitchell and Philip Reed (London: Faber, 1991).
'"For Hedli": Britten and Auden's Cabaret Songs', in W.H. Auden, *The Language of Learning and the Language of Love. Uncollected writings, new interpretations*, ed. by K. Bucknell and N. Jenkins (Oxford: Clarendon, 1994), pp.61−68.
'Benjamin Britten the "Arranger"', sleeve note to *Benjamin Britten: The Folk Songs*, Collins Classic 70392 (1995), p.10.
Cradles of the new: writings on music 1951−1991, ed. by Mervyn Cooke (London: Faber, 1995).
'Violent climates', in *The Cambridge Companion to Benjamin Britten*, ed. by Mervyn Cooke (Cambridge: Cambridge University Press, 1999), pp.188−216.

MITTNER Ladislao
'Da T. Mann a B. Britten', in *Benjamin Britten. "Morte a Venezia"*, programme book (Venezia: Teatro La Fenice, 1973), pp.3−13.

MONELLE Raymond
"The Rape of Lucretia", *Opera* L (1999), p.1349.

MOTOKIYO Zeami
Il segreto del teatro Nô (Milano: Adelphi, 1966).

MURRAY Edward
Varieties of dramatic structures: a study of theory and practice (New York: University Press of America, 1990).

NEWILL Heather
"Paul Bunyan": a critical study of an operetta by W.H. Auden and Benjamin Britten (Bmus, Sheffield University, 1978).

NEWMAN Ernest
"The Rape of Lucretia", *The Times*, 21 July 1946.

NICHOLSON Steve
'Montagu Slater and the theatre of the Thirties', in *Recharting the Thirties*, ed. by Patrick J. Quinn (London: Selinsgrove, 1996), pp.201−220.

NOSKE Frits
The signifier and the signified: studies in the operas of Mozart and Verdi (Oxford: Clarendon, 1990).

OBEY André
Le Viol de Lucrèce (Paris: Nouvelles Editions Latin, 1931).
Théâtre (Paris: Gallimard, 1948).
Noah: a play in five scenes, English text by Arthur Wilmurt; with an introduction by Michel Saint-Denis (London: Heinemann, 1967).

O'DRISCOLL Robert
Yeats and the Theatre, ed. by Robert O'Driscoll and Lorna Reynolds (New York: Maclean -Hunter Press, 1975).

OLIVER Michael
Benjamin Britten (London: Phaidon, 1996).

ORR Buxton
'Some reflections on the operas of Benjamin Britten', in *Benjamin Britten: "Peter Grimes"; "Gloriana"* (London: John Calder, 1983) (ENO Opera Guides) pp.71–74.

OSBORNE Charles
'An interview with Benjamin Britten', *The London Magazine* 3/7 (October 1963), pp.91–97.

PADUANO Guido
Il giro di vite (Firenze: La Nuova Italia, 1992).

PALMER Christopher
The Britten Companion, ed. by Christopher Palmer (London: Faber,1984).
'Britten's Venice orchestra', in *Benjamin Britten:"Death in Venice"*, ed. by Donald Mitchell, (Cambridge: University Press, 1987), pp.129–153.

PARKER Roger
Reading Opera, ed. by Roger Parker and Arthur Groos (Princeton: Princeton University Press, 1988).
Analysing Opera, ed. by Roger Parker and Carolyn Abbate (Berkeley: University of California, 1989).

PAYNE Anthony
'Dramatic use of the tonality in "Peter Grimes"', *Tempo* 66-67 (1963), pp.22–26.
'Britten and the String Quartet', *Tempo* 163 (1987), pp.2–6.

PAULY Reinhard
Music and the theatre: an introduction to opera (Englewood Cliffs: Prentice Hall, 1970).

PETROBELLI Pierluigi
Music in the theater (Princeton: University Press, 1994).

PFISTER Manfred
Theory and analysis of the drama (Cambridge: University Press, 1988).

PINTACUDA Mario
La musica nella tragedia greca (Cefalù: Misuraca, 1978).

PIPER Myfanwy
'Some thoughts on the libretto of "The Turn of the Screw"', in *A tribute to Benjamin Britten on his 50th birthday*, ed. by Anthony Gisford (London: Faber, 1963), pp.78–83.
"Death in Venice": an opera in two acts; libretto (London: Faber, 1973).
'Writing for Britten', in *The operas of Benjamin Britten*, ed. by David Herbert (London: Hamilton, 1979), pp.8–21.
'Creating words for Aschenbach' in: *Benjamin Britten. Death in Venice*, programme book (London: Royal Opera House, 1992), p.20.

PIRIE Peter John
The English Musical Renaissance (London: Gollanz, 1979).

PITT Charles
Benjamin Britten 1913-76 (Paris: Theatre National de l'Opéra, 1981).

PLOMER William
'Notes on the libretto of "Gloriana"', *Tempo* XXVIII (1953), pp.5–13.

POIZAT Michel
The Angel's Cry: Beyond the Pleasure Principle in Opera, translated by Arthur Denner (Ithaca: Cornell University Press 1992).

POLLARD Alfred
English Miracle Plays, Moralities and Interludes (Oxford: Clarendon Press, 1927).

PORTER Gerard
'The World's Ill-Divided: the Communist Party and Progressive Song', in *A Weapon in the Struggle. The Cultural History of the Communist Party in Britain*, ed. by Andy Croft (London: Pluto Press, 1998), pp.171–191.

PORTER Peter
'Benjamin Britten's librettos', in *Benjamin Britten: "Peter Grimes"; "Gloriana"* (London: John Calder, 1983) (ENO Opera Guides), pp.7−14.
'Composer and poet', in *The Britten Companion*, ed. by Christopher Palmer (London: Faber,1984), pp.271−285.

POWELL John
Britten's Church Parables, with particular reference to their Japanese origins (PhD, Cambridge University, 1973).

PUGLIESE Giuseppe
'The ceremony of innocence is drowed', in *Benjamin Britten. "Morte a Venezia"*, programme book, (Venezia: Teatro La Fenice, 1973), pp.15−31.

REDLICH Hans
'The significance of Britten's operatic style', *Music Survey* II (1950), pp.240−245.

REED Philip
The incidental music of Benjamin Britten. A study and catalogue of his music for film, theatre and radio (PhD, University of East Anglia, 1987).
'Johnson over Jordan', programme note in *Britten and the French Connection, Aldeburgh October Festival Programme Book* 1994, pp.52−54.
On Mahler and Britten. Essays in honour of Donald Mitchell on his seventieth birthday, ed. by Philip Reed (Aldeburgh: Britten–Pears Library; Woodbridge: The Boydell Press, 1995) (Aldeburgh Studies in Music 3).
'Britten and Auden at the cinema', *Aldeburgh Festival Programme Book* XLIX (1996), pp.130−133.
'Britten and "The Rescue"', CD booklet Erato 0630-12713-2, (1996), p.7.
'A "Peter Grimes" Chronology, 1941-1945', in *The Making of "Peter Grimes"*, ed. by Paul Banks (Aldeburgh: The Britten Estate; Woodbridge: The Boydell Press, 1996), pp.21−52.
'Britten's American dream' in *Paul Bunyan*, programme book (London: Royal Opera House, 1997), pp.18−22.
'Britten in the cinema: "Coal Face"', in *The Cambridge Companion to Benjamin Britten*, ed. by Mervyn Cooke (Cambridge: Cambridge University Press, 1999), pp.54−77.

REED Thomas J.
Thomas Mann. Der Tod in Venedig, ed. by T.J. Reed (Oxford: Oxford University Press, 1971).
'Thomas Mann's "Death in Venice"', *Aldeburgh Festival Programme Book* XXVI (1973), pp.5–6.
Thomas Mann. The Uses of Tradition (Oxford: Clarendon, 1984).
'Mann and his novella: "Death in Venice"', in *Benjamin Britten: "Death in Venice"*, ed. by Donald Mitchell (Cambridge: CambridgeUniversity Press, 1987), pp.163–167.
Death in Venice. Making and Unmaking a Master (New York: Twaye Publishers, 1994).

RETI Rudolph
Tonality, Atonality, Pantonality (London: Rockliff, 1958).

RICHARD Albert
'La musique. Âme et spiritualitè', ed. by Albert Richard, *La Revue Musicale* 318 (1980).

RINKEL Lewis
The Forms of English Opera: literary and musical responses to a continental genre (PhD, Ritgers University, 1977).

ROBINSON Paul
Opera and ideas (New York: Harper and Row, 1985).

ROGNONI Luigi
'Funzione della musica nel teatro di Bertold Brecht', in *Fenomenologia della musica radicale* (Milano: Garzanti, 1974), pp.276–290.

ROSEBERRY Eric
'Britten's Purcell realizations and Folksong Arrangements', *Tempo* 57 (Spring 1961), p.7–28.
'Tonal ambiguity in "Death in Venice": a symphonic view', in *Benjamin Britten: "Death in Venice"*, ed. by Donald Mitchell (Cambridge: Cambridge University Press, 1987), pp.86–98.

'Old songs in new contexts: Britten as arranger', in *The Cambridge Companion to Benjamin Britten*, ed. by Mervyn Cooke (Cambridge: Cambridge University Press, 1999), pp.292−305.

ROSEN, David
'Cone's and Kivy's "World of opera"', *Cambridge Opera Journal* 4/1 (1992), pp.61−74.

ROTHA Paul
Documentary Film (London: Faber, 1936).

SACKVILLE-WEST Edward
The Rescue (London: Secker and Warburg, 1945).

SAINT-DENIS Michel
Theatre: the rediscovery of style (London: Heinemann, 1960).

SAMSON Ian
'Auden's American awakening' in *Paul Bunyan*, programme book (London: Royal Opera House, 1997), pp.11−14.

SANDERS Ronald
The days grow short: the life and music of Kurt Weill (London: Weidenfeld and Nicolson, 1980).

SCHAFER Murray
British composers in interview (London: Faber, 1963).

SCHMIDGALL Gary
Literature as opera (New York: Oxford University Press, 1977).

SCHOFFMANN Nachum
'Mann decribes Wagner: a literary *coup de maître*', *The Music Review*, 51/2 (1990), pp.77−94.

SEARLE Humphrey
'Britten's Lucretia', *Modern Music* 23 (1946), p.284.

SEGAL Charles
Interpreting Greek tragedy: myth, poetry, text (Ithaca: Cornell University Press, 1986).

SEGRE Cesare
Teatro e romanzo. Due tipi di comunicazione letteraria (Torino: Einaudi, 1984).
Strutturalismo e critica (Milano: Il Saggiatore, 1985).
Avviamento all'analisi del testo letterario (Torino: Einaudi, 1999).

SENIOR Evan
'Is Britten new opera really an opera?', *Music and Musicians* VIII (1960), pp.10–11.

SEYMOUR Claire
The subversive voice: expression and evasion in the operas of Benjamin Britten (PhD, University of Kent, 1998).

SHEPPARD W. Anthony
Revealing Masks: exotic influences and ritualized performance in modernist music theater (Berkeley: University of California Press, 2001).

SIDNELL Michael J.
Dances of Death: The Group Theatre of London in the Thirties (London: Faber, 1984).

SIMEON Ennio
'Le esperienze cinematografiche di Benjamin Britten', *La Cosa Vista* (1988), pp.24–9.

SINCLAIR Frances Teresa
Benjamin Britten's Music for Children: reflections on youth and innocence (DMA, University of North Carolina, 1997).

SMETHURST Mae
The Artistry of Aeschylus and Zeami: A Comparative Study of Greek Tragedy and Nô (Princeton: University Press, 1989).

SMITH Christopher
'André Obey and Benjamin Britten', in *Aldeburgh and around: local studies* ed. by Christopher Smith ([S.l.]: Yara Valley Publishers, 1983).
'André Obey and "The Rape of Lucretia"' in *The Rape of Lucretia*, programme book, (London: English National Opera, 2001).

SMITH Patrick J.
The Tenth Muse. A historical study of the opera libretto (London: Gollancz, 1971).

SMOLDON William
The Music of the Medieval Church Dramas (London: Oxford University Press, 1980).

SOLIE Ruth A.
Musicology and difference: Gender and Sexuality in Music Scholarship (Berkeley: University of California Press, 1993).

SORRELL Neil
A guide to gamelan (London: Faber, 1990).

SPEARS Monroe K.
The poetry of W.H. Auden: the disenchanted island (New York: Oxford University Press, 1965).

SPERANZA Ennio
'"Inglese italianato diavolo incarnato": brevi note, con alcune licenze, su Britten e Michelangelo', *Nuova Rivista Musicale Italiana* NS IV/1 (2000), pp.97–118.

STANSKY Peter
London's Burning: Life, Death and Art in the Second World War (London: Constable, 1994).

STEIN Erwin
'Form in opera: "Albert Herring" examined', *Tempo* V (1947), pp.4–8.
'Benjamin Britten's operas', *Opera* I (1950), pp.16–21.
Orpheus in new guises (London: Rockliff, 1953).

STIMPSON Mansel
'Drama and meaning in "The Turn of the Screw"', *Opera Quarterly* IV (986) pp.75−82.

STROCHER Vicky Pierce
Form and Meaning in Benjamin Britten's Sonnet Cycles (PhD, University of North Texas, 1994).

STUART Charles
'Britten "The Eclectic"', *Music Survey* II/4 (1950), pp.247−250.

SUBOTNIK Rose Rosengard
Developing Variations. Style and Ideology in Western Music (Minneapolis: University of Minnesota Press, 1990).

SUTCLIFFE Tom
'Is it all?', *Musical Times* CXXIII (1992), pp.569−71.

SWANSTON Hamish
In defence of opera (London: Allen Lane, 1978).

SZONDI Peter
Theory of the Modern Drama. A Critical Edition. Edited and translated by Michael Hays (Cambridge: Polity Press, 1987).

TAMBLING Jeremy
Opera, ideology and film (Manchester: University Press, 1987).

TARUSKIN Richard
'Back to whom? Neoclassicism as Ideology', *19th Century Music* 16 (1992-93), pp.286−302.

TAYLOR Desmond Shawe
'"The Rape of Lucretia"' (review), *The New Statesman and Nation*, 20 July 1946.

THORPE Marion
Peter Pears. A tribute on his 75th birthday, ed. by Marion Thorpe (London: Faber, 1985).

TOOGOOD Catherine Mary

An Introductory Study of Benjamin Britten's Children Operas: "Let's Make an Opera" and "Noye's Fludde" (BEd, Exmouth College, n.d.).

TRANCHELL Peter
'Britten and Brittenites', *Music and Letters* XXXIV (1953), pp.124–132.

TRAVIS Roy
'The recurrent figure in the Britten/Piper opera "Death in Venice"', *The Music Forum*, ed. by Felix Salzer (New York: Columbia University Press, 1987), vol.VI, pp. 129–223.

TREND Michael
The music-makers: heirs and rebels of the English musical renaissance (London: Weidenfield, 1985).

VERRIEST Guy
'L'art-lirique: esthétique et defénse', *La Revue Musicale* 300 (1977).

VICENTINI Claudio
La teoria del teatro politico (Firenze: Sansoni, 1981).

VITTOZ Roger
Notes et pensées, ed by P. d'Espiney (Paris, Editions du Levain, 1955).

VOUGA François
Résonance theologiques de la musique (Genève: Labor et Fides, 1983).

WALEY Arthur
The Nô Plays of Japan, [translated by] Arthur Waley (London: Allen & Unwin, 1921).

WALLIS Mick
'Heirs to the Pageant: Mass Spectacle and the Popular Front', in *A Weapon in the Struggle. The Cultural History of the Communist Party in Britain*, ed. by Andy Croft (London: Pluto Press, 1998), pp.48–67.

WALSH Stephen
'Two interpretations of "Gloriana" as a music drama: 2. A new impression', *Tempo* 79 (1966-67), pp.5–9.

WARRACK John
'Benjamin Britten musician of the year in conversation with John Warrack', *Musical America* LXXXIV (1964), pp. 25–29.
'Britten's television opera', *Opera* XXII (1971), pp.371–378.

WATKINS Glenn
Pyramids at the Louvre. Music, Culture and Collage from Stravinsky to the Postmodernists (Cambridge, Mass.: Harvard University Press, 1994).

WATSON Gary
Curlew River as Holy Theatre (MA, University of Sidney, 1985).

WEBSTER James
'To understand Verdi and Wagner we must understand Mozart', *19th-Century Music* 11 (1987-88), pp.175–93.
'Mozart's operas and the myth of musical unity', *Cambridge Opera Journal*, 2 (1990), p.197–218.

WEISSTEIN Ulrich
'Cocteau, Stravinsky, Brecht and the birth of epic opera', *Modern Drama* 5 (1962), pp.142–153.
The essence of opera (New York: Norton, 1964).
'Reflections on a golden style. Auden's theory of opera', *Comparative Literature* XXII/2 (1970), pp.108–124.

WELLEK René
Concepts of criticism (New Haven and London: Yale University Press, 1963).

WHITE Eric Walter
The rise of English opera, introduction by Benjamin Britten (New York: Da Capo, 1972).
Benjamin Britten: his life and operas, 2nd edition, ed. by John Evans (London: Faber, 1983).

A History of English Opera (London: Faber, 1985).

WHITESELL Lloyd Ashley
Images of self in the music of Benjamin Britten (PhD, Stony Brook University, 1993).

WHITING Frank
An Introduction to Theatre (New York: Harper and Row, 1978).

WHITTALL Arnold
'Benjamin Britten', *Music Review* XXIII (1962), pp.314–316.
'A war and a wedding: two modern British operas', *Music and Letters* LV (1974), pp.299–306.
Music since the First World War (London: Dent, 1977).
The music of Britten and Tippett; studies in themes and techniques (Cambridge: Cambridge University Press, 1982, 2/1990).
'Twisted relations: method and meaning in Britten's "Billy Budd"', *Cambridge Opera Journal* II (1990), pp.145–171.
'The Signs of Genre: Britten's version of Pastoral', in *Sundry sorts of music books*, ed. by C. Banks, A. Searle and M. Turner (London: The British Library, 1993), pp.363–374.
'Along the Knife-Edge: The Topic of Transcendence in Britten's Musical Aesthetic', in *On Mahler and Britten. Essays in honour of Donald Mitchell on his seventieth birthday*, ed. by Philip Reed (Aldeburgh: Britten–Pears Library; Woodbridge: Boydell Press, 1995) (Aldeburgh Studies in Music 3), pp.290–298.
'The chamber operas', in *The Cambridge Companion to Benjamin Britten*, ed. by Mervyn Cooke (Cambridge: Cambridge University Press, 1999), pp.95–112.

WILBER, Ken
Up from Eden. A transpersonal view of human evolution (London: Routledge, 1983).

WILCOX Michael
Benjamin Britten's Operas (Bath: Absolute Press, 1997)

WILDER Thornton
Lucrece, translated by Thornton Niven Wilder from "Le viol de Lucrèce" by André Obey (London: Longmans, 1933).

WILLETT John
'"Die Massnahme": the vanishing Lehrstuck', in *Hanns Eisler: a miscellany*, compiled and edited by David Blake (Luxembourg: Harwood Academic Publishers, 1995), pp.79-89.

WILLIAMS Raymond
English Drama: Forms and Development. Essays in Honour of Muriel Clara Bradbrook, ed. by Raymond Williams (Cambridge: Cambridge University Press, 1977).

WIRTH Andrzej
'Brecht and the Asiatic model: the secularization of magical rites', in *Literature East and West (Japanese issue)* XV/-XVI/1-2 (Dec. 1971- June 1972), pp.601-615.

YOUNG Karl
The Drama of the Medieval Church (Oxford: University Press, 1933).

ZINKIN Leonard
'"Death in Venice'. A Jungian view', *The Journal of Analytical Psychology* XXII/4 (1970), pp.354-365.

Music and Books published by Travis & Emery Music Bookshop:

Anon.: Hymnarium Sarisburiense, cum Rubricis et Notis Musicis.
Anon.: Säcularfeier des Geburtstages von Ludwig van Beethoven
Agricola, Johann Friedrich from Tosi: Anleitung zur Singkunst.
Bach, C.P.E.: edited W. Emery: Nekrolog or Obituary Notice of J.S. Bach.
Bateson, Naomi Judith: Alcock of Salisbury
Bathe, William: A Briefe Introduction to the Skill of Song
Bax, Arnold: Symphony #5, Arranged for Piano Four Hands by Walter Emery
Burney, Charles: The Present State of Music in France and Italy
Burney, Charles: The Present State of Music in Germany, The Netherlands …
Burney, Charles: An Account of the Musical Performances … Handel
Burney, Karl: Nachricht von Georg Friedrich Handel's Lebensumstanden.
Burns, Robert: The Caledonian Musical Museum ..The Best Scotch Songs. (1810)
Cobbett, W.W.: Cobbett's Cyclopedic Survey of Chamber Music. (2 vols.)
Corrette, Michel: Le Maitre de Clavecin
Crimp, Bryan: Dear Mr. Rosenthal … Dear Mr. Gaisberg …
Crimp, Bryan: Solo: The Biography of Solomon
Crotch, William: Substance of Several Courses of Lectures on Music
d'Indy, Vincent: Beethoven: Biographie Critique
d'Indy, Vincent: Beethoven: A Critical Biography
d'Indy, Vincent: César Franck (in French)
Diana, B.A.: Benjamin Britten's Holy Theatre
Fischhof, Joseph: Versuch einer Geschichte des Clavierbaues. (Faksimile 1853).
Frescobaldi, Girolamo: D'Arie Musicali per Cantarsi. Primo & Secondo Libro.
Geminiani, Francesco: The Art of Playing the Violin.
Handel; Purcell; Boyce; Geene et al: Calliope or English Harmony: Volume First.
Häuser: Musikalisches Lexikon. 2 vols in one.
Hawkins, John: A General History of the Science and Practice of Music (5 vols.)
Herbert-Caesari, Edgar: The Science and Sensations of Vocal Tone
Herbert-Caesari, Edgar: Vocal Truth
Hopkins, Antony: The Concertgoer's Companion - Bach to Haydn.
Hopkins, Antony: The Concertgoer's Companion – Holst to Webern.
Hopkins, Antony: Music All Around Me
Hopkins, Antony: Sounds of Music / Sounds of the Orchestra
Hopkins, Antony: The Nine Symphonies of Beethoven
Hopkins, Antony: Understanding Music
Hopkins, Edward and Rimboult, Edward: The Organ. Its History & Construction.
Hunt, John: - see separate list of discographies at the end of these titles
Isaacs, Lewis: Hänsel and Gretel. A Guide to Humperdinck's Opera.
Isaacs, Lewis: Königskinder (Royal Children) A Guide to Humperdinck's Opera.
Kastner: Manuel Général de Musique Militaire
Lacassagne, M. l'Abbé Joseph : Traité Général des élémens du Chant.
Lascelles (née Catley), Anne: The Life of Miss Anne Catley.
Mainwaring, John: Memoirs of the Life of the Late George Frederic Handel
Malcolm, Alexander: A Treaty of Music: Speculative, Practical and Historical
Marx, Adolph Bernhard: Die Kunst des Gesanges, Theoretisch-Practisch
May, Florence: The Life of Brahms
May, Florence: The Girlhood Of Clara Schumann: Clara Wieck And Her Time.
Mellers, Wilfrid: Angels of the Night: Popular Female Singers of Our Time

Music and Books published by Travis & Emery Music Bookshop:

Mellers, Wilfrid: Bach and the Dance of God
Mellers, Wilfrid: Beethoven and the Voice of God
Mellers, Wilfrid: Caliban Reborn - Renewal in Twentieth Century Music
Mellers, Wilfrid: Darker Shade of Pale, A Backdrop to Bob Dylan
Mellers, Wilfrid: François Couperin and the French Classical Tradition
Mellers, Wilfrid: Harmonious Meeting
Mellers, Wilfrid: Le Jardin Retrouvé, The Music of Frederic Mompou
Mellers, Wilfrid: Music and Society, England and the European Tradition
Mellers, Wilfrid: Music in a New Found Land: …… American Music
Mellers, Wilfrid: Romanticism and the Twentieth Century (from 1800)
Mellers, Wilfrid: The Masks of Orpheus: …… the Story of European Music.
Mellers, Wilfrid: The Sonata Principle (from c. 1750)
Mellers, Wilfrid: Vaughan Williams and the Vision of Albion
Panchianio, Cattuffio: Rutzvanscad Il Giovine
Pearce, Charles: Sims Reeves, Fifty Years of Music in England.
Pettitt, Stephen: Philharmonia Orchestra: A Record of Achievement, 1948-1985
Pettitt, Stephen (ed. Hunt): Philharmonia Orchestra: Complete Discography 1945-1987
Playford, John: An Introduction to the Skill of Musick.
Purcell, Henry et al: Harmonia Sacra … The First Book, (1726)
Purcell, Henry et al: Harmonia Sacra … Book II (1726)
Quantz, Johann: Versuch einer Anweisung die Flöte traversiere zu spielen.
Rameau, Jean-Philippe: Code de Musique Pratique, ou Methodes.
Rameau, Jean-Philippe: Erreurs sur La Musique dans l'Encyclopédie
Rastall, Richard: The Notation of Western Music.
Rimbault, Edward: The Pianoforte, Its Origins, Progress, and Construction.
Rousseau, Jean Jacques: Dictionnaire de Musique
Rubinstein, Anton : Guide to the proper use of the Pianoforte Pedals.
Sainsbury, John S.: Dictionary of Musicians. (1825). 2 vols.
Serré de Rieux, Jean de : Les dons des Enfans de Latone
Simpson, Christopher: A Compendium of Practical Musick in Five Parts
Spohr, Louis: Autobiography
Spohr, Louis: Grand Violin School
Tans'ur, William: A New Musical Grammar; or The Harmonical Spectator
Terry, Charles Sanford: Bach's Chorals – Parts 1, 2 and 3.
Terry, Charles Sanford: John Christian Bach
Terry, Charles Sanford: J.S. Bach's Original Hymn-Tunes for Congregational Use.
Terry, Charles Sanford: Four-Part Chorals of J.S. Bach. (German & English)
Terry, Charles Sanford: Joh. Seb. Bach, Cantata Texts, Sacred and Secular.
Terry, Charles Sanford: The Origins of the Family of Bach Musicians.
Tosi, Pierfrancesco: Opinioni de' Cantori Antichi, e Moderni
Tosi, Pierfrancesco: Observations on the Florid Song.
Van der Straeten, Edmund: History of the Violoncello, The Viol da Gamba …
Van der Straeten, Edmund: History of the Violin, Its Ancestors… (2 vols.)
Walther, J. G. [Waltern]: Musicalisches Lexikon [Musikalisches Lexicon]
Wagner, Richard: Beethoven (Leipzig 1870)
Wagner, Richard: Lebens-Bericht (Leipzig 1884)
Wagner, Richard: The Music of the Future (Translated by E. Dannreuther).
Zwirn, Gerald: Stranded Stories From The Operas

Discographies by John Hunt.

3 Italian Conductors and 7 Viennese Sopranos: 10 Discographies: Arturo Toscanini, Guido Cantelli, Carlo Maria Giulini, Elisabeth Schwarzkopf, Irmgard Seefried, Elisabeth Gruemmer, Sena Jurinac, Hilde Gueden, Lisa Della Casa, Rita Streich.

A Gallic Trio: 3 Discographies: Charles Muench, Paul Paray, Pierre Monteux.

A Notable Quartet: 4 Discographies: Gundula Janowitz, Christa Ludwig, Nicolai Gedda, Dietrich Fischer-Dieskau.

American Classics: The Discographies of Leonard Bernstein and Eugene Ormand

Antal Dorati 1906-1988: Discography and Concert Register.

Back From The Shadows: 4 Discographies: Willem Mengelberg, Dimitri Mitropoulos, Hermann Abendroth, Eduard Van Beinum.

Carlo Maria Giulini: Discography and Concert Register.

Columbia 33CX Label Discography.

Concert Hall Discography: Concert Hall Society and Concert Hall Record Club

Conductors On The Yellow Label: 8 Discographies: Fritz Lehmann, Ferdinand Leitner, Ferenc Fricsay, Eugen Jochum, Leopold Ludwig, Artur Rother, Franz Konwitschny, Igor Markevitch.

Dirigenten der DDR: Conductors of the German Democratic Republic

From Adam to Webern: the Recordings of von Karajan.

Giants of the Keyboard: 6 Discographies: Wilhelm Kempff, Walter Gieseking, Edwin Fischer, Clara Haskil, Wilhelm Backhaus, Artur Schnabel.

Gramophone Stalwarts: 3 Separate Discographies: Bruno Walter, Erich Leinsdorf, Georg Solti.

Great Violinists: 3 Discographies: David Oistrakh, Wolfgang Schneiderhan, Arthur Grumiaux.

Hans Knappertsbusch: Kna: Concert Register and Discography of Hans Knappertsbusch, 1888-1965. Second Edition.

Her Master's Voice: Concert Register and Discography of Dame Elisabeth Schwarzkopf [Third Edition].

Hungarians in Exile: 3 Discographies: Fritz Reiner, Antal Dorati, George Szell.

Leopold Stokowski (1882-1977): Discography and Concert Register

Leopold Stokowski: Discography and Concert Listing.

Leopold Stokowski: Second Edition of the Discography.

Makers of the Philharmonia: 11 Discographies Alceo Galliera, Walter Susskind, Paul Kletzki, Nicolai Malko, Issay Dobrowen, Lovro Von Matacic, Efrem Kurtz, Otto Ackermann, Anatole Fistoulari, George Weldon, Robert Irving.

Makers of the Philharmonia: 11 Discographies: Alceo Galliera, Walter Susskind, Paul Kletzki, Nicolai Malko, Issay Dobrowen, Lovro Von Matacic, Efrem Kurtz, Otto Ackermann, Anatole Fistoulari, George Weldon, Robert Irving.

Metropolitan Sopranos: 4 Discographies: Rosa Ponselle, Eleanor Steber, Zinka Milanov, Leontyne Price.

Mezzo and Contraltos: 5 Discographies: Janet Baker, Margarete Klose, Kathleen Ferrier, Giulietta Simionato, Elisabeth Hoengen.

Mid-Century Conductors and More Viennese Singers: 10 Discographies: Karl Boehm, Victor De Sabata, Hans Knappertsbusch, Tullio Serafin, Clemens Krauss, Anton Dermota, Leonie Rysanek, Eberhard Waechter, Maria Reining, Erich Kunz.

More 20th Century Conductors: 7 Discographies: Eugen Jochum, Ferenc Fricsay, Carl Schuricht, Felix Weingartner, Josef Krips, Otto Klemperer, Erich Kleiber.

More Giants of the Keyboard: 5 Discographies: Claudio Arrau, Gyorgy Cziffra, Vladimir Horowitz, Dinu Lipatti, Artur Rubinstein.

More Musical Knights: 4 Discographies: Hamilton Harty, Charles Mackerras, Simon Rattle, John Pritchard.

Musical Knights: 6 Discographies: Henry Wood, Thomas Beecham, Adrian Boult, John Barbirolli, Reginald Goodall, Malcolm Sargent.

Philharmonic Autocrat 1: Discography of: Herbert Von Karajan [Third Edition]

Philharmonic Autocrat 2: Concert Register of Herbert Von Karajan Second Ed.

Philips Minigroove: Second Extended Version of the European Discography.

Pianists For The Connoisseur: 6 Discographies: Arturo Benedetti Michelangeli, Alfred Cortot, Alexis Weissenberg, Clifford Curzon, Solomon, Elly Ney.

Sächsische Staatskapelle Dresden: Complete Discography.

Singers of the Third Reich: 5 Discographies: Helge Roswaenge, Tiana Lemnitz, Franz Voelker, Maria Mueller, Max Lorenz.

Singers on the Yellow Label: 7 Discographies: Maria Stader, Elfriede Troetschel, Annelies Kupper, Wolfgang Windgassen, Ernst Haefliger, Josef Greindl, Kim Borg

Six Wagnerian Sopranos: 6 Discographies: Frieda Leider, Kirsten Flagstad, Astrid Varnay, Martha Moedl, Birgit Nilsson, Gwyneth Jones.

Sviatoslav Richter: Pianist of the Century: Discography.

Teachers and Pupils: 7 Discographies: Elisabeth Schwarzkopf, Maria Ivoguen, Maria Cebotari, Meta Seinemeyer, Ljuba Welitsch, Rita Streich, Erna Berger

Tenors in a Lyric Tradition: 3 Discographies: Peter Anders, Walther Ludwig, Fritz Wunderlich.

The Art of the Diva: 3 Discographies: Claudia Muzio, Maria Callas, Magda Olivero.

The Furtwaengler Sound Sixth Edition: Discography and Concert Listing.

The Great Dictators: 3 Discographies: Evgeny Mravinsky, Artur Rodzinski, Sergiu Celibidache.

The Lyric Baritone: 5 Discographies: Hans Reinmar, Gerhard Huesch, Josef Metternich, Hermann Uhde, Eberhard Waechter.

The Post-War German Tradition: 5 Discographies: Rudolf Kempe, Joseph Keilberth, Wolfgang Sawallisch, Rafael Kubelik, Andre Cluytens.

Wagner Im Festspielhaus: Discography of the Bayreuth Festival.

Wiener Philharmoniker 1 - Vienna Philharmonic and Vienna State Opera Orchestras: Discography Part 1 1905-1954.

Wiener Philharmoniker 2 - Vienna Philharmonic and Vienna State Opera Orchestras: Discography Part 2 1954-1989.

Available from: Travis & Emery at 17 Cecil Court, London, UK.
(+44) 20 7 240 2129.   email on sales@travis-and-emery.com .
© Travis & Emery 2011

www.ingramcontent.com/pod-product-compliance
Lightning Source LLC
Chambersburg PA
CBHW071704160426
43195CB00012B/1573